Holt McDougal Algebra 2

Practice and Problem Solving Workbook

COMMON CORE EDITION

HOLT McDOUGAL

HOUGHTON MIFFLIN HARCOURT

Printed in the U.S.A.

ISBN 978-0-547-70998-7

11 12 13 14 15 0304 22 21 20 19 18

4500701148 D E F G

Contents

Practice

Problem Solving

Name ______________________ Date ______________ Class ______________

LESSON 1-1

Practice

Exploring Transformations

Perform the given translation on the point (2, 5) and give the coordinates of the translated point.

1. left 3 units ____________

2. down 6 units ____________

3. right 4 units, up 2 units ____________

Use the table to perform each transformation of $y = f(x)$. Use the same coordinate plane as the original function.

4. translation left 1 unit, down 5 units

	x	y	
	–3	3	
	–1	1	
	1	2	
	2	1	
	3	2	

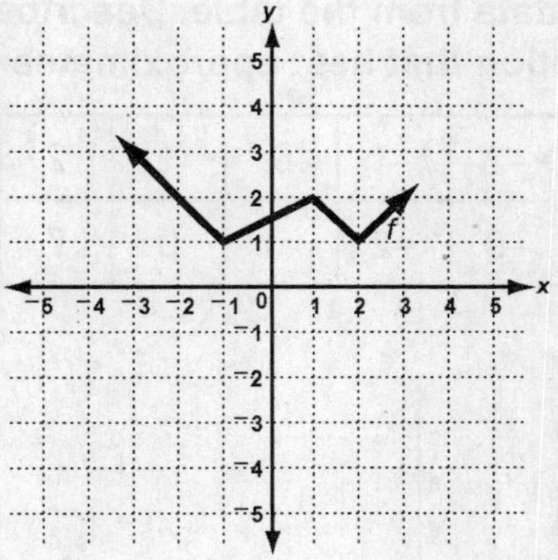

5. vertical stretch factor of $\frac{3}{2}$

x	y	
–3	3	
–1	1	
1	2	
2	1	
3	2	

6. horizontal compression factor of $\frac{1}{2}$

	x	y
	–3	3
	–1	1
	1	2
	2	1
	3	2

7. reflection across x-axis

x	y	
–3	3	
–1	1	
1	2	
2	1	
3	2	

Solve.

8. George has a goal for the number of computers he wants to sell each month for the next 6 months at his computer store. He draws a graph to show his projected profits for that period. Then he decides to discount the prices by 10%. How will this affect his profits? Identify the transformation to his graph and describe how to find the ordered pairs for the transformation.

____

Name ______________________ Date ____________ Class ____________

LESSON 1-2

Practice

Introduction to Parent Functions

Identify the parent function for *h* from its function rule. Then graph *h* on your calculator and describe what transformation of the parent function it represents.

1. $h(x) = \sqrt{x+4}$

2. $h(x) = (x-4)^3$

3. $h(x) = 4x^2$

________________ ________________ ________________

________________ ________________ ________________

Graph the data from the table. Describe the parent function and the transformation that best approximates the data set.

4.

x	−2	−1	0	1	2
y	−9	−2	−1	0	7

5.

x	0	2	8	18	32
y	0	1	2	3	4

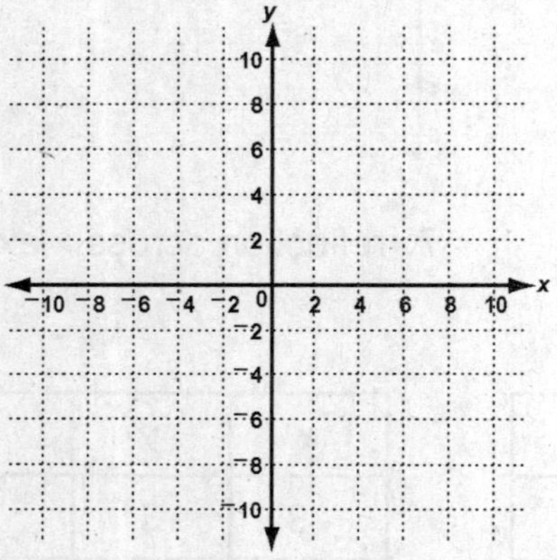

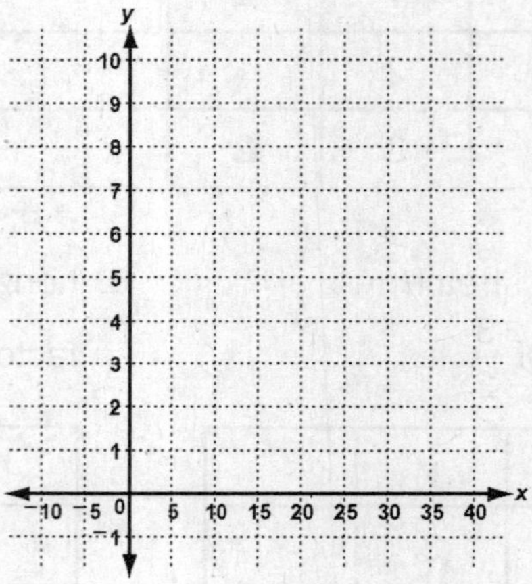

________________________________ ________________________________

6. Compare the domain and the range for the parent quadratic function to the domain and the range for the parent linear function.

____

____

____

7. Compare the domain and the range for the parent square-root function to the domain and the range for the parent cubic function.

____

____

____

Name ______________________ Date ______________ Class______________

LESSON 1-3

Practice

Transforming Linear Functions

Let $g(x)$ be the indicated transformation of $f(x)$. Write the rule for $g(x)$.

1. 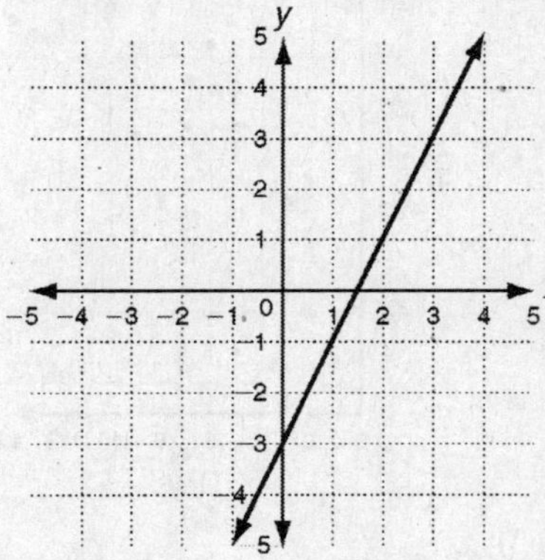

horizontal translation left 3 units

____

2. 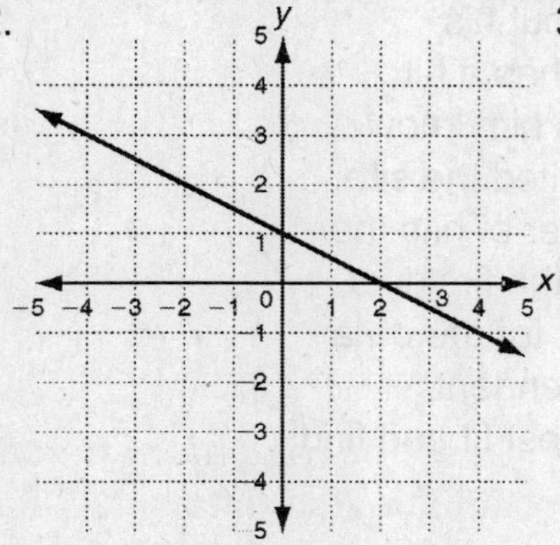

vertical compression by a factor of $\frac{1}{5}$

____

3. 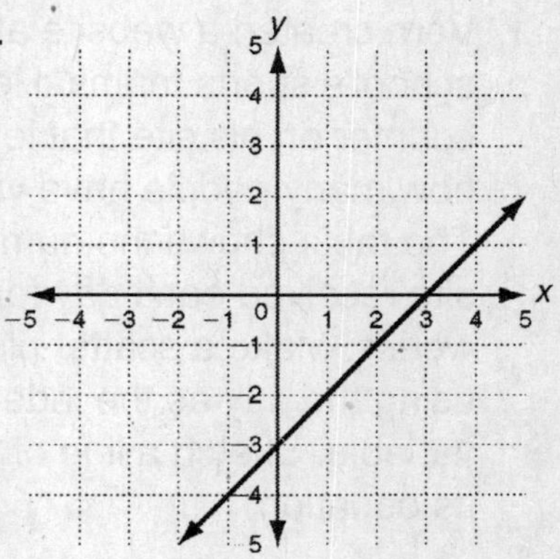

reflection across the y-axis

____

4. linear function defined by the table; horizontal stretch by a factor of 2.3

x	–5	0	7
y	–3	7	21

____

5. $f(x) = 1.7x - 3$; vertical compression by a factor of 0.7 ______________

Let $g(x)$ be the indicated combined transformation of $f(x) = x$. Write the rule for $g(x)$.

6. vertical translation down 2 units followed by a horizontal compression by a factor of $\frac{2}{5}$ ______________

7. horizontal stretch by a factor of 3.2 followed by a horizontal translation right 3 units ______________

Solve.

8. The Red Cab Taxi Service used to charge $1.00 for the first $\frac{1}{5}$ mile and $0.75 for each additional $\frac{1}{5}$ mile. The company just raised its rates by a factor of 1.5.

a. Write a new price function $g(x)$ for a taxi ride.

____

b. Describe the transformation(s) that have been applied.

____

Name ______________________ Date ____________ Class ____________

LESSON 1-4

Practice

Curve Fitting with Linear Models

Solve.

1. Vern created a website about his school's sports teams. He has a hit counter on his site that lets him know how many people have visited the site. The table shows the number of hits the site received each day for the first two weeks. Make a scatter plot for the data using the day as the independent variable. Sketch a line of best fit and find its equation.

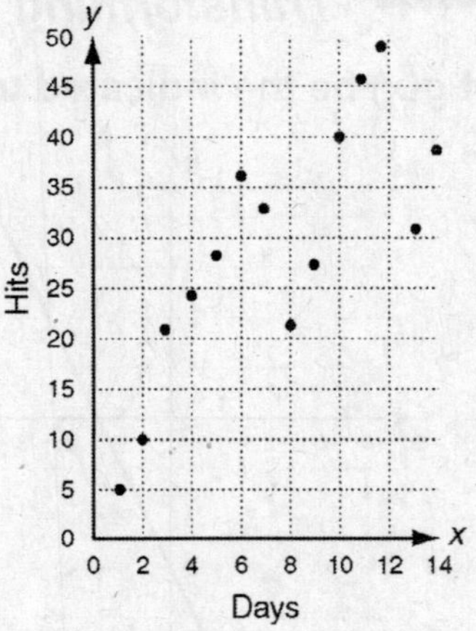

Lincoln High Website

Day	1	2	3	4	5	6	7	8	9	10	11	12	13	14
Hits	5	10	21	24	28	36	33	21	27	40	46	50	31	38

____

2. A photographer hiked through the Grand Canyon. Each day she filled a photo memory card with images. When she returned from the trip, she deleted some photos, saving only the best. The table shows the number of photos she kept from all those taken for each memory card.

Grand Canyon Photos

Photos Taken	**Photos Kept**
117	25
128	31
140	39
157	52
110	21
188	45
170	42

a. Use a graphing calculator to make a scatter plot of the data. Use the number of photos taken as the independent variable.

b. Find the correlation coefficient.

____

c. Write the equation of the line of best fit.

____

d. Predict the number of photos this photographer will keep if she takes 200 photos.

____

3. What is the relationship between the slope of a line and its correlation coefficient?

____

____

Name ______________________ Date ______________ Class ______________

LESSON 2-1

Practice

Using Transformations to Graph Quadratic Functions

Graph the function by using a table.

1. $f(x) = x^2 + 2x - 1$

x	$f(x) = x^2 + 2x - 1$	$(x, f(x))$
−2		
−1		
0		
1		
2		

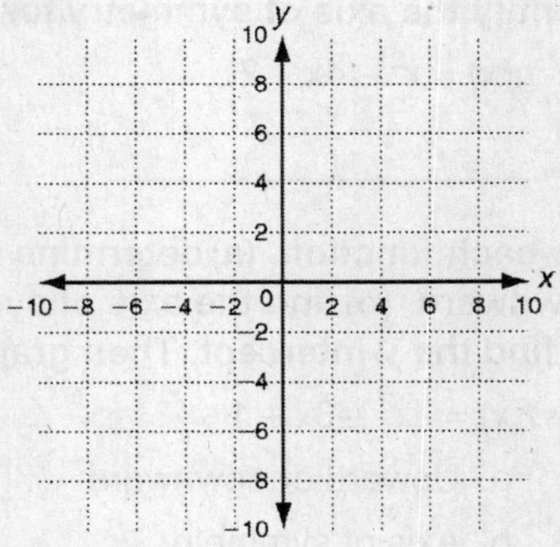

Using the graph of $f(x) = x^2$ as a guide, describe the transformations, and then graph each function. Label each function on the graph.

2. $h(x) = (x - 2)^2 + 2$

____

3. $h(x) = -(3x)^2$

____

4. $h(x) = \left(\frac{1}{2}x\right)^2$

____

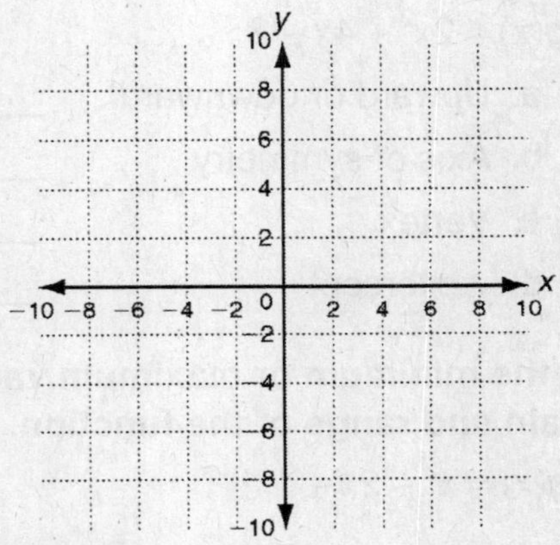

Use the description to write a quadratic function in vertex form.

5. The parent function $f(x) = x^2$ is reflected across the x-axis, horizontally stretched by a factor of 3 and translated 2 units down to create function g.

____

6. A ball dropped from the top of tower A can be modeled by the function $h(t) = -9.8t^2 + 400$, where t is the time after it is dropped and $h(t)$is its height at that time. A ball dropped from the top of tower B can be modeled by the function $h(t) = -9.8t^2 + 200$. What transformation describes this change? What does this transformation mean?

____

Name ______________________ Date ______________ Class ______________

LESSON 2-2

Practice

Properties of Quadratic Functions in Standard Form

Identify the axis of symmetry for the graph of each function.

1. $g(x) = x^2 - 4x + 2$
2. $h(x) = -8x^2 + 12x - 11$
3. $k(x) = -4(x + 3)^2 + 9$

______________ ______________ ______________

For each function, (a) determine whether the graph opens upward or downward, (b) find the axis of symmetry, (c) find the vertex, and (d) find the *y*-intercept. Then graph the function.

4. $f(x) = -x^2 + 3x + 1$
   a. Upward or downward ______________
   b. Axis of symmetry ______________
   c. Vertex ______________
   d. *y*-intercept ______________

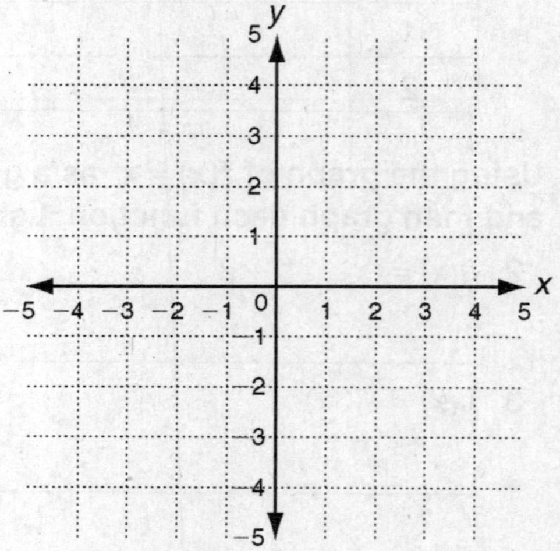

5. $g(x) = 2x^2 + 4x - 2$
   a. Upward or downward ______________
   b. Axis of symmetry ______________
   c. Vertex ______________
   d. *y*-intercept ______________

Find the minimum or maximum value of each function. Then state the domain and range of the function.

6. $g(x) = x^2 - 2x + 1$
7. $h(x) = -5x^2 + 15x - 3$

______________ ______________

Solve.

8. A record label uses the following function to model the sales of a new release.

$$a(t) = -90t^2 + 8100t$$

The number of albums sold is a function of time, *t*, in days. On which day were the most albums sold? What is the maximum number of albums sold on that day?

____

Name ____________________ Date ______________ Class ______________

LESSON 2-3

Practice

Solving Quadratic Equations by Graphing and Factoring

Find the zeros of each function by using a graph and a table.

1. $f(x) = x^2 + 5x + 6$

x	−4	−3	−2	−1	0
f(x)					

____

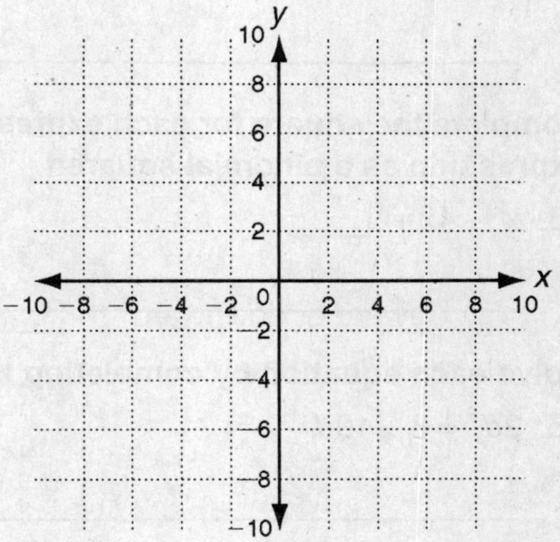

2. $g(x) = -x^2 + 4x + 5$

x	−2	0	2	4	6
f(x)					

____

Find the zeros of each function by factoring.

3. $h(x) = -x^2 - 6x - 9$

____

4. $f(x) = 2x^2 + 9x + 4$

____

5. $g(x) = x^2 + x - 20$

____

Find the roots of each equation by factoring.

6. $12x = 9x^2 + 4$

____

7. $16x^2 = 9$

____

Write a quadratic function in standard form for each given set of zeros.

8. −2 and 7

____

9. 1 and −8

____

Solve.

10. The quadratic function that approximates the height of a javelin throw is $h(t) = -0.08t^2 + 4.48$, where t is the time in seconds after it is thrown and h is the javelin's height in feet. How long will it take for the javelin to hit the ground?

____

Name ______________________ Date ______________ Class ______________

LESSON 2-4

Practice

Completing the Square

Solve each equation.

1. $2x^2 - 6 = 42$

2. $x^2 - 14x + 49 = 18$

Complete the square for each expression. Write the resulting expression as a binomial squared.

3. $x^2 - 4x +$ _____

4. $x^2 + 12x +$ _____

Solve each equation by completing the square.

5. $2d^2 = 8 + 10d$

6. $x^2 + 2x = 3$

7. $-3x^2 + 18x = -30$

8. $4x^2 = -12x + 4$

Write each function in vertex form, and identify its vertex.

9. $f(x) = x^2 - 6x - 2$

10. $f(x) = x^2 - 4x + 1$

11. $h(x) = 3x^2 - 6x - 15$

12. $f(x) = -2x^2 - 16x + 4$

Solve.

13. Nathan made a triangular pennant for the band booster club. The area of the pennant is 80 square feet. The base of the pennant is 12 feet shorter than the height.

    a. What are the lengths of the base and height of the pennant?

    b. What are the dimensions of the pennant if the base is only 6 feet shorter than the height?

Name ______________________ Date ______________ Class ______________

LESSON 2-5

Practice

Complex Numbers and Roots

Express each number in terms of *i*.

1. $\sqrt{-32}$

2. $2\sqrt{-18}$

3. $\sqrt{-\frac{1}{9}}$

Solve each equation.

4. $3x^2 + 81 = 0$

5. $4x^2 = -28$

6. $\frac{1}{4}x^2 + 12 = 0$

7. $6x^2 = -126$

Find the values of *x* and *y* that make each equation true.

8. $2x - 20i = 8 - (4y)i$

9. $5i - 6x = (10y)i + 2$

Find the zeros of each function.

10. $f(x) = x^2 - 2x + 4$

11. $g(x) = x^2 + 6x + 14$

Find each complex conjugate.

12. $i - 3$

13. $3i - 4$

14. $11i$

Solve.

15. The impedance of an electrical circuit is a way of measuring how much the circuit impedes the flow of electricity. The impedance can be a complex number. A circuit is being designed that must have an impedance that satisfies the function $f(x) = 2x^2 - 12x + 40$, where x is a measure of the impedance. Find the zeros of the function.

Name ______________________ Date ______________ Class ______________

LESSON 2-6

Practice

The Quadratic Formula

Find the zeros of each function by using the Quadratic Formula.

1. $f(x) = x^2 + 10x + 9$

2. $g(x) = 2x^2 + 4x - 12$

3. $h(x) = 3x^2 - 3x + \frac{3}{4}$

4. $f(x) = x^2 + 2x - 3$

5. $g(x) = 2x^2 + 3x + 1$

6. $g(x) = x^2 + 5x + -3$

Find the type and number of solutions for each equation.

7. $x^2 - 3x = -8$

8. $x^2 + 4x = -3$

9. $2x^2 - 12x = -18$

Solve.

10. A newspaper delivery person in a car is tossing folded newspapers from the car window to driveways. The speed of the car is 30 feet per second, and the driver does not slow down. The newspapers are tossed horizontally from a height of 4 feet above the ground. The height of the papers as they are thrown can be modeled by $y = -16t^2 + 4$, and the distance they travel to the driveway is $d = 30t$.

    a. How long does it take for a newspaper to land?

    b. From how many feet before the driveway must the papers be thrown?

    c. The delivery person starts to throw the newspapers at an angle and the height of the papers as they travel can now be modeled by $y = -16t^2 + 12t + 4$. How long does it take the papers to reach the ground now?

Name ______________________ Date ______________ Class ______________

LESSON 2-7

Practice

Solving Quadratic Inequalities

Graph each inequality.

1. $y < x^2 - 2x + 6$

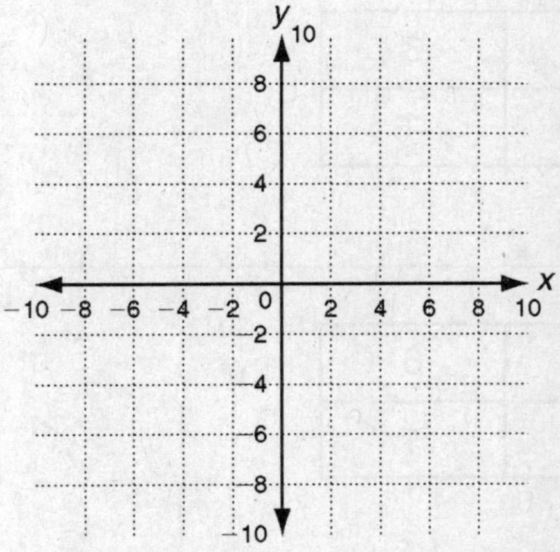

2. $y > 2x^2 - x - 7$

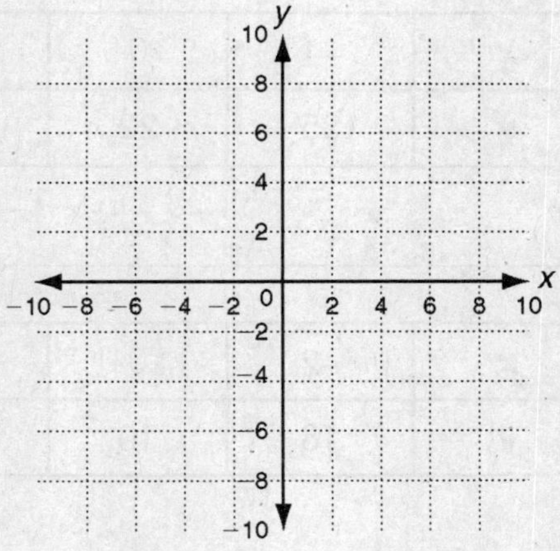

Solve each inequality by using tables or graphs.

3. $x^2 + 3x - 14 \le 14$

____

4. $x^2 - 9x > -18$

____

Solve each inequality by using algebra.

5. $x^2 - x - 3 > x$

____

6. $x^2 + 6x + 3 < -2$

____

7. $3 \le x^2 - 8x + 15$

____

8. $3x^2 + x + 8 \le 12$

____

Solve.

9. An online music service that sells song downloads models its profit using the function $P(d) = -5d^2 + 450d - 1000$, where d is the number of downloads sold and P is the profit. How many downloads does it need to sell to make a profit of more than $8000?

____

Name ______________________ Date ______________ Class ______________

LESSON 2-8

Practice

Curve Fitting with Quadratic Models

Determine whether each data set could represent a quadratic function. Explain.

1.

x	−1	0	1	2	3
y	35	22	11	2	−5

____

2.

x	−2	0	2	4	6
y	18	10	6	2	1

____

Write a quadratic equation that fits each set of points.

3. (0, −8), (2, 0), and (−3, −5)

____

4. (−1, −16), (2, 5), and (5, 8)

____

5. (−2, 6), (0, −6), and (3, −9)

____

6. (1, 4), (−2, 13), and (0, 3)

____

Solve.

7. The data table shows the energy, *E,* of a certain object in joules at a given velocity, *v,* in meters per second.

Energy (joules)	4.5	12.5	24.5	40.5
Velocity (m/s)	1.5	2.5	3.5	4.5

a. Find the quadratic relationship between the energy and velocity of the object. ________________________

b. What is the energy of an object with a speed of 5 m/s? ________________________

c. What is the velocity of the object if the energy is 128 joules? ________________________

Name ______________________________ Date ________________ Class______________

LESSON 2-9

Practice

Operations with Complex Numbers

Graph each complex number.

1. -6
2. $4i$
3. $6 + 7i$
4. $-8 - 5i$
5. $-3i$

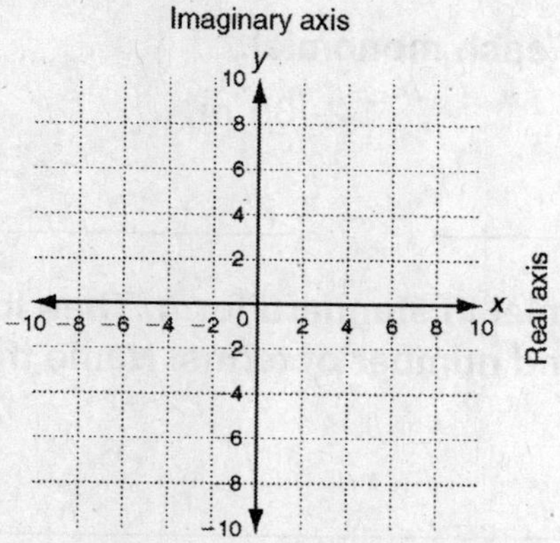

Find each absolute value.

6. $|4 + 2i|$ ________________

7. $|5 - i|$ ________________

8. $|-3i|$ ________________

Add or subtract. Write the result in the form *a* + *bi*.

9. $(-1 + 2i) + (6 - 9i)$ ________________

10. $(3 - 3i) - (4 + 7i)$ ________________

11. $(-5 + 2i) + (-2 + 8i)$ ________________

Multiply. Write the result in the form *a* + *bi*.

12. $3i(2 - 3i)$ ________________

13. $(4 + 5i)(2 + i)$ ________________

14. $(-1 + 6i)(3 - 2i)$ ________________

Simplify.

15. $\dfrac{2 + 4i}{3i}$ ________________

16. $\dfrac{3 + 2i}{4 + i}$ ________________

17. $2i^{11}$ ________________

Solve.

18. In electronics, the total resistance to the flow of electricity in a circuit is called the impedance, *Z*. Impedance is represented by a complex number. The total impedance in a series circuit is the sum of individual impedances. The impedance in one part of a circuit is $Z_1 = 3 + 4i$. In another part of a circuit, the impedance is $Z_1 = 5 - 2i$. What is the total impedance of the circuit?

____

Name ______________________ Date ____________ Class ____________

LESSON 3-1

Practice

Polynomials

Identify the degree of each monomial.

1. $6x^2$ ____________
2. $3p^3m^4$ ____________
3. $2x^8y^3$ ____________

Rewrite each polynomial in standard form. Then identify the leading coefficient, degree, and number of terms. Name the polynomial.

4. $6 + 7x - 4x^3 + x^2$

____

5. $x^2 - 3 + 2x^5 + 7x^4 - 12x$

____

Add or subtract. Write your answer in standard form.

6. $(2x^2 - 2x + 6) + (11x^3 - x^2 - 2 + 5x)$ ____________
7. $(x^2 - 8) - (3x^3 - 6x - 4 + 9x^2)$ ____________
8. $(5x^4 + x^2) + (7 + 9x^2 - 2x^4 + x^3)$ ____________
9. $(12x^2 + x) - (6 - 9x^2 + x^7 - 8x)$ ____________

Graph each polynomial function on a calculator. Describe the graph, and identify the number of real zeros.

10. $f(x) = x^3 + 2x^2 - 3$

____

____

11. $f(x) = x^4 - 5x^2 + 1$

____

____

Solve.

12. The height, *h*, in feet, of a baseball after being struck by a bat can be approximated by $h(t) = -16t^2 + 100t + 5$, where *t* is measured in seconds.

a. Evaluate *h(t)* for $t = 3$ and $t = 5$. ____________

b. Describe what the values of the function from part a represent.

____

Name ______________________ Date ______________ Class ______________

LESSON 3-2

Practice

Multiplying Polynomials

Find each product.

1. $4x^2(3x^2 + 1)$

2. $-9x(x^2 + 2x + 4)$

3. $-6x^2(x^3 + 7x^2 - 4x + 3)$

4. $x^3(-4x^3 + 10x^2 - 7x + 2)$

5. $-5m^3(7n^4 - 2mn^3 + 6)$

6. $(x + 2)(y^2 + 2y - 12)$

7. $(p + q)(4p^2 - p - 8q^2 - q)$

8. $(2x^2 + xy - y)(y^2 + 3x)$

Expand each expression.

9. $(3x - 1)^3$

10. $(x - 4)^4$

11. $3(a - 4b)^2$

12. $5\left(x^2 - 2y^3\right)^3$

Solve.

13. A biologist has found that the number of branches on a certain rare tree in its first few years of life can be modeled by the polynomial $b(y) = 4y^2 + y$. The number of leaves on each branch can be modeled by the polynomial $l(y) = 2y^3 + 3y^2 + y$, where y is the number of years after the tree reaches a height of 6 feet. Write a polynomial describing the total number of leaves on the tree.

Name ________________________ Date ______________ Class ______________

LESSON 3-3

Practice

Dividing Polynomials

Divide by using long division.

1. $(x^2 - x - 6) \div (x - 3)$

2. $(2x^3 - 10x^2 + x - 5) \div (x - 5)$

3. $(-3x^2 + 20x - 12) \div (x - 6)$

4. $(3x^3 + 9x^2 - 14) \div (x + 3)$

Divide by using synthetic division.

5. $(3x^2 - 8x + 4) \div (x - 2)$

6. $(5x^2 - 4x + 12) \div (x + 3)$

7. $(9x^2 - 7x + 3) \div (x - 1)$

8. $(-6x^2 + 5x - 10) \div (x + 7)$

Use synthetic substitution to evaluate the polynomial for the given value.

9. $P(x) = 4x^2 - 9x + 2$ for $x = 3$

10. $P(x) = -3x^2 + 10x - 4$ for $x = -2$

Solve.

11. The total number of dollars donated each year to a small charitable organization has followed the trend $d(t) = 2t^3 + 10t^2 + 2000t + 10{,}000$, where d is dollars and t is the number of years since 1990. The total number of donors each year has followed the trend $p(t) = t^2 + 1000$. Write an expression describing the average number of dollars per donor.

Name ______________________ Date ______________ Class ______________

LESSON 3-4

Practice

Factoring Polynomials

Determine whether the given binomial is a factor of the polynomial *P*(*x*).

1. $(x-4)$; $P(x) = x^2+8x-48$

2. $(x+5)$; $P(x) = 2x^2 - 6x - 1$

______________________ ______________________

3. $(x-6)$; $P(x) = -2x^2 + 15x - 18$

4. $(x+3)$; $P(x) = 2x^2 - x + 7$

______________________ ______________________

Factor each expression.

5. $2x^4 + 2x^3 - x^2 - x$

6. $4x^3 + x^2 - 8x - 2$

______________________ ______________________

7. $5x^6 - 5x^4 + x^3 - x$

8. $2x^4 + 54x$

______________________ ______________________

9. $64x^3 - 1$

10. $3x^4 + 24x$

______________________ ______________________

Solve.

11. Since 2006, the water level in a certain pond has been modeled by the polynomial $d(x) = -x^3 + 16x^2 - 74x + 140$, where the depth d, is measured in feet over x years. Identify the year that the pond will dry up. Use the graph to factor $d(x)$.

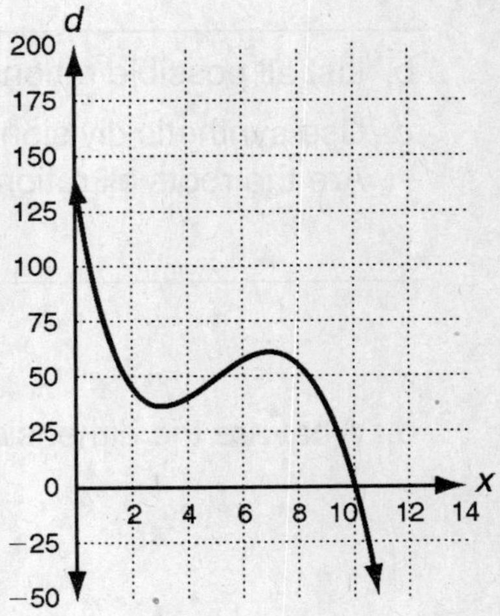

____

Name ______________________ Date ______________ Class ______________

LESSON 3-5

Practice

Finding Real Roots of Polynomial Equations

Solve each polynomial equation by factoring.

1. $9x^3 - 3x^2 - 3x + 1 = 0$

____

2. $x^5 - 2x^4 - 24x^3 = 0$

____

3. $3x^5 + 18x^4 - 21x^3 = 0$

____

4. $-x^4 + 2x^3 + 8x^2 = 0$

____

Identify the roots of each equation. State the multiplicity of each root.

5. $x^3 + 3x^2 + 3x + 1 = 0$

____

6. $x^3 + 5x^2 - 8x - 48 = 0$

____

Identify all the real roots of each equation.

7. $x^3 + 10x^2 + 17x = 28$

____

8. $3x^3 + 10x^2 - 27x = 10$

____

Solve.

9. An engineer is designing a storage compartment in a spacecraft. The compartment must be 2 meters longer than it is wide and its depth must be 1 meter less than its width. The volume of the compartment must be 8 cubic meters.

a. Write an equation to model the volume of the compartment.

____

b. List all possible rational roots. _________________________

c. Use synthetic division to find the roots of the polynomial equation. Are the roots all rational numbers?

____

d. What are the dimensions of the storage compartment? _________________________

Name ______________________ Date ______________ Class ______________

LESSON 3-6

Practice

Fundamental Theorem of Algebra

Write the simplest polynomial function with the given roots.

1. 1, 4, and –3

2. $\frac{1}{2}$, 5, and –2

3. $2i$, $\sqrt{3}$, and 4

4. $\sqrt{2}$, –5, and $-3i$

Solve each equation by finding all roots.

5. $x^4 - 2x^3 - 14x^2 - 2x - 15 = 0$

6. $x^4 - 16 = 0$

7. $x^4 + 4x^3 + 4x^2 + 64x - 192 = 0$

8. $x^3 + 3x^2 + 9x + 27 = 0$

Solve.

9. An electrical circuit is designed such that its output voltage, V, measured in volts, can be either positive or negative. The voltage of the circuit passes through zero at $t = 1$, 2, and 7 seconds. Write the simplest polynomial describing the voltage $V(t)$.

Name ____________________ Date ______________ Class ______________

LESSON 3-7

Practice

Investigating Graphs of Polynomial Functions

Identify the leading coefficient, degree, and end behavior.

1. $P(x) = 2x^5 - 6x^3 + x^2 - 2$

____

2. $Q(x) = -4x^2 + x - 1$

____

Identify whether the function graphed has an odd or even degree and a positive or negative leading coefficient.

3. 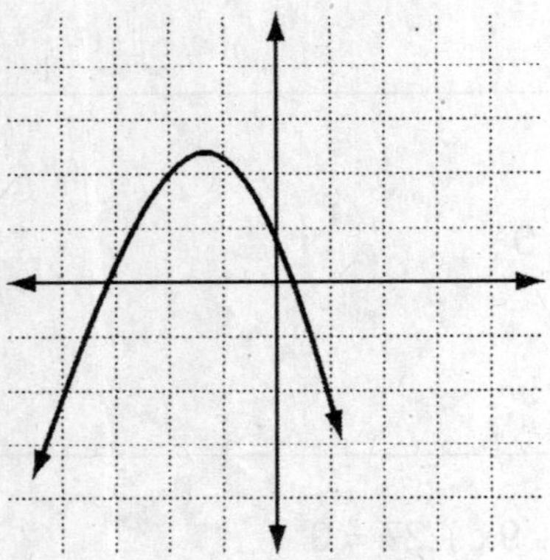

4. 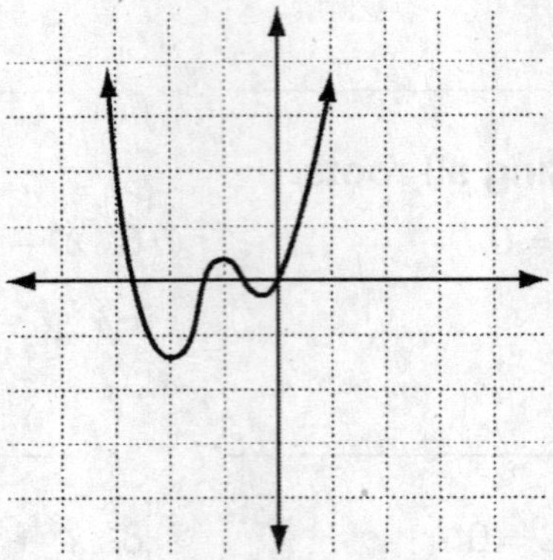

5. 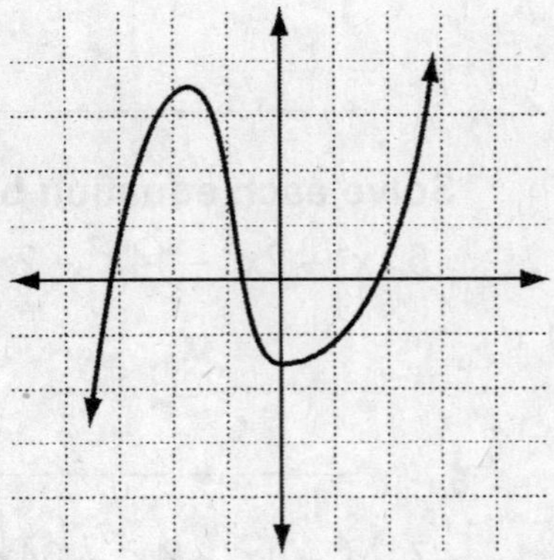

________________ ________________ ________________

Graph the function $P(x) = x^3 + 6x^2 + 5x - 12$.

6. Identify the possible rational roots.

____

7. Identify the zeros.

____

8. Describe the end behavior of the function.

____

9. Sketch the graph of the function.

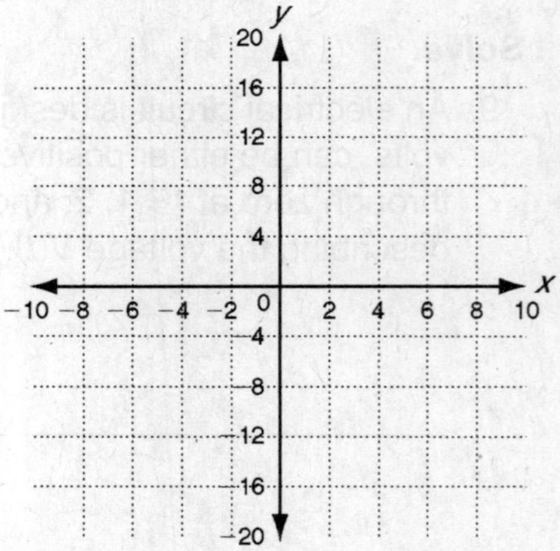

Solve.

10. The number, $N(y)$, of subscribers to a local magazine can be modeled by the function $N(y) = 0.1y^4 - 3y^3 + 10y^2 - 30y + 10{,}000$, where y is the number of years since the magazine was founded. Graph the polynomial on a graphing calculator and find the minimum number of subscribers and the year in which this occurs.

____

Name ______________________ Date ______________ Class ______________

LESSON 3-8

Practice

Transforming Polynomial Functions

For $f(x) = x^3 + 1$, write the rule for each function and sketch its graph.

1. $g(x) = f(x + 4)$

____

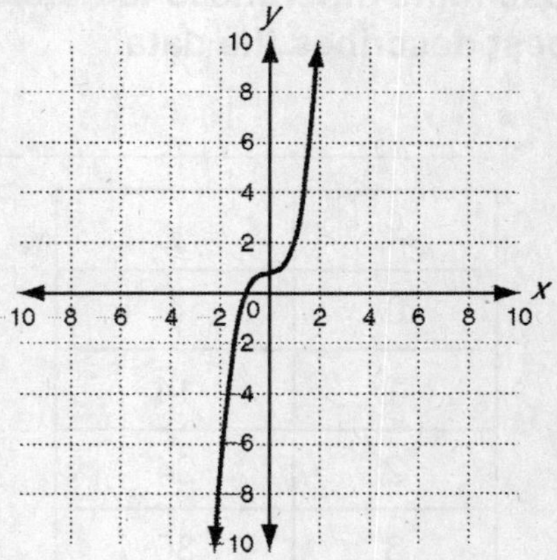

2. $g(x) = 3f(x)$

____

3. $g(x) = f\left(\dfrac{1}{2}x\right)$

____

Let $f(x) = -x^3 + 4x^2 - 5x + 12$. Write a function $g(x)$ that performs each transformation.

4. Reflect $f(x)$ across the y-axis

____

5. Reflect $f(x)$ across the x-axis

____

Let $f(x) = x^3 + 2x^2 - 3x - 6$. Describe $g(x)$ as a transformation of $f(x)$ and graph.

6. $g(x) = \dfrac{1}{4}f(x)$

____

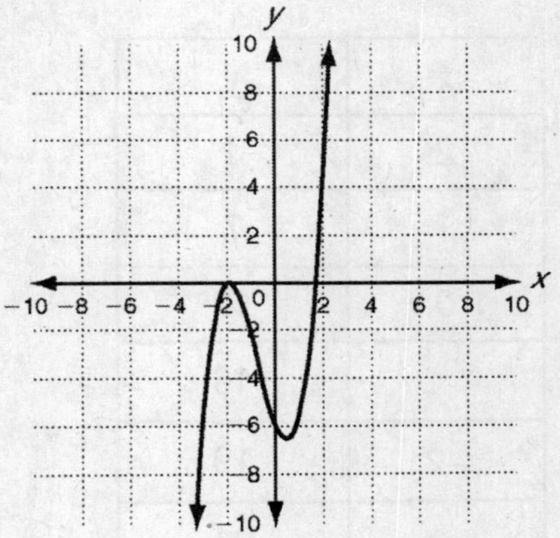

7. $g(x) = f(x - 6)$

____

Write a function that transforms $f(x) = x^3 + 4x^2 - x + 5$ in each of the following ways. Support your solution by using a graphing calculator.

8. Move 6 units up and reflect across the y-axis. _______________________

9. Compress vertically by a factor of 0.25 and move 3 units right. _______________________

Solve.

10. The number of participants, N, in a new Internet political forum during each month of the first year can be modeled by $N(t) = 4t^2 - t + 2000$, where t is the number of months since January. In the second year, the number of forum participants doubled compared to the same month in the previous year. Write a function that describes the number of forum participants in the second year.

____

Name ______________________ Date ______________ Class ______________

LESSON 3-9

Practice

Curve Fitting with Polynomial Models

Use finite differences to determine the degree of the polynomial that best describes the data.

1. ______________________

x	*y*
0	4
1	14
2	24
3	30
4	30
5	24

2. ______________________

x	*y*
−2	70
−1	35
0	15
1	7
2	8
3	15

3. ______________________

x	*y*
2	1
1	7
0	12
−1	16
−2	19
−3	21

4. ______________________

x	*y*
−6	−31
−5	0
−4	16
−3	19
−2	11
−1	−6

Solve.

5. The data set shows the average price for a luxury commodity for the years since 1998.

Year	1998	1999	2000	2001	2002	2003	2004	2005
Price ($)	1000	2027	4472	7507	10,472	12,875	14,392	14,867

a. Write a polynomial function for the data.

____

b. Predict the price of the item in 2008.

____

Name ____________________ Date ____________ Class ____________

LESSON 4-1

Practice

Exponential Functions, Growth, and Decay

Tell whether the function shows growth or decay. Then graph.

1. $g(x) = -(2)^x$

____

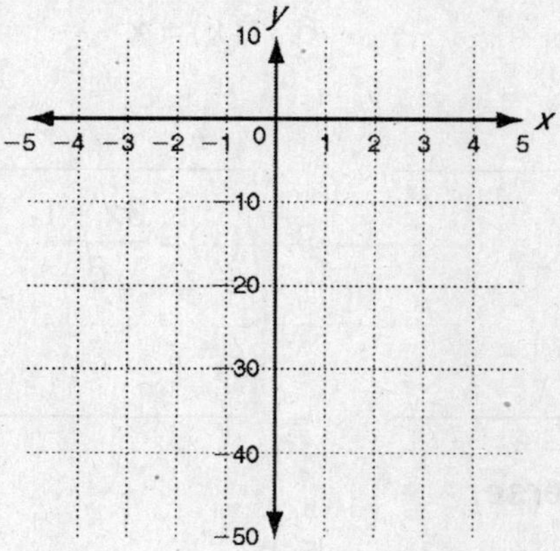

2. $h(x) = -0.5(0.2)^x$

____

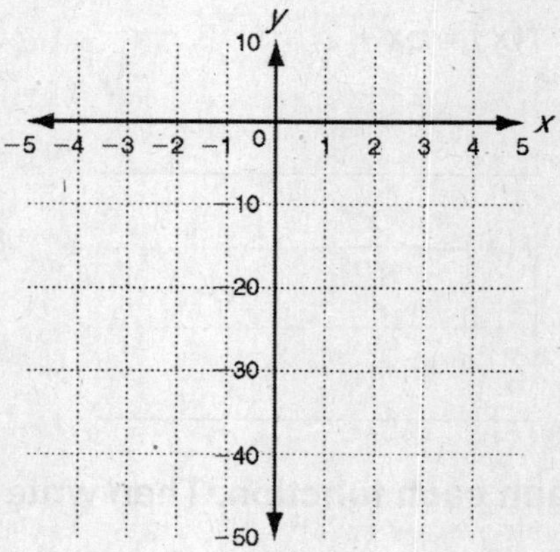

3. $j(x) = -2(0.5)^x$

____

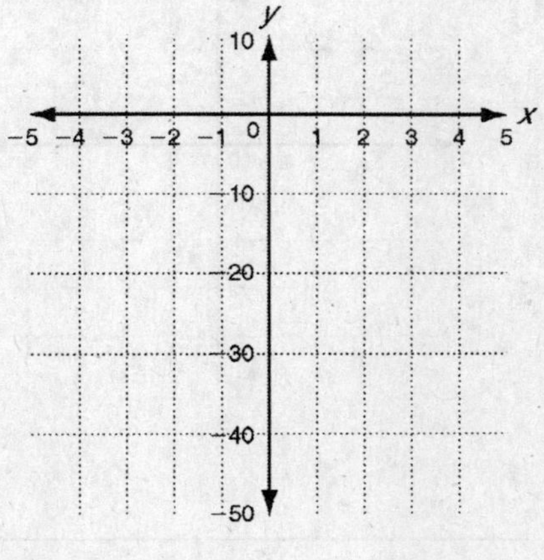

4. $p(x) = 4(1.4)^x$

____

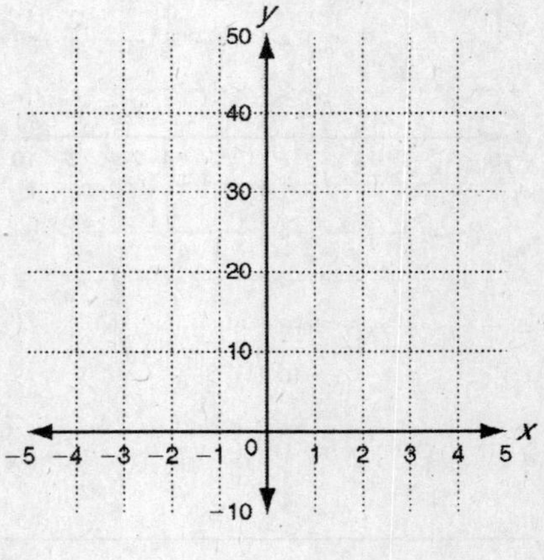

Solve.

5. A certain car depreciates about 15% each year.

   a. Write a function to model the depreciation in value for a car valued at $20,000.

   ____

   b. Graph the function.

   c. Suppose the car was worth $20,000 in 2005. What is the first year that the value of this car will be worth less than half of that value?

   ____

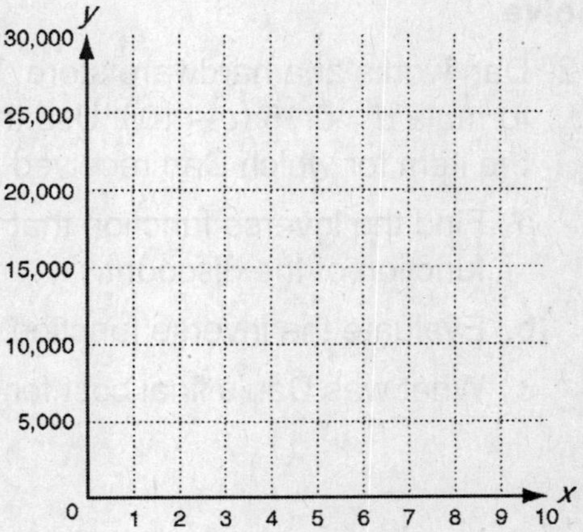

Name ______________________ Date ______________ Class ______________

LESSON 4-2

Practice

Inverses of Relations and Functions

Use inverse operations to write the inverse of each function.

1. $f(x) = 15x - 10$ ______
2. $f(x) = 10 - 4x$ ______
3. $f(x) = 12 - 9x$ ______
4. $f(x) = 5x + 2$ ______
5. $f(x) = x + 6$ ______
6. $f(x) = x + \frac{1}{2}$ ______
7. $f(x) = -\frac{x}{12}$ ______
8. $f(x) = \frac{x - 12}{4}$ ______
9. $f(x) = \frac{3x + 1}{6}$ ______

Graph each function. Then write and graph its inverse.

10. $f(x) = 2x - 4$

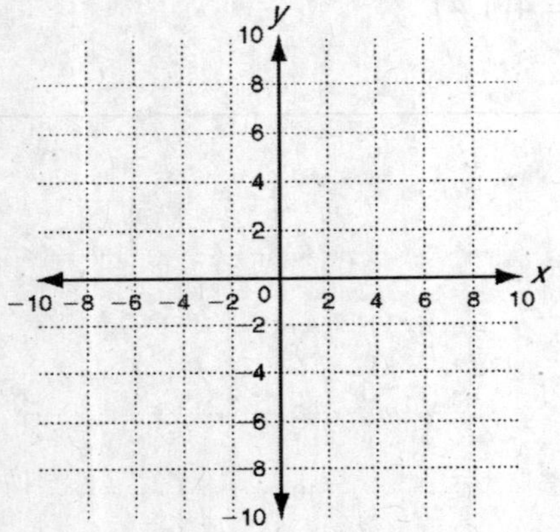

______

11. $f(x) = \frac{5}{2}x - 2$

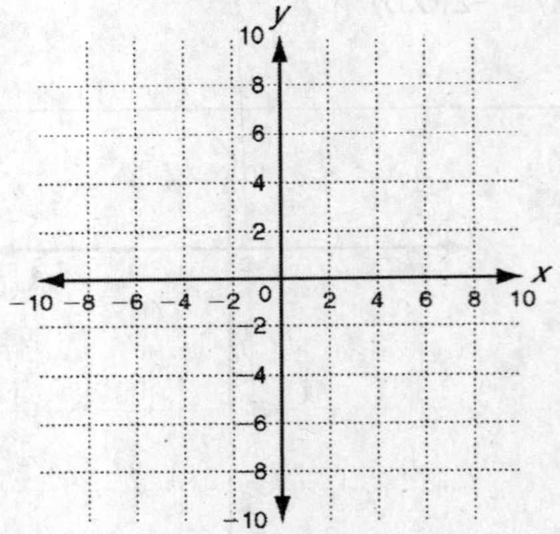

______

Solve.

12. Dan works at a hardware store. The employee discount is determined by the formula $d = 0.15(c - 10)$. Use the inverse of this function to find the cost of the item for which Dan received an $18.00 discount.

    a. Find the inverse function that models cost as a function of the discount. ______

    b. Evaluate the inverse function for $d = 18$. ______

    c. What was Dan's final cost for this item? ______

Name ______________________ Date ____________ Class ____________

LESSON 4-3

Practice

Logarithmic Functions

Write each exponential equation in logarithmic form.

1. $3^7 = 2187$ ____________
2. $12^2 = 144$ ____________
3. $5^3 = 125$ ____________

Write each logarithmic equation in exponential form.

4. $\log_{10} 100{,}000 = 5$ ____________
5. $\log_4 1024 = 5$ ____________
6. $\log_9 729 = 3$ ____________

Evaluate by using mental math.

7. log 1,000,000 ____________
8. log 10 ____________
9. log 1 ____________
10. $\log_4 16$ ____________
11. $\log_8 1$ ____________
12. $\log_5 625$ ____________

Use the given *x*-values to graph each function. Then graph its inverse. Describe the domain and range of the inverse function.

13. $f(x) = 2^x$; $x = -2, -1, 0, 1, 2, 3, 4$

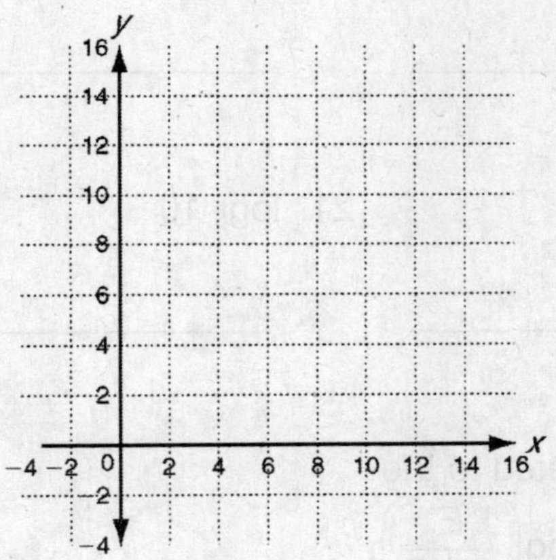

____

14. $f(x) = \left(\frac{1}{2}\right)^x$; $x = -3, -2, -1, 0, 1, 2, 3$

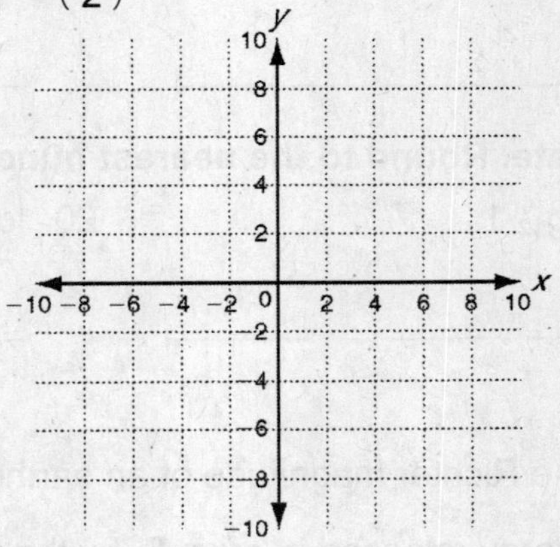

____

Solve.

15. The hydrogen ion concentration in moles per liter for a certain brand of tomato-vegetable juice is 0.000316.

 a. Write a logarithmic equation for the pH of the juice. ____________

 b. What is the pH of the juice? ____________

Name ______________________ Date ______________ Class______________

LESSON 4-4

Practice

Properties of Logarithms

Express as a single logarithm. Simplify, if possible.

1. $\log_3 9 + \log_3 27$ ________
2. $\log_2 8 + \log_2 16$ ________
3. $\log_{10} 80 + \log_{10} 125$ ________
4. $\log_6 8 + \log_6 27$ ________
5. $\log_3 6 + \log_3 13.5$ ________
6. $\log_4 32 + \log_4 128$ ________

Express as a single logarithm. Simplify, if possible.

7. $\log_2 80 - \log_2 10$ ________
8. $\log_{10} 4000 - \log_{10} 40$ ________
9. $\log_4 384 - \log_4 6$ ________
10. $\log_2 1920 - \log_2 30$ ________
11. $\log_3 486 - \log_3 2$ ________
12. $\log_6 180 - \log_6 5$ ________

Simplify, if possible.

13. $\log_4 4^6$ ________
14. $\log_5 5^{x-5}$ ________
15. $7^{\log_7 30}$ ________
16. $12^{\log_{12} 1}$ ________
17. $\log_8 8^5$ ________
18. $\log_3 9^4$ ________

Evaluate. Round to the nearest hundredth.

19. $\log_{12} 1$ ________
20. $\log_3 30$ ________
21. $\log_5 10$ ________

Solve.

22. The Richter magnitude of an earthquake, M, is related to the energy released in ergs, E, by the formula $M = \frac{2}{3}\log\left(\frac{E}{10^{11.8}}\right)$.
Find the energy released by an earthquake of magnitude 4.2. ________

Name ______________________ Date ______________ Class ______________

LESSON 4-5

Practice

Exponential and Logarithmic Equations and Inequalities

Solve and check.

1. $5^{2x} = 20$ ______________

2. $12^{2x-8} = 15$ ______________

3. $2^{x+6} = 4$ ______________

4. $16^{5x} = 64^{x+7}$ ______________

5. $243^{0.2x} = 81^{x+5}$ ______________

6. $25^{x} = 125^{x-2}$ ______________

7. $\left(\frac{1}{2}\right)^{x} = 16^{2}$ ______________

8. $\left(\frac{1}{32}\right)^{2x} = 64$ ______________

9. $\left(\frac{1}{27}\right)^{x-6} = 27$ ______________

Solve.

10. $\log_4 x^5 = 20$ ______________

11. $\log_3 x^6 = 12$ ______________

12. $\log_4 (x-6)^3 = 6$ ______________

13. $\log x - \log 10 = 14$ ______________

14. $\log x + \log 5 = 2$ ______________

15. $\log (x+9) = \log (2x-7)$ ______________

16. $\log (x+4) - \log 6 = 1$ ______________

17. $\log x^2 + \log 25 = 2$ ______________

18. $\log (x-1)^2 = \log (-5x-1)$ ______________

Use a table and graph to solve.

19. $2^{x-5} < 64$ ______________

20. $\log x^3 = 12$ ______________

21. $2^x 3^x = 1296$ ______________

Solve.

22. The population of a small farming community is declining at a rate of 7% per year. The decline can be expressed by the exponential equation $P = C(1 - 0.07)^t$, where P is the population after t years and C is the current population. If the population was 8,500 in 2004, when will the population be less than 6,000?

____

Name ________________ Date ____________ Class ____________

LESSON 4-6

Practice

The Natural Base, e

Graph.

1. $f(x) = e^{2x}$

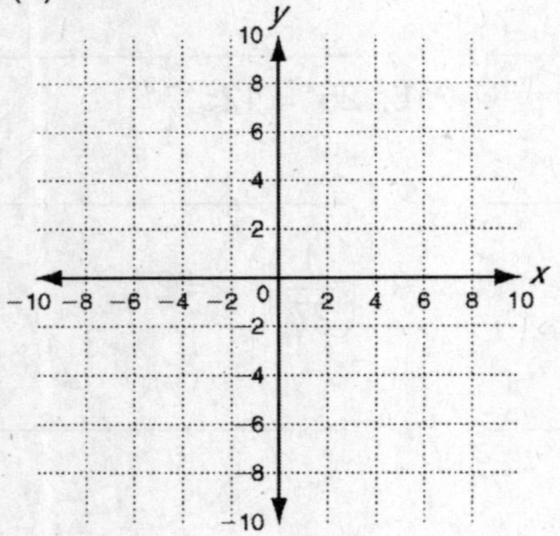

2. $f(x) = e^{0.5x}$

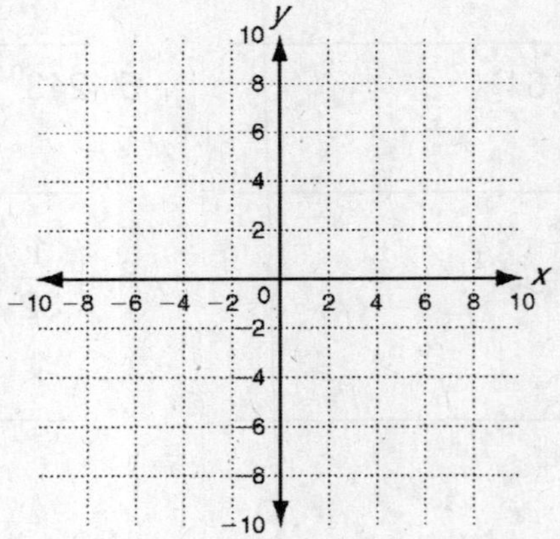

3. $f(x) = e^{1+x}$

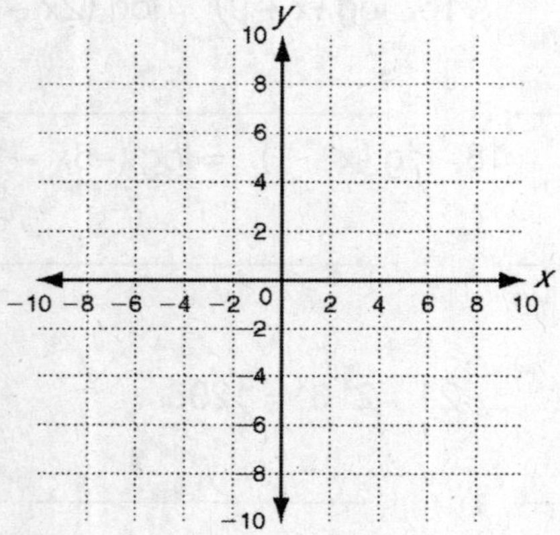

4. $f(x) = e^{2-x}$

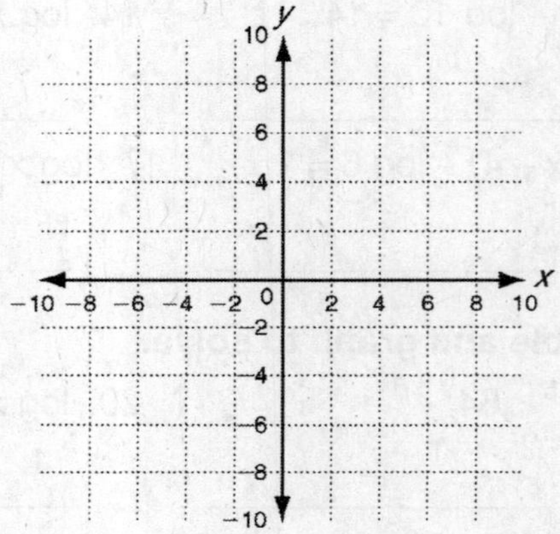

Simplify.

5. $\ln e^{x+2}$

6. $e^{\ln 2x}$

7. $e^{7 \ln x}$

8. $\ln e^{3x+1}$

9. $\ln e$

10. $\ln e^{2x+y}$

Solve.

11. Use the formula $A = Pe^{rt}$ to compute the total amount for an investment of $4500 at 5% interest compounded continuously for 6 years.

____

12. Use the natural decay function, $N(t) = N_0 e^{-kt}$, to find the decay constant for a substance that has a half-life of 1000 years.

____

Name ________________________ Date ______________ Class ______________

LESSON 4-7

Practice

Transforming Exponential and Logarithmic Functions

Graph each function. Find the asymptote. Tell how the graph is transformed from the graph of its parent function.

1. $f(x) = 5(2^x)$

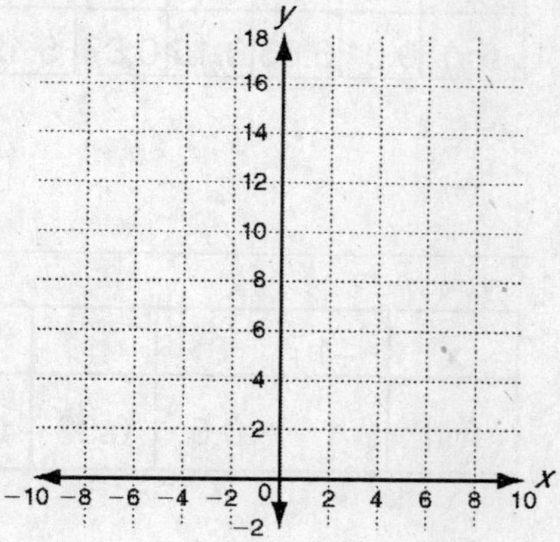

____

2. $f(x) = 5^{\frac{x}{4}}$

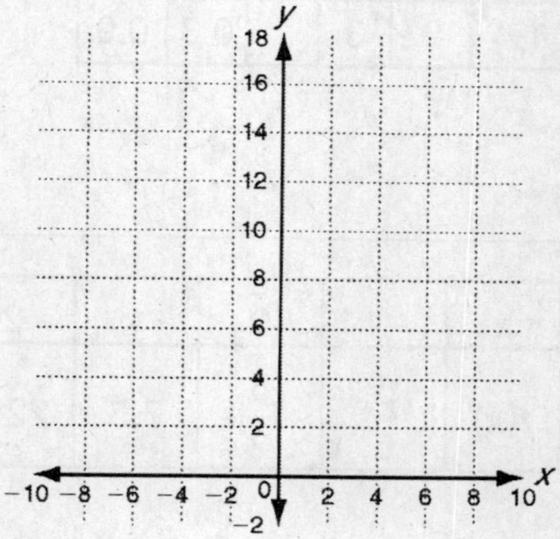

____

3. $f(x) = \log(x + 5)$

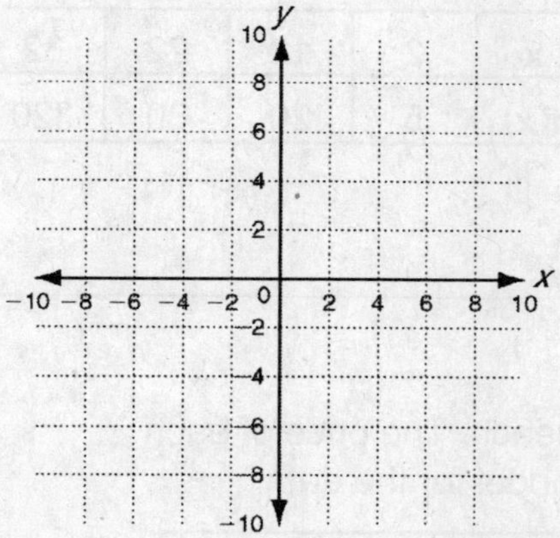

____

4. $f(x) = 3 + \ln x$

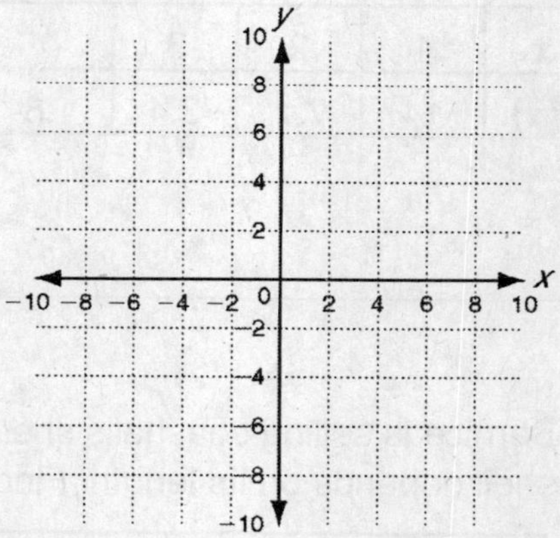

____

Write each transformed function.

5. The function $f(x) = \log(x + 1)$ is reflected across the *y*-axis and translated down 4 units. ______________________________

6. The function $f(x) = -8^{x-3}$ is reflected across the *x*-axis, compressed horizontally by a factor of 0.2, and stretched vertically by a factor of 2. ______________________________

Solve.

7. The function $A(t) = Pe^{rt}$ can be used to calculate the growth of an investment in which the interest is compounded continuously at an annual rate, *r*, over *t* years. What annual rate would double an investment in 8 years?

____

Name ______________________ Date ______________ Class ______________

LESSON 4-8

Practice

Curve Fitting with Exponential and Logarithmic Models

Determine whether *f* is an exponential function of *x*. If so, find the constant ratio.

1.

x	−1	0	1	2	3
f(*x*)	9	3	1	0.3	0.9

____

2.

x	−1	0	1	2	3
f(*x*)	0.01	0.03	0.15	0.87	5.19

____

3.

x	−1	0	1	2	3
f(*x*)	$\frac{5}{6}$	$\frac{5}{2}$	7.5	22.5	67.5

____

4.

x	−1	0	1	2	3
f(*x*)	1	0.5	0.33	0.25	0.2

____

Use exponential regression to find a function that models the data.

5.

x	1	2	3	4	5
f(*x*)	14	7.1	3.4	1.8	0.8

____

6.

x	2	12	22	32	42
f(*x*)	5	20	80	320	1280

____

Solve.

7. a. Bernice is selling seashells she has found at the beach. The price of each shell depends on its length. Find an exponential model for the data.

Length of Shell (cm)	5	8	12	20	25
Price ($)	2	3.5	5	18	40

____

b. What is the length of a shell selling for $9.00? ______________________

c. If Bernice found a 40 cm Conch shell. How much could she sell it for? ______________________

8. a. Use logarithmic regression to find a function that models this data.

Time (min)	1	2	3	4	5
Speed (m/s)	1.5	6.2	10.6	12.9	14.8

____

b. When will the speed exceed 20 m/s? ______________________

c. What will the speed be after 1 hour? ______________________

Name ______________________ Date ______________ Class ______________

LESSON 5-1

Practice

Variation Functions

Write and graph each function.

1. *y* varies directly as *x*, and $y = 30$ when $x = -6$.

____

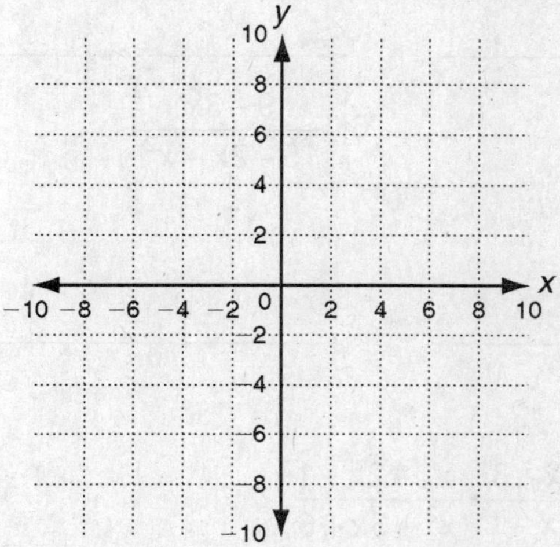

2. *y* varies inversely as *x*, and $y = 5$ when $x = 3$.

____

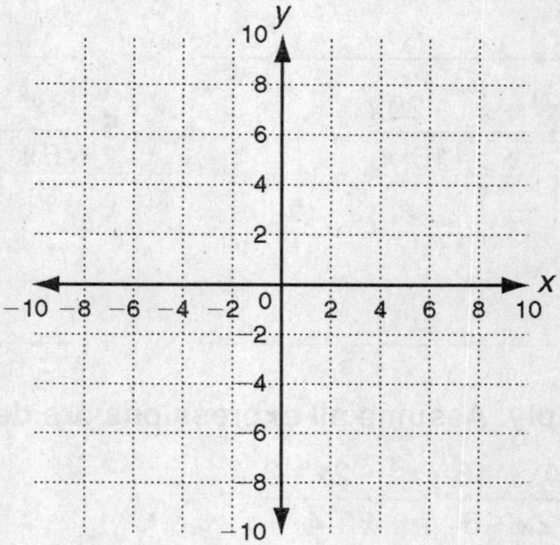

Determine whether each data set represents a direction variation, an inverse variation, or neither.

3.

x	8	12	16
y	2	3	4

____

4.

x	3	1	0.5
y	5	15	30

____

Solve.

5. The number of chaperones, *c*, needed for the class trip varies directly as the number of students, *s*, going on the trip, and $c = 7$ when $s = 56$. How many chaperones are needed if 104 students go on the class trip?

____

6. The owner of a bookstore developed a model for determining the price of rare comic books. The price, *P*, of each book should vary directly with the number of people, *N*, that have requested the book and inversely to the number of such books in existence, *M*. If $N = 10$ people, $M = 10{,}000$ copies, and $P = \$5$, then find *P* for $N = 200$ people and $M = 100$ copies.

____

Name ______________________ Date ____________ Class ____________

LESSON 5-2

Practice

Multiplying and Dividing Rational Expressions

Simplify. Identify any *x*-values for which the expression is undefined.

1. $\frac{x^2+3x+2}{x^2-3x-4}$

2. $\frac{4x^6}{2x^4}$

3. $\frac{x^2-x^3}{2x^2-5x+3}$

________________ ________________ ________________

4. $\frac{x^3+x^2-20x}{x^2-16}$

5. $\frac{3x^2-9x-12}{6x^2+9x+3}$

6. $\frac{9-3x}{15-2x-x^2}$

________________ ________________ ________________

Multiply. Assume all expressions are defined.

7. $\frac{4x+16}{2x+6} \bullet \frac{x^2+2x-3}{x+4}$

8. $\frac{x+3}{x-1} \bullet \frac{x^2-2x+1}{x^2+5x+6}$

________________ ________________

Divide. Assume all expressions are defined.

9. $\frac{5x^6}{x^2y} \div \frac{10x^2}{y}$

10. $\frac{x^2-2x-8}{x^2-2x-15} \div \frac{2x^2-8x}{2x^2-10x}$

________________ ________________

Solve. Check your solution.

11. $\frac{x^2+x-12}{x-3} = 15$

12. $\frac{2x^2+8x-10}{2x^2+14x+20} = 4$

________________ ________________

Solve.

13. The distance, *d*, traveled by a car undergoing constant acceleration, *a*, for a time, *t*, is given by $d = v_0t + \frac{1}{2}at^2$, where v_0 is the initial velocity of the car. Two cars are side by side with the same initial velocity. One car accelerates, $a = A$, and the other car does not accelerate, $a = 0$. Write an expression for the ratio of the distance traveled by the accelerating car to the distance traveled by the nonaccelerating car as a function of time.

____

Name ______________________ Date ______________ Class ______________

LESSON 5-3

Practice

Adding and Subtracting Rational Expressions

Find the least common multiple for each pair.

1. $3x^2y^6$ and $5x^3y^2$

2. $x^2 + x - 2$ and $x^2 - x - 6$

Add or subtract. Identify any *x*-values for which the expression is undefined.

3. $\dfrac{2x-3}{x+4} + \dfrac{4x-5}{x+4}$

4. $\dfrac{x+12}{2x-5} - \dfrac{3x-2}{2x-5}$

5. $\dfrac{x+4}{x^2-x-12} + \dfrac{2x}{x-4}$

6. $\dfrac{3x^2-1}{x^2-3x-18} - \dfrac{x+2}{x-6}$

7. $\dfrac{x+2}{x^2-2x-15} + \dfrac{x}{x+3}$

8. $\dfrac{x+6}{x^2-7x-18} - \dfrac{2x}{x-9}$

Simplify. Assume all expressions are defined.

9. $\dfrac{\dfrac{x-1}{x+5}}{\dfrac{x+6}{x-3}}$

10. $\dfrac{\dfrac{12}{x+3}}{\dfrac{x^2+1}{x-2}}$

Solve.

11. A messenger is required to deliver 10 packages per day. Each day, the messenger works only for as long as it takes to deliver the daily quota of 10 packages. On average, the messenger is able to deliver 2 packages per hour on Saturday and 4 packages per hour on Sunday. What is the messenger's average delivery rate on the weekend?

Name ________________________ Date ______________ Class ______________

LESSON 5-4

Practice

Rational Functions

Using the graph of $f(x)=\frac{1}{x}$ as a guide, describe the transformation and graph the function.

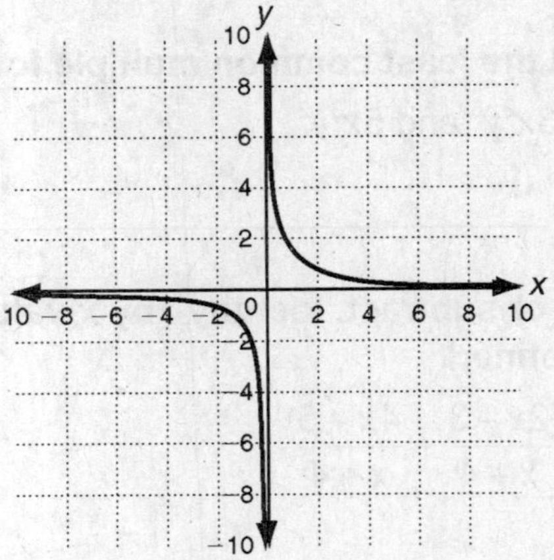

1. $g(x)=\dfrac{2}{x+4}$

____

Identify the asymptotes, domain, and range of each function.

2. $g(x)=\dfrac{1}{x-3}+5$ ________________________

____

3. $g(x)=\dfrac{1}{x+8}-1$ ________________________

____

Identify the zeros and asymptotes of the function. Then graph.

4. $f(x)=\dfrac{x^2+4x-5}{x+1}$

a. Zeros:

____

b. Vertical asymptote:

____

c. Horizontal asymptote:

____

d. Graph.

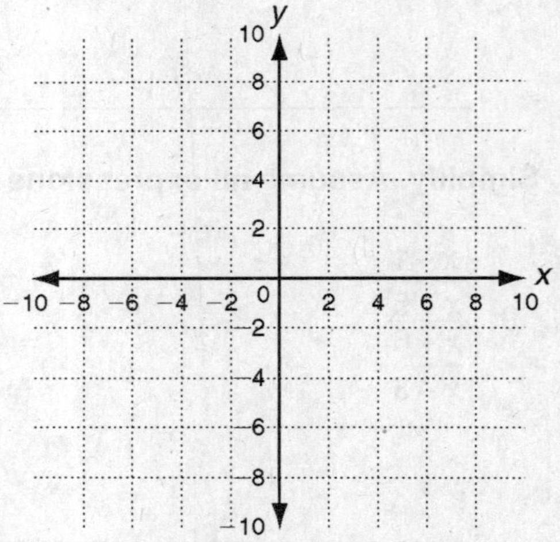

Solve.

5. The number, n, of daily visitors to a new store can be modeled by the function $n=\dfrac{(250x+1000)}{x}$, where x is the number of days the store has been open.

a. What is the asymptote of this function and what does it represent? ________________________

b. To the nearest integer, how many visitors can be expected on day 30? ________________________

Name ________________________ Date ______________ Class ______________

LESSON 5-5

Practice

Solving Rational Equations and Inequalities

Solve each equation.

1. $x - \frac{6}{x} = 5$

____

2. $\frac{15}{4} = \frac{6}{x} + 3$

____

3. $x = \frac{3}{x} + 2$

____

4. $\frac{4}{x^2 - 4} = \frac{1}{x - 2}$

____

Solve each inequality by using a graphing calculator and a table.

5. $\frac{6}{x + 1} < -3$

____

6. $\frac{x}{x - 2} \geq 0$

____

7. $\frac{2x}{x + 5} \leq 0$

____

8. $\frac{-x}{x - 3} \geq 0$

____

Solve each inequality algebraically.

9. $\frac{12}{x + 4} \leq 4$

____

10. $\frac{7}{x + 3} < -5$

____

11. $\frac{x}{x - 2} > 9$

____

12. $\frac{2x}{x - 5} \geq 3$

____

Solve.

13. The time required to deliver and install a computer at a customer's location is $t = 4 + \frac{d}{r}$, where t is time in hours, d is the distance, in miles, from the warehouse to the customer's location, and r is the average speed of the delivery truck. If it takes 6.2 hours for the employee to deliver and install a computer for a customer located 100 miles from the warehouse, what is the average speed of the delivery truck?

____

Name ______________________ Date ______________ Class ______________

LESSON 5-6

Practice

Radical Expressions and Rational Exponents

Simplify each expression. Assume all variables are positive.

1. $\sqrt[3]{125x^9}$ ________

2. $\sqrt[4]{\dfrac{x^8}{81}}$ ________

3. $\sqrt[3]{\dfrac{64x^3}{8}}$ ________

Write each expression in radical form, and simplify.

4. $64^{\frac{5}{6}}$ ________

5. $27^{\frac{2}{3}}$ ________

6. $(-8)^{\frac{4}{3}}$ ________

Write each expression by using rational exponents.

7. $\sqrt[5]{51^4}$ ________

8. $\left(\sqrt{169}\right)^3$ ________

9. $\sqrt[7]{36^{14}}$ ________

Simplify each expression.

10. $4^{\frac{3}{2}} \cdot 4^{\frac{5}{2}}$ ________

11. $\dfrac{27^{\frac{4}{3}}}{27^{\frac{2}{3}}}$ ________

12. $\left(125^{\frac{2}{3}}\right)^{\frac{1}{2}}$ ________

13. $(27 \cdot 64)^{\frac{2}{3}}$ ________

14. $\left(\dfrac{1}{243}\right)^{\frac{1}{5}}$ ________

15. $64^{-\frac{1}{3}}$ ________

16. $\left(-27x^6\right)^{\frac{1}{3}}$ ________

17. $\dfrac{(25x)^{\frac{3}{2}}}{5 \cdot x^{\frac{1}{2}}}$ ________

18. $(4x)^{-\frac{1}{2}} \cdot (9x)^{\frac{1}{2}}$ ________

Solve.

19. In every atom, electrons orbit the nucleus with a certain characteristic velocity known as the Fermi–Thomas velocity, equal to $\dfrac{Z^{\frac{2}{3}}}{137}$ c, where Z is the number of protons in the nucleus and c is the speed of light. In terms of c, what is the characteristic Fermi-Thomas velocity of the electrons in Uranium, for which $Z = 92$?

____

Name ______________________ Date ______________ Class ______________

LESSON 5-7

Practice

Radical Functions

Graph each function, and identify its domain and range.

1. $f(x)=\sqrt{x-4}$

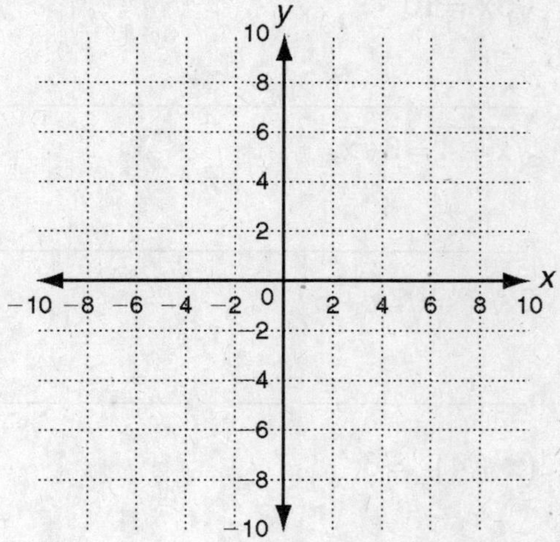

Domain: ______________

Range: ______________

2. $f(x)=\sqrt[3]{x}+1$

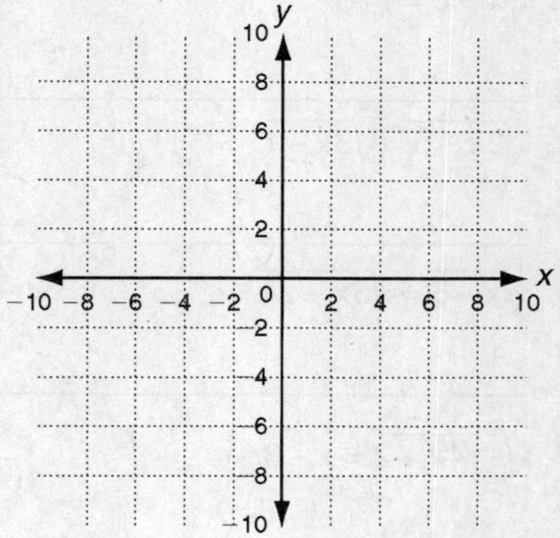

Domain: ______________

Range: ______________

Using the graph of $f(x)=\sqrt{x}$ as a guide, describe the transformation.

3. $g(x)=4\sqrt{x+8}$ ______________

4. $g(x)=-\sqrt{3x}+2$ ______________

Use the description to write the square root function *g*.

5. The parent function $f(x)=\sqrt{x}$ is reflected across the *y*-axis, vertically stretched by a factor of 7, and translated 3 units down. ______________

6. The parent function $f(x)=\sqrt{x}$ is translated 2 units right, compressed horizontally by a factor of $\frac{1}{2}$, and reflected across the *x*-axis. ______________

Solve.

7. For a gas with density, *n*, measured in atoms per cubic centimeter, the average distance, *d*, between atoms is given by $d=\left(\frac{3}{4\pi n}\right)^{\frac{1}{3}}$. The gas in a certain region of space has a density of just 10 atoms per cubic centimeter. Find the average distance between the atoms in that region of space.

____

Name ______________________ Date ______________ Class ______________

LESSON 5-8

Practice

Solving Radical Equations and Inequalities

Solve each equation.

1. $\sqrt{x+6}=7$

2. $\sqrt{5x}=10$

3. $\sqrt{2x+5}=\sqrt{3x-1}$

4. $\sqrt{x+4}=3\sqrt{x}$

5. $\sqrt[3]{x-6}=\sqrt[3]{3x+24}$

6. $3\sqrt[3]{x}=\sqrt[3]{7x+5}$

7. $\sqrt{-14x+2}=x-3$

8. $(x+4)^{\frac{1}{2}}=6$

9. $4(x-3)^{\frac{1}{2}}=8$

10. $4(x-12)^{\frac{1}{3}}=-16$

Solve each inequality.

11. $\sqrt{3x+6}\le 3$

12. $\sqrt{x-4}+3>9$

13. $\sqrt{x+7}\ge\sqrt{2x-1}$

14. $\sqrt{2x-7}>9$

Solve.

15. A biologist is studying two species of animals in a habitat. The population, p_1, of one of the species is growing according to $p_1=500t^{\frac{3}{2}}$ and the population, p_2, of the other species is growing according to $p_2=100t^2$ where time, t, is measured in years. After how many years will the populations of the two species be equal?

Name ______________________ Date ______________ Class ______________

LESSON 6-1

Practice

Multiple Representations of Functions

Match each situation to its corresponding graph. Sketch a possible graph of the situation if it does not match any of the given graphs.

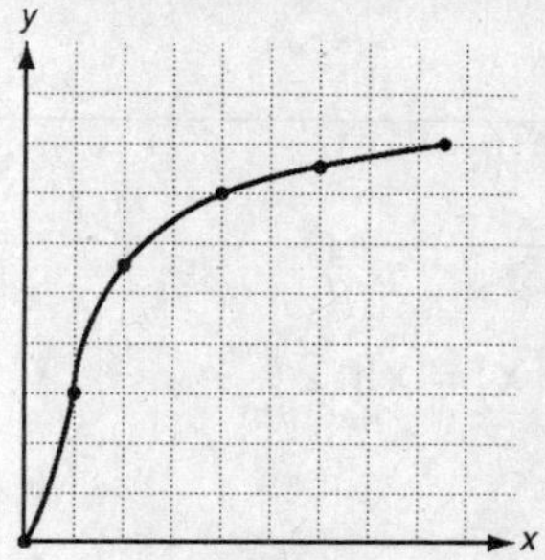

Graph A

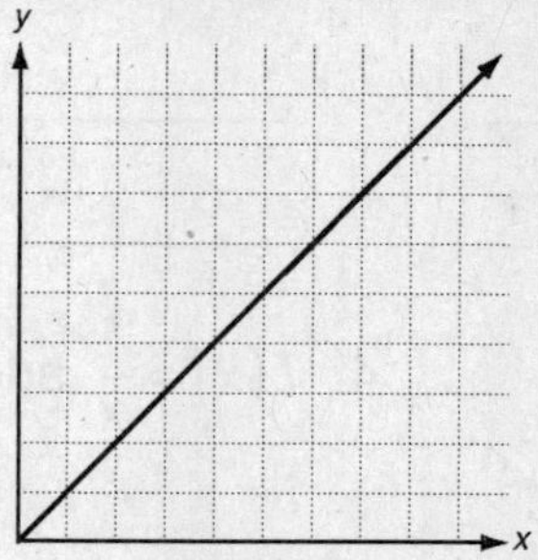

Graph B

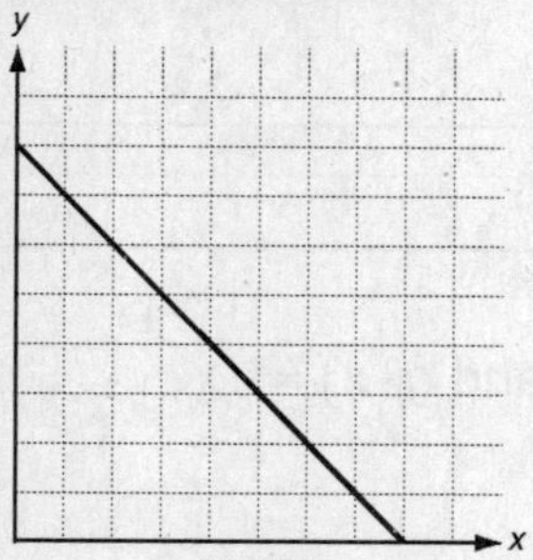

Graph C

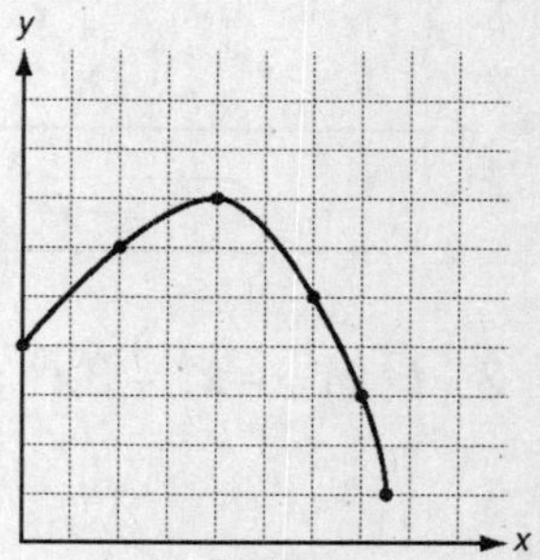

Graph D

1. A train is approaching its destination. ____________
2. The temperature on an autumn day increases until late afternoon and then drops dramatically by late evening. ____________
3. A helium balloon is released by a running child on a calm day. ____________
4. A golf ball hit by a golfer flies over the trees and disappears into the woods. ____________

Solve.

5. A bicyclist leaves a rest stop at 1:00 and heads directly for home at a constant rate. The table shows how far, *d*, he is from home in miles as a function of time, *t*. Create a graph and an equation to predict the time he will arrive home.

t	1:00	1:10	1:20	1:30	1:40
d	18.5	16.0	13.5	11.0	8.5

____

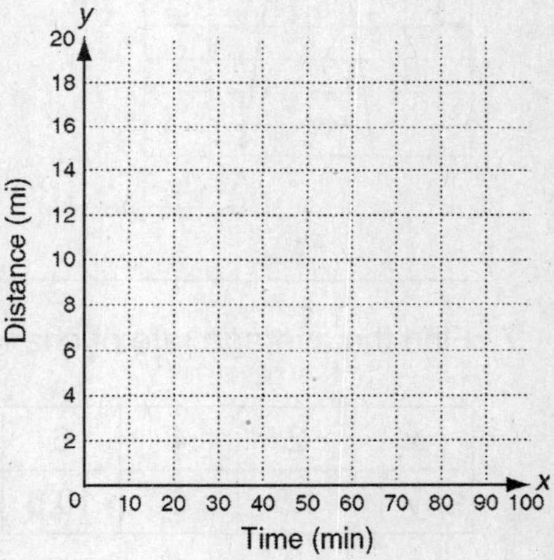

6. New members at a fitness club pay $200 to start and then $20 per month for life. Create a table, a graph, and an equation that represent the total cost of enrollment, *c*, as a function of months, *m*, of participation.

m			
c			

____

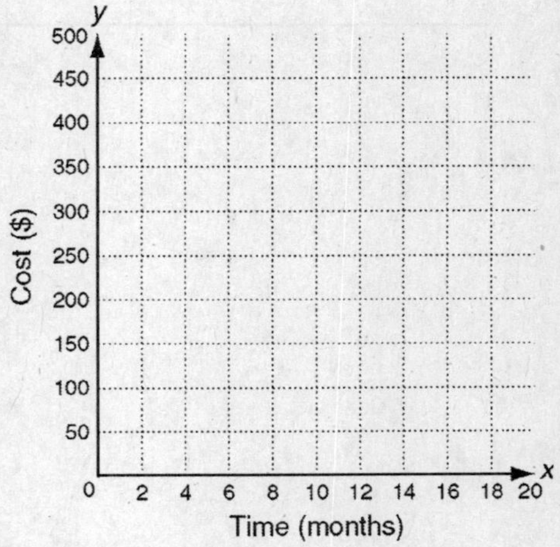

Name ______________________ Date ______________ Class ______________

LESSON 6-2

Practice B

Comparing Functions

Compare the end behavior for each pair of functions.

1. $f(x) = x^4 - x^2 + 4x$ and $g(x) = -5x + 2$

____

____

2. $f(x) = x^3$ and $g(x) = -x^2$

____

____

3. $f(x) = -x^4 - 3x^3$ and $g(x) = \sqrt{x}$

____

____

4. $f(x) = \frac{1}{x}$ and $g(x) = x\ln 2$

____

____

Determine which function matches the graphical representation shown.

5.

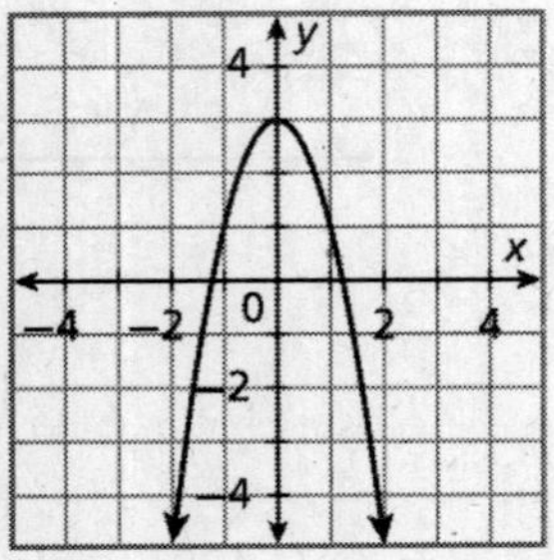

____

6.

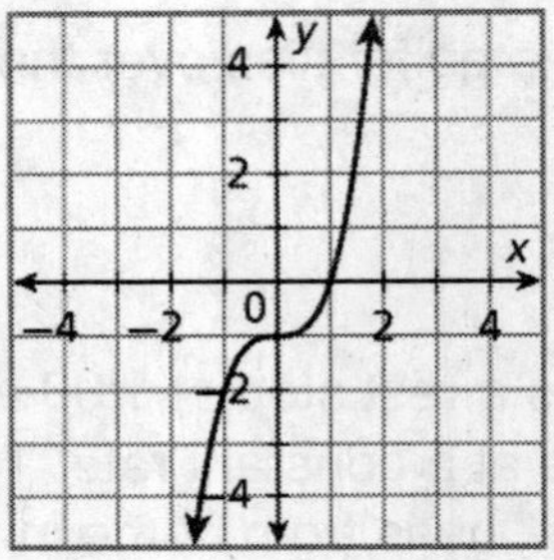

____

7. Find the average rate of change for the data in the following chart.

x	2	4	6	8	10	12	14
y	1.5	6	10.5	15	19.5	24	28.5

____

Name ______________________ Date ____________ Class ____________

LESSON 6-3

Practice

Piecewise Functions

Evaluate each piecewise function for $x = -8$ and $x = 5$.

1. $f(x) = \begin{cases} 2x & \text{if } x < 0 \\ 0 & \text{if } x \geq 0 \end{cases}$

____

2. $g(x) = \begin{cases} 2 - x & \text{if } x \leq 5 \\ -x^2 & \text{if } 5 < x < 8 \\ 6 & \text{if } 8 \leq x \end{cases}$

____

3. $h(x) = \begin{cases} 2x + 4 & \text{if } x \leq -8 \\ -1 & \text{if } -8 < x < 5 \\ x^2 & \text{if } 5 \leq x \end{cases}$

____

4. $k(x) = \begin{cases} 15 & \text{if } x \leq -5 \\ x & \text{if } -5 < x < 1 \\ 7 - \frac{x}{2} & \text{if } 1 < x \end{cases}$

____

Graph each function.

5. $f(x) = \begin{cases} 6 & \text{if } x < -2 \\ 3x & \text{if } -2 \leq x \end{cases}$

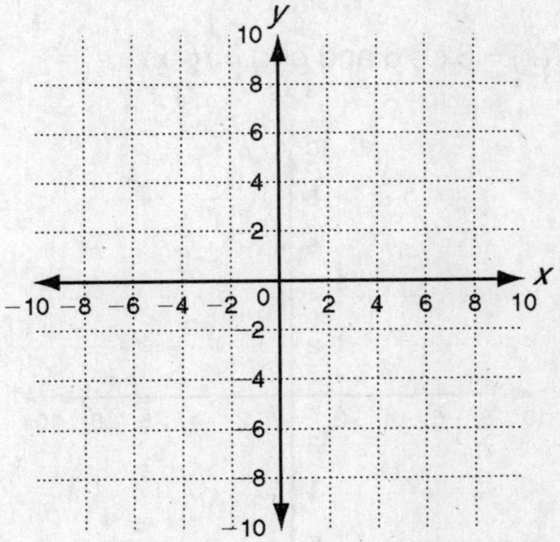

6. $g(x) = \begin{cases} 12 - x & \text{if } x \leq 5 \\ x + 2 & \text{if } 5 < x \end{cases}$

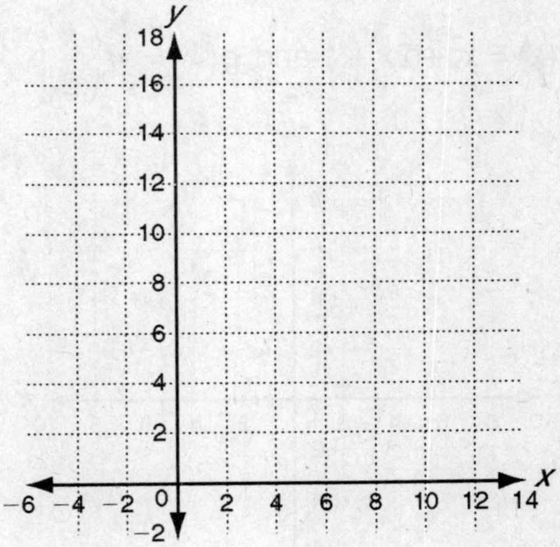

Solve.

7. An airport parking garage costs \$20 per day for the first week. After that, the cost decreases to \$17 per day.

   a. Write a piecewise function for the cost of parking a car for x days. ________________________

   b. What is the cost to park for 10 days? ________________________

   c. Ms. Anderson went on two trips. On the first, she parked at the garage for 5 days; on the second, she parked at the garage for 8 days. What was the difference in the cost of parking between the two trips? ________________________

Name ______________________ Date ______________ Class ______________

LESSON 6-4

Practice

Transforming Functions

Given $f(x) = \begin{cases} x^2 - 9x - 1 & \text{if } x < 0 \\ 10 - x & \text{if } x \geq 0 \end{cases}$, write the rule for each function.

1. $h(x)$, a reflection of $f(x)$ across the y-axis ______________

2. $k(x)$, a vertical stretch of $f(x)$ by a factor of 2 ______________

3. $g(x)$, a horizontal translation 2 units right ______________

Identify the *x*- and *y*-intercepts of $f(x)$. Then identify the *x*- and *y*-intercepts of $g(x)$.

4. $f(x) = x^2 - 36$ ______________ $g(x) = f(2x)$ ______________

5. $f(x) = -3x + 12$ ______________ $g(x) = -2f(x)$ ______________

Given $f(x)$, graph $g(x)$.

6. $f(x) = x^2 + 2x + 1$ and $g(x) = -f\left(\dfrac{x}{2}\right)$

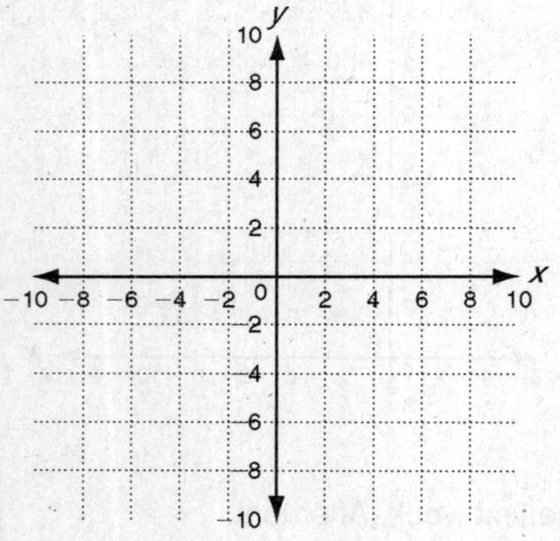

7. $f(x) = 3x - 6$ and $g(x) = f(-x)$

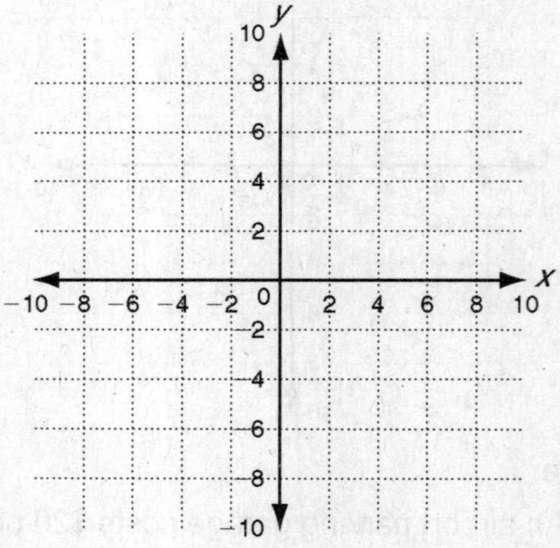

Solve.

8. Ron walks from his house to the parking garage at a rate of 8 feet per second. The parking garage is 3960 feet from the house. The distance can be represented by the function $D(x) = 8x$, where x is the time, in seconds. Walking back to his house, Ron increases his speed by 25%.

   a. Write a function to show the distance Ron is from the house as he walks back from the parking garage. ______________

   b. How far is Ron from his house 2 minutes after leaving the parking garage? ______________

Name ______________________ Date ______________ Class ______________

LESSON 6-5

Practice

Operations with Functions

Use the following functions for Exercises 1–18.

$f(x) = \dfrac{1}{2x}$ $\quad g(x) = x^2$ $\quad h(x) = x - 8$ $\quad k(x) = \sqrt{x}$

Find each function.

1. $(gk)(x)$ ______________
2. $(g + h)(x)$ ______________
3. $(g - h)(x)$ ______________
4. $(fg)(x)$ ______________
5. $(gh)(x)$ ______________
6. $\left(\dfrac{f}{g}\right)(x)$ ______________

Find each value.

7. $g(k(9))$ ______________
8. $h(g(-3))$ ______________
9. $g(h(-3))$ ______________
10. $k(h(12))$ ______________
11. $f(g(4))$ ______________
12. $f(h(1))$ ______________

Write each composite function. State the domain of each.

13. $f(g(x))$ ______________
14. $h(g(x))$ ______________
15. $h(k(x))$ ______________
16. $f(k(x))$ ______________
17. $k(g(x))$ ______________
18. $k(h(x))$ ______________

Solve.

19. A retail shoe store manager sets the price of shoes at twice his cost. The shoe store is now offering a 40% discount on all shoes.

    a. Write a composite function for the price of a pair of shoes after the discount. ______________

    b. If a pair of shoes cost the manager $25, what is the sale price? ______________

Name ______________________ Date ____________ Class ____________

LESSON 6-6

Practice

Functions and Their Inverses

Find the inverse of each function. Determine whether the inverse is a function and state its domain and range.

1. $k(x) = 10x + 5$

2. $d(x) = 6 - 2x$

3. $f(x) = (x - 5)^2$

4. $g(x) = \dfrac{4 - x}{2}$

5. $h(x) = \sqrt{x^2 - 9}$

6. $b(x) = 2\log x$

Determine by composition whether each pair of functions are inverses.

7. $g(x) = \sqrt{x} - 4$ and $r(x) = x^2 + 4$ for $x \geq 0$

8. $s(x) = \dfrac{2}{x - 2}$ and $t(x) = \dfrac{x + 2}{-2}$

9. $u(x) = \dfrac{x^2}{4} - 1$ for $x \geq -1$ and $v(x) = \pm 2\sqrt{x + 1}$

10. $A(x) = \log (x - 1)^4$ and $B(x) = 1 + \log^{-1}\left(\dfrac{x}{4}\right)$

Solve.

11. So far, Rhonda has saved \$3000 for her college expenses. She plans to save \$30 each month. Her college fund can be represented by the function $f(x) = 30x + 3000$.

    a. Find the inverse of $f(x)$.

    b. What does the inverse represent?

    c. When will the fund reach \$3990?

    d. How long will it take her to reach her goal of \$4800?

Name ______________________ Date ______________ Class ______________

LESSON 6-7

Practice

Modeling Real-World Data

Use constant differences or ratios to determine which parent function would best model the given data set.

1.

x	12	16	20	24	28
y	0.8	3.6	16.2	72.9	328.05

____

2.

x	13	19	25	31	37	43
y	–1	17	35	53	71	89

____

3.

x	2	7	12	17	22
y	–100	–55	40	185	380

____

4.

x	0.10	0.37	0.82	1.45	2.26
y	0.3	0.6	0.9	1.2	1.5

____

Write a function that models the data set.

5.

x	2.2	2.6	3.0	3.4	3.8
y	0.68	4.52	9.0	14.12	19.88

____

6.

x	–5	0	5	10	15	20
y	8	6	4	2	0	–2

____

7.

x	0.3	0.7	1.1	1.5	1.9
y	2.5	3	3.6	4.32	5.184

____

8.

x	0.06	0.375	0.96	1.815	2.94
y	0.2	0.5	0.8	1.1	1.4

____

9.

x	–6	1	8	15	22
y	15	1	30.12	102.36	217.72

____

10.

x	0.32	2.07	4.8	8.51	13.2
y	0.9	1.6	2.3	3.0	3.7

____

Solve.

11. The table shows the population growth of a small town.

Years after 1974	1	6	11	16	21	26	31
Population	662	740	825	908	1003	1095	1200

a. Write a function that models the data. ________________________

b. Use your model to predict the population in 2020. ________________________

Name ______________________ Date ______________ Class ______________

LESSON 7-1

Practice

Permutations and Combinations

Use the Fundamental Counting Principle.

1. The soccer team is silk-screening T-shirts. They have 4 different colors of T-shirts and 2 different colors of ink. How many different T-shirts can be made using one ink color on a T-shirt? ________________

2. A travel agent is offering a vacation package. Participants choose the type of tour, a meal plan, and a hotel class from the table below.

Tour	Meal	Hotel
Walking	Restaurant	4-Star
Boat	Picnic	3-Star
Bicycle		2-Star
		1-Star

How many different vacation packages are offered? ________________

Evaluate.

3. $\frac{3!6!}{3!}$

4. $\frac{10!}{7!}$

5. $\frac{9!-6!}{(9-6)!}$

________________ ________________ ________________

Solve.

6. In how many ways can the debate team choose a president and a secretary if there are 10 people on the team? ________________

7. A teacher is passing out first-, second-, and third-place prizes for the best student actor in a production of *Hamlet*. If there are 14 students in the class, in how many different ways can the awards be presented? ________________

Evaluate.

8. ${}_5P_4$

9. ${}_3C_2$

10. ${}_8P_3$

________________ ________________ ________________

Solve.

11. Mrs. Marshall has 11 boys and 14 girls in her kindergarten class this year.

a. In how many ways can she select 2 girls to pass out a snack? ________________

b. In how many ways can she select 5 boys to pass out new books? ________________

c. In how many ways can she select 3 students to carry papers to the office? ________________

Name ______________________ Date ______________ Class ______________

LESSON 7-2

Practice

Theoretical and Experimental Probability

Solve.

1. A fruit bowl contains 4 green apples and 7 red apples. What is the probability that a randomly selected apple will be green? ______________

2. When two number cubes labeled 1–6 are rolled, what is the probability that the result will be two 4's? ______________

3. Joanne is guessing which day in November is Bess's birthday. Joanne knows that Bess's birthday does not fall on an odd-numbered day. What is the probability that Joanne will guess the correct day on her first try? ______________

4. Tom has a dollar's worth of dimes and a dollar's worth of nickels in his pocket.
   a. What is the probability he will randomly select a nickel from his pocket? ______________
   b. What is the probability he will randomly select a dime from his pocket? ______________

5. Clarice has 7 new CDs; 3 are classical music and the rest are pop music. If she randomly grabs 3 CDs to listen to in the car on her way to school, what is the probability that she will select only classical music? ______________

6. Find the probability that a point chosen at random inside the larger circle shown here will also fall inside the smaller circle.

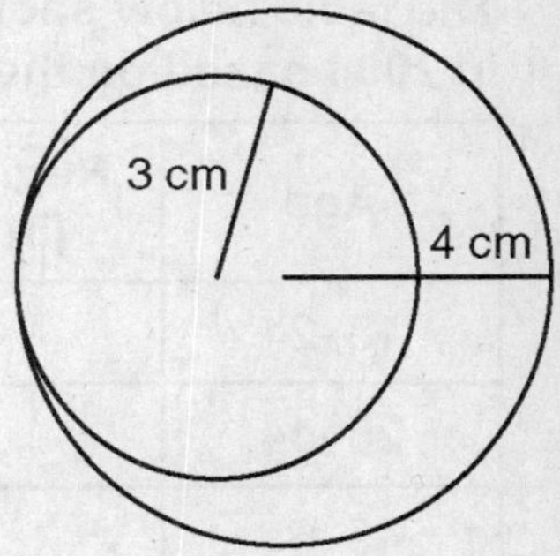

____

Frank is playing darts. The results of his throws are shown in the table below. Assume that his results continue to follow this trend.

Color Hit	Number of Throws
Blue	12
Red	5
White	2

Find the experimental probability of each event.

7. Frank's next throw will hit white. ______________

8. Frank's next throw will hit blue. ______________

9. Frank's next throw will hit either red or white. ______________

10. Frank's next throw will NOT hit red. ______________

Name ______________________ Date ______________ Class ______________

LESSON 7-3

Practice

Independent and Dependent Events

Find each probability.

1. A bag contains 5 red, 3 green, 4 blue, and 8 yellow marbles. Find the probability of randomly selecting a green marble, and then a yellow marble if the first marble is replaced. ______________
2. A sock drawer contains 5 rolled-up pairs of each color of socks, white, green, and blue. What is the probability of randomly selecting a pair of blue socks, replacing it, and then randomly selecting a pair of white socks? ______________

Two 1–6 number cubes are rolled—one is black and one is white.

3. The sum of the rolls is greater than or equal to 6 and the black cube shows a 3.
   a. Explain why the events are dependent.
   ____
   b. Find the probability. ______________
4. The white cube shows an even number, and the sum is 8.
   a. Explain why the events are dependent.
   ____
   b. Find the probability. ______________

The table below shows numbers of registered voters by age in the United States in 2004 based on the census. Find each probability in decimal form.

Age	Registered Voters (in thousands)	Not Registered to Vote (in thousands)
18–24	14,334	13,474
25–44	49,371	32,763
45–64	51,659	19,355
65 and over	26,706	8,033

5. A randomly selected person is registered to vote, given that the person is between the ages of 18 and 24. ______________
6. A randomly selected person is between the ages of 45 and 64 and is not registered to vote. ______________
7. A randomly selected person is registered to vote and is at least 65 years old. ______________

A bag contains 12 blue cubes, 12 red cubes, and 20 green cubes. Determine whether the events are independent or dependent, and find each probability.

8. A green cube and then a blue cube are chosen at random with replacement. ______________
9. Two blue cubes are chosen at random without replacement. ______________

Name ______________________ Date ______________ Class ______________

LESSON 7-4

Practice

Two-Way Tables

1. The table shows the results of a customer satisfaction survey of 100 randomly selected shoppers at the mall who were asked if they would shop at an earlier time if the mall opened earlier. Make a table of joint and marginal relative frequencies.

	Ages 10–20	Ages 21–45	Ages 46–65	65 and Older
Yes	13	2	8	24
No	25	10	15	3

	Ages 10–20	Ages 21–45	Ages 46–65	65 and Older	Total
Yes					
No					
Total					

2. Jerrod collected data on 100 randomly selected students, and summarized the results in a table.

		Owns an MP3 Player	
		Yes	No
Owns a Smart phone	Yes	28	12
	No	34	26

a. Make a table of the joint relative frequencies and marginal relative frequencies. Round to the nearest hundredth where appropriate.

		Owns an MP3 player		
		Yes	No	Total
Owns a Smart Phone	Yes			
	No			
	Total			

b. If you are given that a student owns an MP3 player, what is the probability that the student also owns a smart phone? Round your answer to the nearest hundredth.

____

c. If you are given that a student owns a smart phone, what is the probability that the student also owns an MP3 player? Round your answer to the nearest hundredth.

____

Name ______________________ Date ______________ Class ______________

LESSON 7-5

Practice

Compound Events

A can of vegetables with no label has a $\frac{1}{8}$ chance of being green beans and a $\frac{1}{5}$ chance of being corn.

1. Explain why the events "green beans" or "corn" are mutually exclusive.

____

2. What is the probability that an unlabeled can of vegetables is either green beans or corn? ______________

Ben rolls a 1–6 number cube. Find each probability.

3. Ben rolls a 3 or a 4. ______________

4. Ben rolls a number greater than 2 or an even number. ______________

5. Ben rolls a prime number or an odd number. ______________

Of the 400 doctors who attended a conference, 240 practiced family medicine and 130 were from countries outside the United States. One-third of the family medicine practitioners were not from the United States.

6. What is the probability that a doctor practices family medicine or is from the United States? ______________

7. What is the probability that a doctor practices family medicine or is not from the United States? ______________

8. What is the probability that a doctor does not practice family medicine or is from the United States? ______________

Use the data to fill in the Venn diagram. Then solve.

9. Of the 220 people who came into the Italian deli on Friday, 104 bought pizza and 82 used a credit card. Half of the people who bought pizza used a credit card. What is the probability that a customer bought pizza or used a credit card?

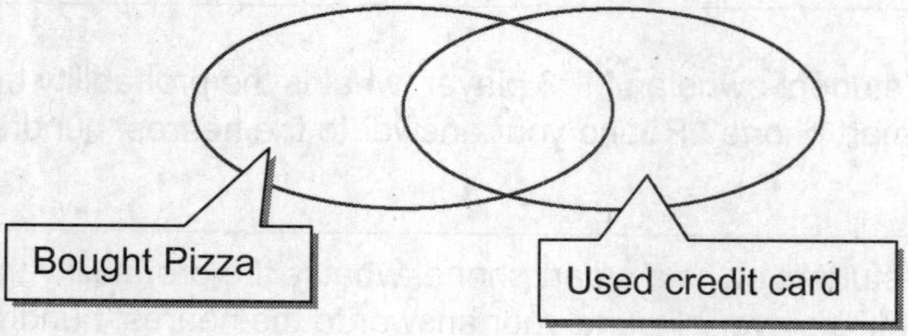

____

Solve.

10. There are 6 people in a gardening club. Each gardener orders seeds from a list of 11 different types of seeds available. What is the probability that 2 gardeners will order the same type of seeds? ______________

Name ________________________ Date ______________ Class ______________

LESSON 8-1

Practice

Measures of Central Tendency and Variation

Find the mean, median, and mode of each data set.

1. { 12, 11, 17, 3, 9, 14, 16, 2 }
   a. Mean ______________
   b. Median ______________
   c. Mode ______________

2. { 6, 9, 9, 20, 4, 5, 9, 13, 10, 1 }
   a. Mean ______________
   b. Median ______________
   c. Mode ______________

Make a box-and-whisker plot of the data. Find the interquartile range.

3. { 3, 7, 7, 3, 10, 1, 6, 6 }

____

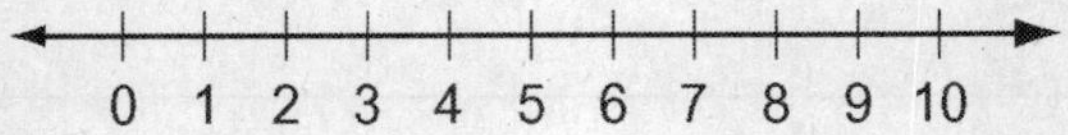

4. { 1, 2, 3, 5, 3, 5, 8, 2 }

____

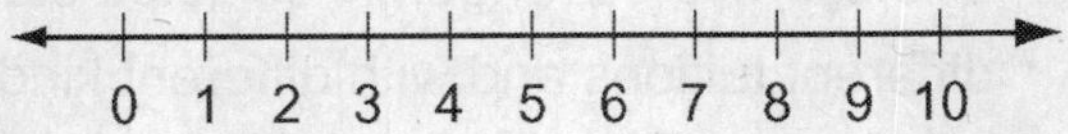

Find the variance and standard deviation.

5. { 7, 4, 3, 9, 2 } ______________

6. { 35, 67, 21, 16, 24, 51, 18, 32 } ______________

7. { 19, 23, 17, 20, 25, 19, 15, 22 } ______________

8. { 5, 12, 10, 13, 8, 11, 15, 12 } ______________

Solve.

9. The probability distribution for the amount of rain that falls on Boston in May each year is given below. Find the expected amount of rain for Boston in May. ______________

Inches of Rain, *n*	5	6	7	8
Probability	0.05	0.10	0.64	0.21

10. A biologist is growing bacteria in the lab. For a certain species of bacteria, she records these doubling times: 41 min, 45 min, 39 min, 42 min, 38 min, 88 min, 43 min, 40 min, 44 min, 39 min, 42 min, and 40 min.
    a. Find the mean of the data. ______________
    b. Find the standard deviation. ______________
    c. Identify any outliers. ______________
    d. Describe how any outlier affects the mean and the standard deviation.

____

Name ______________________ Date ______________ Class ______________

LESSON 8-2

Practice

Data Gathering

Decide which sampling method, A or B, is less likely to result in a biased sample.

1. A representative of a mall wants to know whether the mall's customers would shop at a new audio equipment store in the mall.
   A. He asks every 5th person walking into an electronics store if they would shop at a new audio equipment store in the mall.
   B. He asks every 5th person walking into the main mall entrance if they would shop at a new audio equipment store in the mall.

____

2. A researcher wants to know the average amount of debt college students expect to have.
   A. She surveys 50 randomly-selected students on several college campuses with different tuitions and with different kinds of programs.
   B. She surveys 100 randomly-selected students at an expensive medical school.

____

Decide which survey is more likely to result in a sample that is representative of the population.

3. The manager of a movie theater wants to know what type of movies his customers prefer.
   A. He asks every 3rd customer coming out of a comedy movie.
   B. He asks every 10th customer who enters the theater during a day when the theater is showing an assortment of movie types.

____

4. The chef at a restaurant wants to get feedback on the quality of his food.
   A. He has each server at the restaurant survey 5 customers during each shift for a week.
   B. He has the servers at the restaurant survey every customer on a night when family members of employees get a discount.

____

100 students out of 1000 at a school were surveyed. The results are recorded in each problem below. Predict the number of students in the entire population that would answer similarly.

5. 50 ride the bus to school.

____

6. 10 transferred from another school.

____

____

Name ______________________ Date ______________ Class ______________

LESSON 8-3

Practice

Surveys, Experiments, and Observational Studies

Explain whether each situation is an experiment or an observational study. The first problem has been completed for you.

1. A park ranger measures the change in height of all trees of a similar species and age over a month. Half the trees are within a quarter of a mile from a large lake and half are further away.

   Observational study; the park ranger gathers data without controlling the individuals or applying a treatment.

2. A park ranger plants 10 trees within a quarter of a mile from a large lake and 10 trees of a similar species and age further than half of a mile from the lake. He then measures the growth of all trees over a month.

   ____

3. A caretaker at a zoo records the sleeping habits of the wildcats at the zoo for a month.

   ____

The study described below is a randomized comparative experiment. Describe the treatment, the treatment group, and the control group. The first problem has been completed for you.

4. A researcher feeds one group of rats high-fat and high-calorie foods like cheesecake, bacon, and pastries. She feeds a second group of rats a normal, nutritious diet. For two weeks, the researcher records how many calories each rat eats daily, as well as how often it goes to its feeding bowl. She compares the data from the one group to the data from the other and finds that the rats that eat the nutritious food get hungry less often and eat a smaller number of calories overall.

   The treatment is *feeding high-fat and high-calorie foods.* The treatment group is the rats that were fed the diet that was not nutritious. The control group is the rats that were fed the nutritious diet.

5. A college professor wants to know if students learn as well in an online class as in person. He decides to offer the same course both online and in a classroom. Students who sign up for the course are told they will be assigned to either class randomly. The professor then gives the same test to both classes and compares the scores.

   ____

Explain whether the research topic is best addressed through an experiment or an observational study. Then explain how you would set up the experiment or observational study.

6. Does being a smoker cause people to get minor sicknesses more often?

   ____

   ____

Name ______________________ Date ______________ Class ______________

LESSON 8-4

Practice

Significance of Experimental Results

Use the information below to answer the questions. The first problem has been answered for you.

1. The makers of a light bulb claim that their light bulbs last longer than the leading brand. A researcher decides to test this claim by seeing how many hours 5 light bulbs of each kind last before burning out. State the null hypothesis for the experiment.

   The light bulbs will burn out in the same amount of time, so any difference in how long the bulbs in each group last is caused by chance.

2. Mr. Kaplan is supervising an experiment in his science class in order to find out whether adding salt to water causes the water to boil more quickly. Each student in the class records how long it takes his or her beaker of water to boil when placed on a burner. Half of the students do not add salt to the water (control group) and half add a teaspoon of salt to the water (treatment group). The time, in seconds, that it takes each beaker of water to boil is shown in the chart below.

Control	65	78	64	71	75
Treatment	61	70	73	69	64

   a. State the null hypothesis for the experiment.

   ____

   b. Compare the results for the control group and the treatment group. How different are the numbers in the one group when compared to the other? Is there enough evidence to reject the null hypothesis?

   ____

   ____

3. Carly's friend claims that if Carly takes a new route, she can get to school in 15 (so $\mu = 15$) minutes, which is less than the time it usually takes her. Carly uses the new route for 9 (so $n = 9$) school days and finds that the average amount of time it takes her to get to school with the new route is 16 minutes (so $\bar{x} = 16$), with a standard deviation of 1 minute (so $\sigma = 1$).

   b. Use the formula $z = \dfrac{\bar{x} - \mu}{\frac{\sigma}{\sqrt{n}}}$ to find the z-score: ______________

   c. Compare the z-score to 1.96 in order to explain whether it is likely that Carly's claim is true.

   ____

   ____

Name ______________________ Date ______________ Class______________

LESSON 8-5

Practice

Sampling Distributions

Classify each sample as *simple random*, *systematic*, *stratified*, *cluster*, *convenience*, or *self-selected*. The first problem has been completed for you.

1. The business manager at a gym calls every 20th member on the complete list of members to find out whether they would use a childcare service during their workouts.

   Solution: systematic

2. A hair salon surveys every customer on a busy Saturday and on a slow Monday about whether the services took longer than the customer expected.

   ____

3. A college newspaper reporter surveys 50 randomly selected students on campus to see if they are happy with the college.

   ____

4. A school's counselor asks the first 10 students she meets with on a Monday if they are planning to attend a job fair.

   ____

5. The junior class president wants to know what theme song her classmates would like at junior prom. She is deciding between three different survey methods:
   a. Survey all juniors in her math class.
   b. Survey every 10th junior on the junior class roster.
   c. Survey 50 randomly selected students at a meeting that every junior is required to attend.

   Which method would represent the opinion of the junior class most accurately? Explain.

   ____

   ____

Does each survey indicate the majority's preference? Explain your response.

6. A news group polls citizens about whether they are in favor of a new school. 58% are in favor of the new school and 42% are not. The survey's margin of error is ±3%.

   ____

   ____

7. Hilary and Michael are running for class president. A poll taken a week before the election shows that 47% of the students favor Hilary and 53% favor Michael. The survey's margin of error is ±4%.

   ____

   ____

Name ______________________ Date ______________ Class ______________

LESSON 8-6

Practice

Binomial Distributions

Use the Binomial Theorem to expand each binomial.

1. $(x + y)^3$

____

2. $(2x + y)^4$

____

3. $(m + 3n)^3$

____

4. $(p + q)^5$

____

Solve.

5. Of the new cars in a car dealer's lot, 1 in 6 are white. Today, 4 cars were sold.
   a. What is the probability that 3 of the cars sold were white?

   ____

   b. What is the probability that at least 2 of the cars sold were white?

   ____

6. At a small college, $\frac{1}{3}$ of all of the students are vegetarians. There are 5 students in line at the cafeteria.
   a. What is the probability that all 5 students are vegetarians?

   ____

   b. What is the probability that just 1 of the students is a vegetarian?

   ____

7. Ellen plays 8 hands of a card game with her friends. She has a 1 in 3 chance of winning each hand. What is the probability that she will win exactly half of the hands played?

____

8. In a lottery, each ticket buyer has a 1 in 10 chance of winning a prize. If Chip buys 10 tickets, what is the probability that he will win at least 1 prize?

____

Name ________________ Date ____________ Class ____________

LESSON 8-7

Practice

Fitting to a Normal Distribution

1. In a plant shop, the heights of young plants are normally distributed with a mean of 50 mm and a standard deviation of 4 mm. Count grid squares in the graph to estimate the probability that a plant chosen at random by a customer will be less than 54 mm tall.

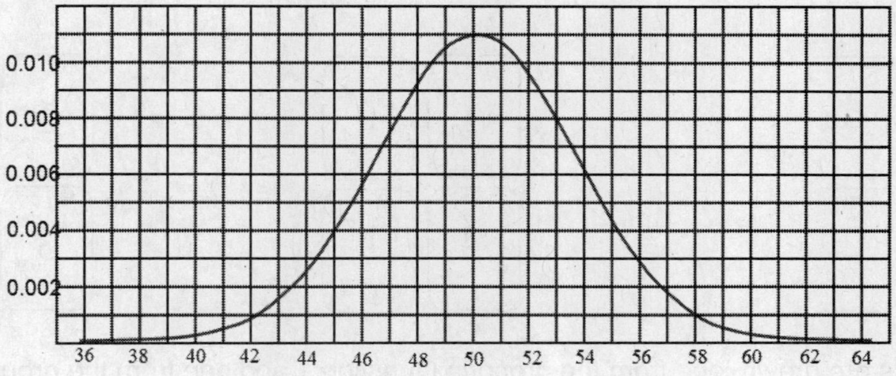

Scores on a test are normally distributed with a mean of 80 and a standard deviation of 5. Use the table below to find each probability. The first probability has been found for you.

$z = \dfrac{x - \mu}{\sigma}$	−2	−1	0	1	2
Area Under Standard Normal Curve	0.02	0.16	0.5	0.84	0.98

2. A randomly selected student scored below 80. $z = \dfrac{80 - 80}{5} = 0$, so P(below 80) = 0.5

3. A randomly selected student scored above 90. ________

4. A randomly selected student scored below 75. ________

5. A randomly selected student scored between 75 and 85. ________

6. The wait times, in minutes, of 10 customers in line at a grocery store are given below. The mean wait time is 7 minutes. How many data points fall below the mean? Use your answer to explain whether the data appear to be normally distributed.

16	15	10	7	5
5	4	3	3	2

Name ______________________ Date ______________ Class ______________

LESSON 8-8

Practice

Analyzing Decisions

In each of the problems below, a card will be drawn at random from the four cards shown. Find the expected value for each group of cards. The first problem has been completed for you.

1. $EV = 6\left(\frac{3}{4}\right) + 2\left(\frac{1}{4}\right) = 5$

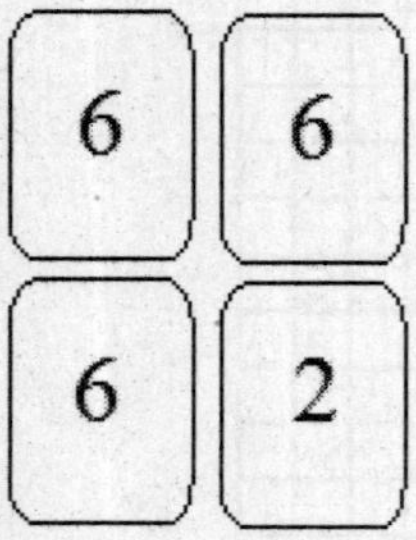

2. ______________________

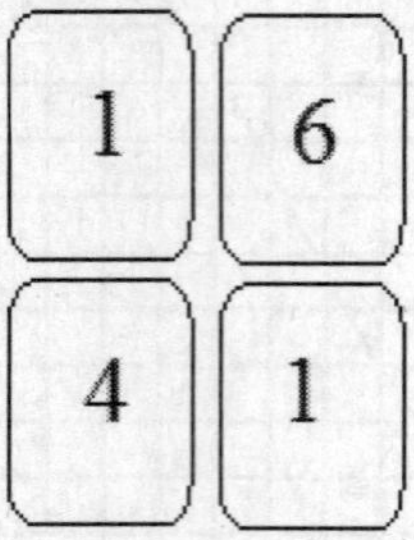

3. ______________________

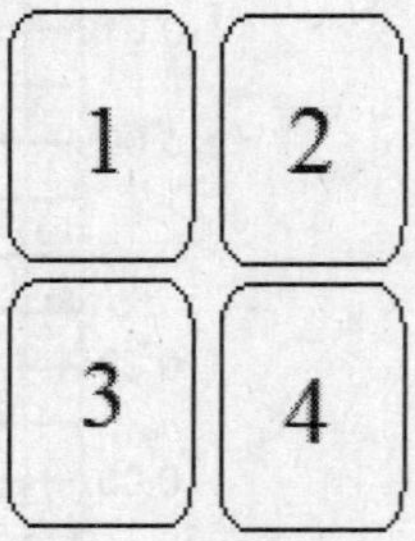

4. Two cards are drawn, one from the group in Question 1 and one from the group in Question 2. Find the expected value for the sum of the two cards.

____

5. Chris can take two routes to get to the mall. Route A takes 22 minutes. Route B takes 18 minutes without traffic, and 26 minutes with traffic. He estimates a 25% chance of encountering traffic on Route B. Based on the expected values for Route A and Route B, which route would you recommend Chris take? Explain.

Hint: For Route B, find the expected value by multiplying 18 minutes by the chance of no traffic. Then multiply 26 minutes by the chance of having traffic, and add the two products together.

____

____

6. Chelsea has been offered two jobs. Her pay rate at either job will be determined by how well she does on a test. At Company A, she has an 80% chance of getting a pay rate of $12 and a 20% chance of getting a pay rate of $15 an hour. At Company B, she has a 60% chance of getting a pay rate of $10 an hour and a 40% chance of getting a pay rate of $15 an hour. At which company is she more likely to get a higher pay rate? Explain.

____

____

Name ______________________ Date ______________ Class ______________

LESSON 9-1

Practice

Introduction to Sequences

Find the first 5 terms of each sequence.

1. $a_1 = 1, a_n = 3(a_{n-1})$ ______________

2. $a_1 = 2, a_n = 2(a_{n-1} + 1) - 5$ ______________

3. $a_1 = -2, a_n = (a_{n-1})^2 - 1$ ______________

4. $a_1 = 1, a_n = 6 - 2(a_{n-1})$ ______________

5. $a_1 = -1, a_n = (a_{n-1} - 1)^2 - 3$ ______________

6. $a_1 = -2, a_n = \dfrac{2 - a_{n-1}}{2}$ ______________

7. $a_n = (n - 2)(n + 1)$ ______________

8. $a_n = n(2n - 1)$ ______________

9. $a_n = n^3 - n^2$ ______________

10. $a_n = \left(\dfrac{1}{2}\right)^{n-3}$ ______________

11. $a_n = (-2)^{n-1}$ ______________

12. $a_n = n^2 - 2n$ ______________

Write a possible explicit rule for the *n*th term of each sequence.

13. 8, 16, 24, 32, 40, ... ______________

14. 0.1, 0.4, 0.9, 1.6, 2.5, ... ______________

15. 3, 6, 11, 18, 27, ... ______________

16. $\dfrac{3}{2}, \dfrac{3}{4}, \dfrac{3}{8}, \dfrac{3}{16}, \dfrac{3}{32}, \ldots$ ______________

17. −2, 1, 4, 7, 10, ... ______________

18. 5, 1, 0.2, 0.04, 0.008, ... ______________

Solve.

19. Find the number of line segments in the next two iterations. ______________

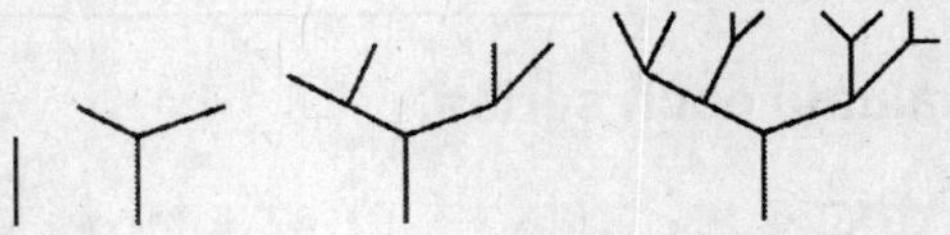

20. Jim charges $50 per week for lawn mowing and weeding services. He plans to increase his prices by 4% each year.

a. Graph the sequence.

b. Describe the pattern.

____

c. To the nearest dollar, how much will he charge per week in 5 years?

____

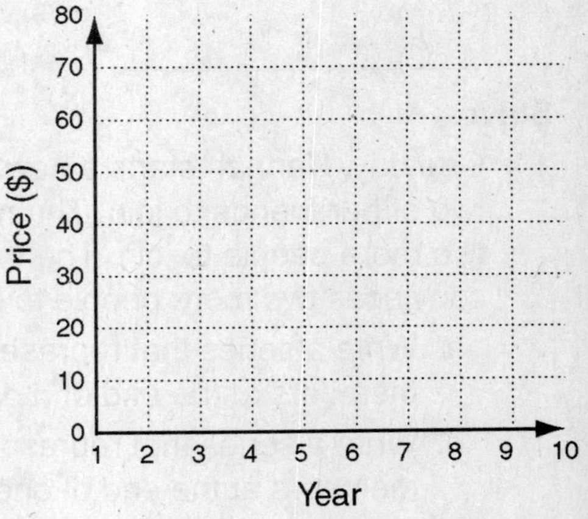

Name ________________________ Date ______________ Class ______________

LESSON 9-2

Practice

Series and Summation Notation

Write each series in summation notation.

1. $-2 + 4 - 8 + 16 - 32$
____

2. $\frac{1}{10} + \frac{1}{100} + \frac{1}{1{,}000} + \frac{1}{10{,}000}$
____

3. $-6 - 1 + 4 + 9 + 14 + 19$
____

4. $\frac{1}{3} + \frac{1}{6} + \frac{1}{9} + \frac{1}{12} + \frac{1}{15} + \frac{1}{18}$
____

5. $7 + 13 + 19 + 25 + 31$
____

6. $-1 + 1 - 1 + 1 - 1 + 1 - 1$
____

Expand each series and evaluate.

7. $\sum_{k=4}^{8} \frac{k}{4}$
   a. Expand. ______________________
   b. Simplify. ______________________

8. $\sum_{k=1}^{4} 5^{k-2}$
   a. Expand. ______________________
   b. Simplify. ______________________

9. $\sum_{k=2}^{6} \left(-2^k\right)$
   a. Expand. ______________________
   b. Simplify. ______________________

10. $\sum_{k=30}^{39} (70 - 2k)$
   a. Expand. ______________________
   b. Simplify. ______________________

Evaluate each series.

11. $\sum_{k=12}^{20} 3$
____

12. $\sum_{k=1}^{40} k$
____

13. $\sum_{k=1}^{10} k^2$
____

Solve.

14. One day, Hannah starts a new online Internet club by convincing two of her friends to join. The next day, each member convinces two more people to join. The third day of the club, each member convinces two more people to join, and so on for a full week.
   a. Write a series that represents the number of club members at the end of *n* days. ______________________
   b. Write a series that represents the number of club members at the end of one week. ______________________
   c. How many members will the club have at the end of a week? ______________________

Name ________________________ Date ______________ Class ______________

LESSON 9-3

Practice

Arithmetic Sequences and Series

Determine whether each sequence could be arithmetic. If so, find the common difference and the next term.

1. 41, 24, 7, –10, –27, ...

2. 6, –6, 6, –6, 6, –6, 6, –6, ...

3. $\frac{4}{5}, \frac{13}{10}, \frac{9}{5}, \frac{23}{10}, \frac{14}{5}, \ldots$

4. 2, 4, 8, 16, 32, 64, ...

Find the 12th term of each arithmetic sequence.

5. 21, 32, 43, 54, 65, ...

6. 3.7, 3.3, 2.9, 2.5, 2.1, ...

7. 1.8, –1.1, –4, –6.9, –9.8, ...

8. –8, –2.75, 2.5, 7.75, 13, ...

Find the missing terms in each arithmetic sequence.

9. 3, __, __, __, 59, ...

10. –4, __, __, 23, ...

11. 7, __, __, __, __, 62, ...

12. 35, __, __, __, __, __, __, –7, ...

Find the 10th term of each arithmetic sequence.

13. $a_4 = 12$ and $a_7 = 20.4$

14. $a_3 = 37$ and $a_{17} = -12$

15. $a_{13} = -5$ and $a_{18} = -51$

16. $a_{25} = 18$ and $a_{41} = 62$

Solve.

17. A banquet hall uses tables that seat 4, one person on each side. For a large party, the tables are positioned end to end in a long row. Two tables will seat 6, three tables will seat 8, and four tables will seat 10. How many tables should be set end to end to seat 40?

Name ______________________ Date ______________ Class ______________

LESSON 9-4

Practice

Geometric Sequences and Series

Determine whether each sequence could be geometric or arithmetic. If possible, find the common ratio or difference.

1. 1.1, –3.3, 9.9, –29.7, 89.1, ...

2. –18, –7, 4, 15, 26, ...

3. 1, 2, 6, 24, 120, 720, ...

4. 3125, 2500, 2000, 1600, 1280, ...

Find the 10th term of each geometric sequence.

5. 1600, 800, 400, 200, ...

6. 0.0000001, 0.00001, 0.001, 0.1, ...

7. –64, 96, –144, 216, ...

8. 2, –6, 18, –54, ...

Find the 8th term of each geometric sequence with the given terms.

9. $a_3 = 12$ and $a_6 = 96$

10. $a_{15} = 100$ and $a_{17} = 25$

11. $a_{11} = -4$ and $a_{13} = -36$

12. $a_3 = -4$ and $a_5 = -36$

Find the geometric mean of each pair of numbers.

13. 2 and 8

14. 4 and 25

15. 2 and 3

Find the indicated sum for each geometric series.

16. S_7 for 14, 42, 126, 378, ...

17. $\sum_{k=1}^{8} (-4)^{k-1}$

Solve.

18. Deanna received an e-mail asking her to forward it to 10 other people. Assume that no one breaks the chain and that there are no duplicate recipients. How many e-mails will have been sent after 8 generations, including Deanna's?

Name ______________________ Date ______________ Class ______________

LESSON 9-5

Practice

Mathematical Induction and Infinite Geometric Series

Determine whether each geometric series converges or diverges.

1. $\frac{81}{625}+\frac{27}{125}+\frac{9}{25}+\frac{3}{5}+1+\cdots$

2. $1-\frac{3}{5}+\frac{9}{25}-\frac{27}{125}+\frac{81}{625}-\cdots$

Find the sum of each infinite geometric series, if it exists.

3. $7+\frac{7}{4}+\frac{7}{16}+\frac{7}{64}+\cdots$

4. $500-300+180-108+\ldots$

5. $\sum_{k=1}^{\infty}\frac{1}{4}\left(\frac{4}{3}\right)^{k}$

6. $\sum_{k=1}^{\infty}99\left(-\frac{4}{9}\right)^{k}$

Write each repeating decimal as a fraction in simplest form.

7. $0.\overline{16}$

8. $0.\overline{016}$

9. $0.0\overline{16}$

10. $0.0\overline{45}$

11. $0.\overline{1}$

12. $0.\overline{123}$

Identify a counterexample to disprove each statement.

13. $2^{-n} < n^2$

14. $n^3 \geq 3n$

Solve.

15. Ron won a prize that pays \$200,000 the first year and half of the previous year's amount each year for the rest of his life.

a. Write the first 4 terms of a series to represent the situation.

b. Write a general rule for a geometric sequence that models his prize each year.

c. Estimate Ron's total prize in the first 10 years.

d. If Ron lives forever, what is the total of his winnings?

Name ______________________ Date ______________ Class ______________

LESSON 10-1

Practice

Right-Angle Trigonometry

Find the value of the sine, cosine, and tangent functions for θ.

1.

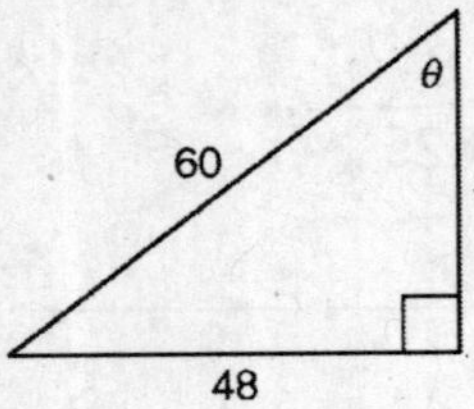

2.

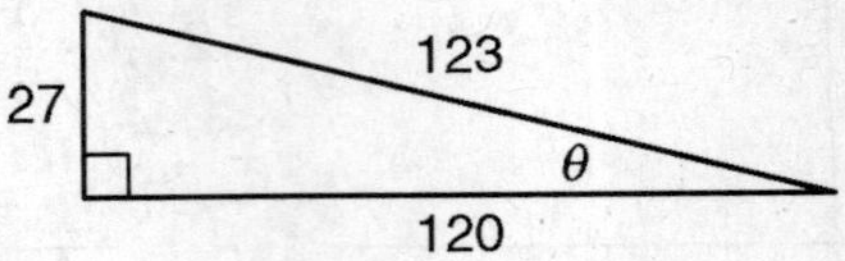

3.

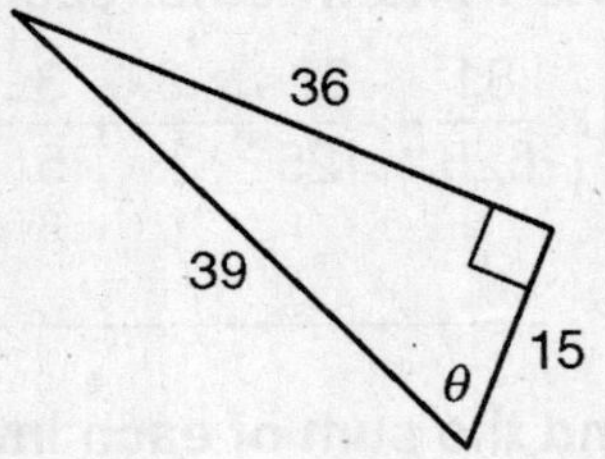

______________________ ______________________ ______________________

Use a trigonometric function to find the value of x.

4.

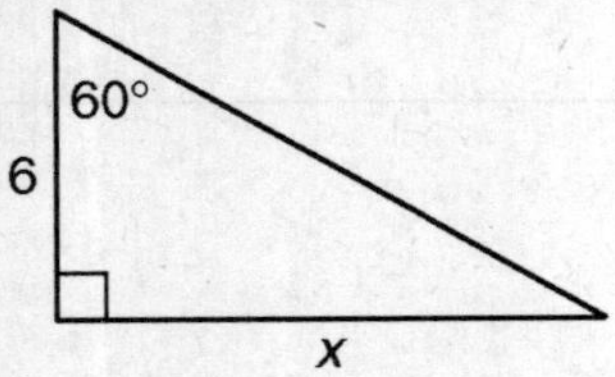

5.

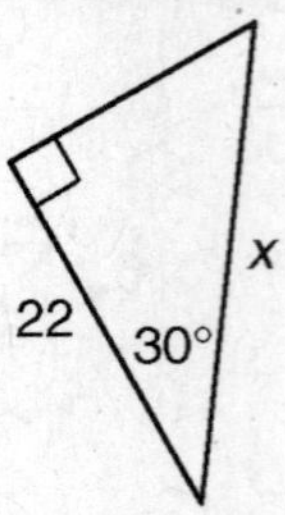

6.

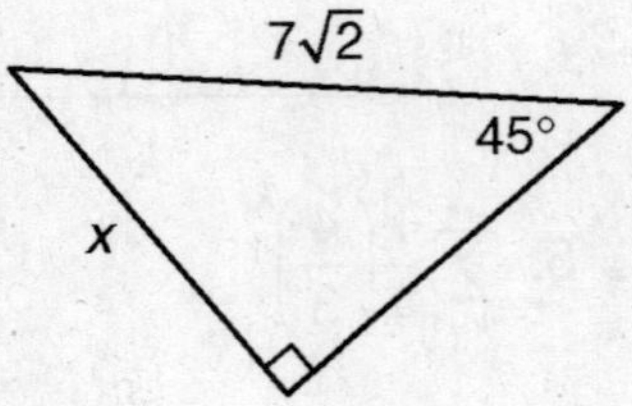

______________________ ______________________ ______________________

Find the values of the six trigonometric functions for θ.

7.

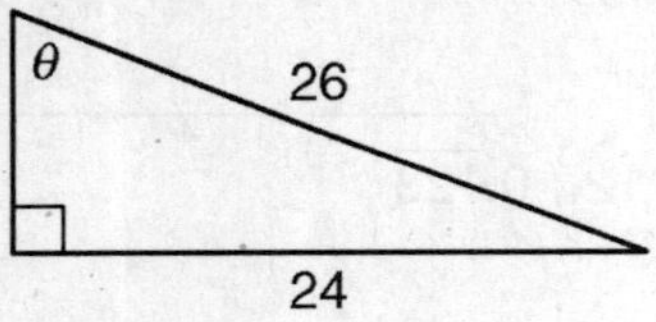

8.

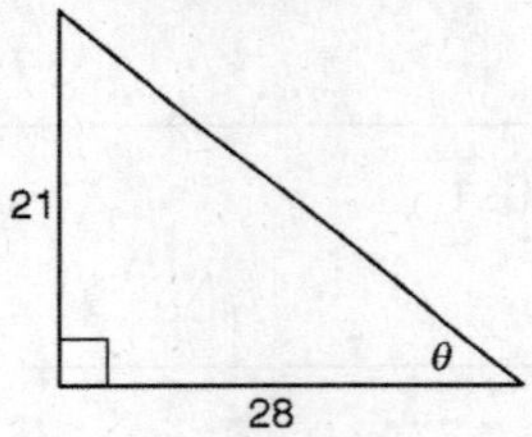

9.

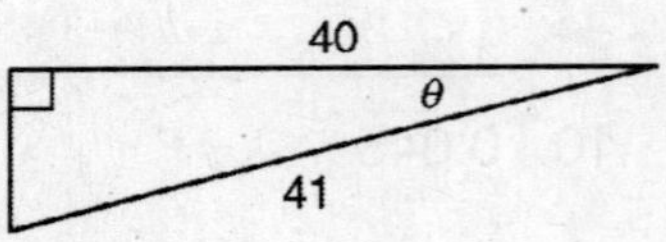

______________________ ______________________ ______________________

______________________ ______________________ ______________________

Solve.

10. A water slide is 26 feet high. The angle between the slide and the water is 33.5°. What is the length of the slide? ______________________

11. A surveyor stands 150 feet from the base of a viaduct and measures the angle of elevation to be 46.2°. His eye level is 6 feet above the ground. What is the height of the viaduct to the nearest foot? ______________________

12. The pilot of a helicopter measures the angle of depression to a landing spot to be 18.8°. If the pilot's altitude is 1640 meters, what is the horizontal distance to the landing spot to the nearest meter? ______________________

Name ______________________ Date ______________ Class ______________

LESSON 10-2

Practice

Angles of Rotation

Draw an angle with the given measure in standard position.

1. –420°

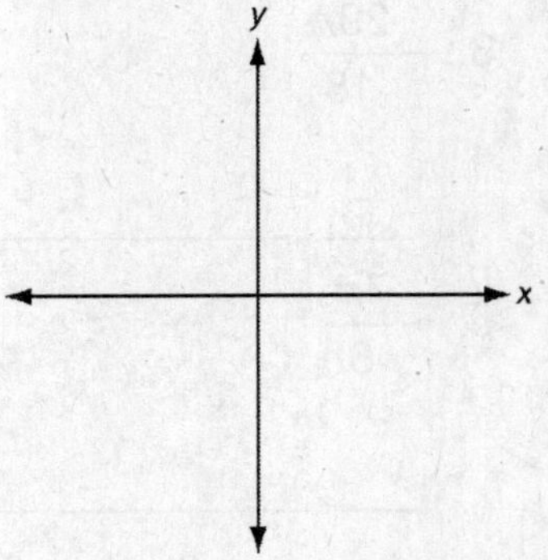

2. 405°

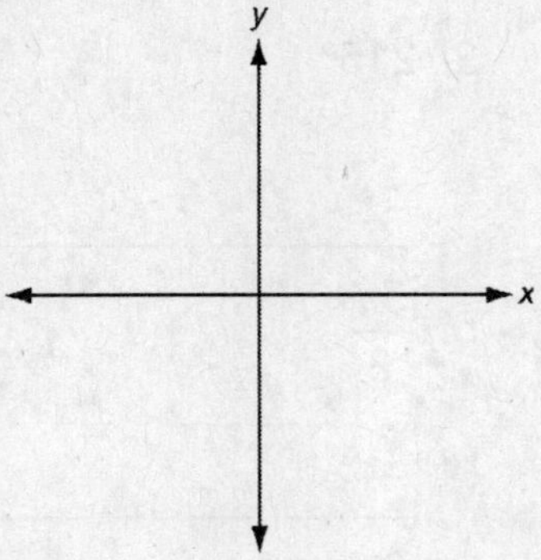

3. –450°

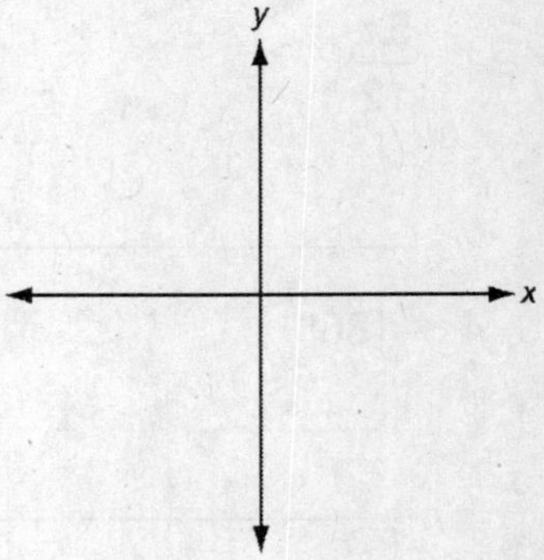

Find the measures of a positive angle and a negative angle that are coterminal with each given angle.

4. $\theta = 425°$ ______________

5. $\theta = -316°$ ______________

6. $\theta = -800°$ ______________

7. $\theta = 281°$ ______________

8. $\theta = -4°$ ______________

9. $\theta = 743°$ ______________

Find the measure of the reference angle for each given angle.

10. $\theta = 211°$ ______________

11. $\theta = -755°$ ______________

12. $\theta = -555°$ ______________

13. $\theta = 119°$ ______________

14. $\theta = -160°$ ______________

15. $\theta = 235°$ ______________

***P* is a point on the terminal side of θ in standard position. Find the exact value of the six trigonometric functions for θ.**

16. $P(-5, 5)$

17. $P(2, 9)$

18. $P(-7, -5)$

Solve.

19. A circus performer trots her pony into the ring. The pony circles the ring 22 times as the performer flips and turns on the pony's back. At the end of the act, the pony exits on the side of the ring opposite its point of entry. Through how many degrees does the pony trot during the entire act? ______________

Name ______________________ Date ______________ Class ______________

LESSON 10-3

Practice

The Unit Circle

Convert each measure from degrees to radians or from radians to degrees.

1. $\frac{5\pi}{12}$ ______

2. 215° ______

3. $-\frac{29\pi}{18}$ ______

4. –180° ______

5. $\frac{5\pi}{3}$ ______

6. $-\frac{7\pi}{6}$ ______

7. 400° ______

8. $\frac{3\pi}{10}$ ______

9. 35° ______

Use the unit circle to find the exact value of each trigonometric function.

10. $\cos\frac{2\pi}{3}$ ______

11. $\tan\frac{5\pi}{4}$ ______

12. $\tan\frac{5\pi}{6}$ ______

13. sin 315° ______

14. cos 225° ______

15. tan 60° ______

Use a reference angle to find the exact value of the sine, cosine, and tangent of each angle.

16. 150° ______

17. –225° ______

18. –300° ______

19. $\frac{11\pi}{6}$ ______

20. $-\frac{2\pi}{3}$ ______

21. $\frac{5\pi}{4}$ ______

Solve.

22. San Antonio, Texas, is located about 30° north of the equator. If Earth's radius is about 3959 miles, approximately how many miles is San Antonio from the equator?

______

Name ______________________ Date ______________ Class ______________

LESSON 10-4

Practice

Inverses of Trigonometric Functions

Find all possible values of each expression.

1. $\sin^{-1}\left(-\frac{\sqrt{3}}{2}\right)$ ______
2. $\cos^{-1}\left(-\frac{1}{2}\right)$ ______
3. $\tan^{-1}0$ ______
4. $\sin^{-1}\left(-\frac{\sqrt{2}}{2}\right)$ ______
5. $\cos^{-1}\left(-\frac{\sqrt{2}}{2}\right)$ ______
6. $\tan^{-1}\left(\frac{\sqrt{3}}{3}\right)$ ______

Evaluate each inverse trigonometric function. Give your answer in both radians and degrees.

7. $\text{Sin}^{-1}(-1)$ ______
8. $\text{Tan}^{-1}\left(-\sqrt{3}\right)$ ______
9. $\text{Cos}^{-1}1$ ______
10. $\text{Sin}^{-1}\left(\frac{\sqrt{3}}{2}\right)$ ______
11. $\text{Tan}^{-1}\left(-\frac{\sqrt{3}}{3}\right)$ ______
12. $\text{Cos}^{-1}\left(\frac{\sqrt{2}}{2}\right)$ ______

Solve each equation to the nearest tenth. Use the given restrictions.

13. $\sin\theta = 0.45$, for $0° < \theta < 90°$ ______
14. $\sin\theta = 0.801$, for $90° < \theta < 270°$ ______
15. $\tan\theta = 2.42$, for $180° < \theta < 360°$ ______
16. $\cos\theta = -0.334$, for $0° < \theta < 180°$ ______
17. $\cos\theta = -0.181$, for $180° < \theta < 360°$ ______
18. $\tan\theta = -10$, for $90° < \theta < 270°$ ______

Solve.

19. A 21-foot ladder is leaning against a building. The base of the ladder is 7 feet from the base of a building. To the nearest degree, what is the measure of the angle that the ladder makes with the ground? ______

Name ______________________ Date ______________ Class ______________

LESSON 10-5

Practice

The Law of Sines

Find the area of each triangle. Round to the nearest tenth.

1.

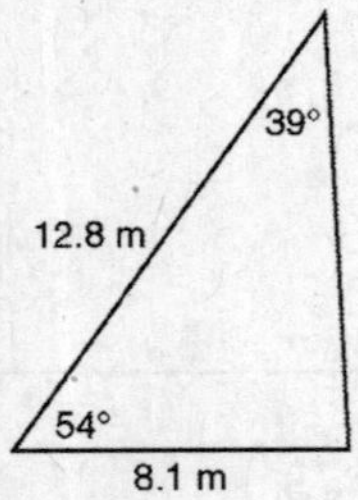

____

2.

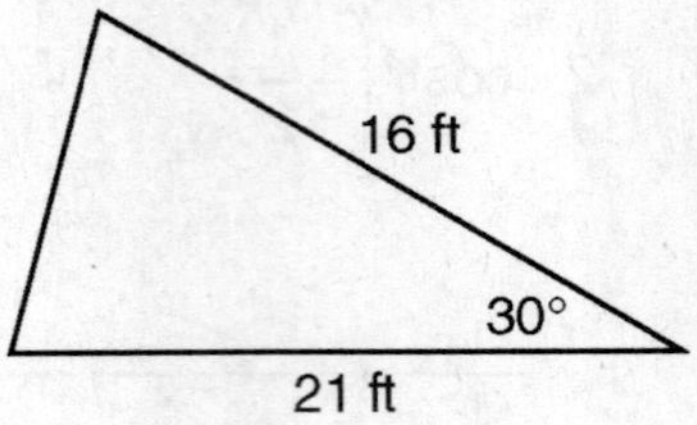

____

3.

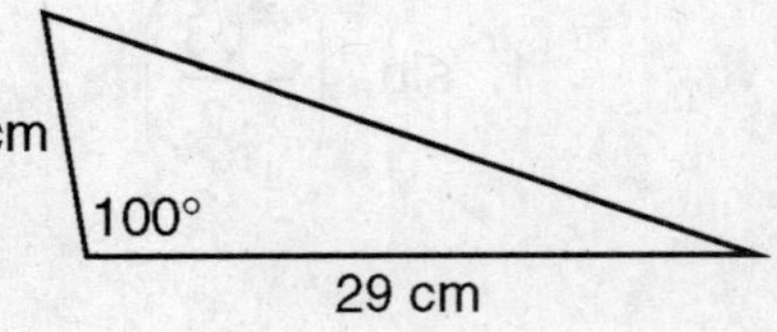

____

Solve each triangle. Round to the nearest tenth.

4.

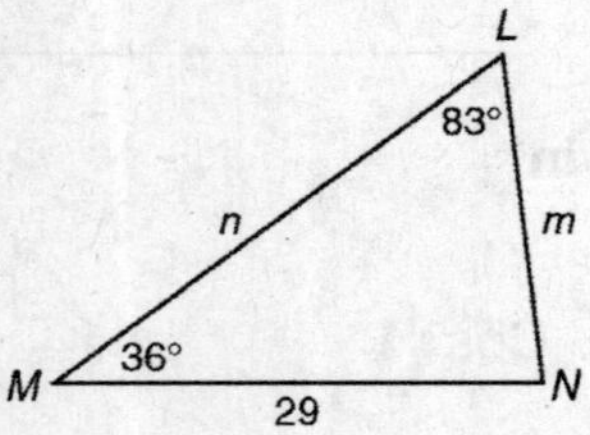

____

5.

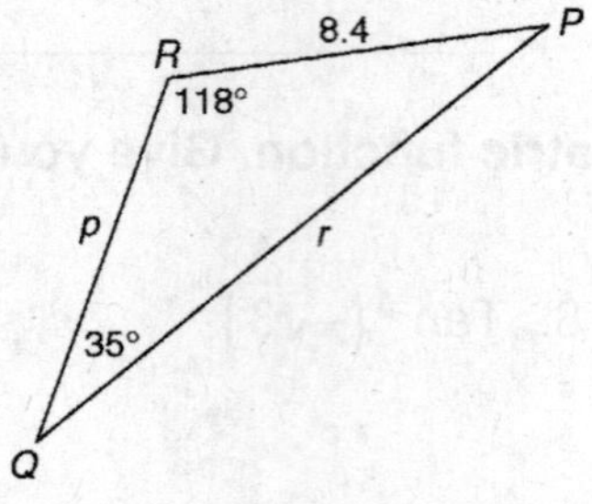

____

6.

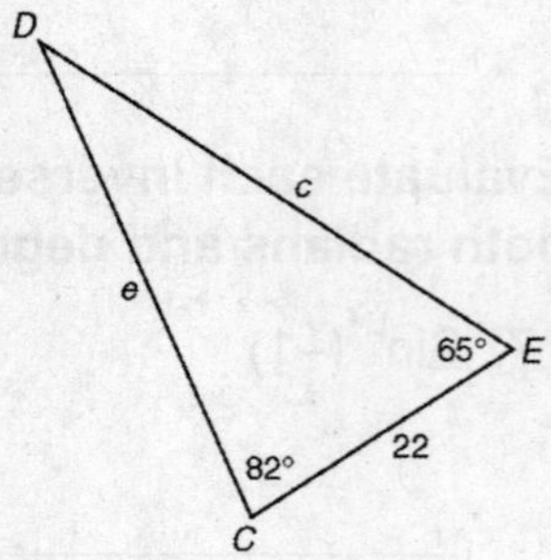

____

7.

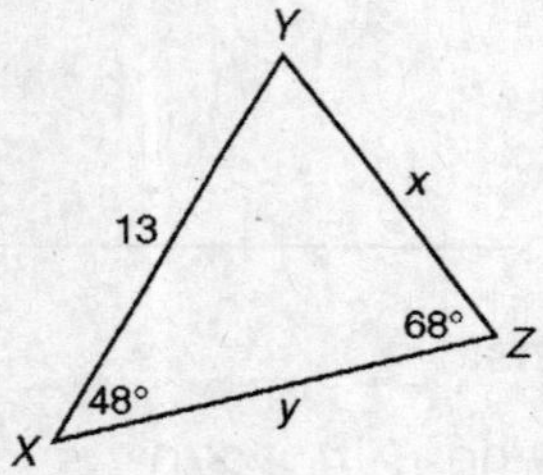

____

8.

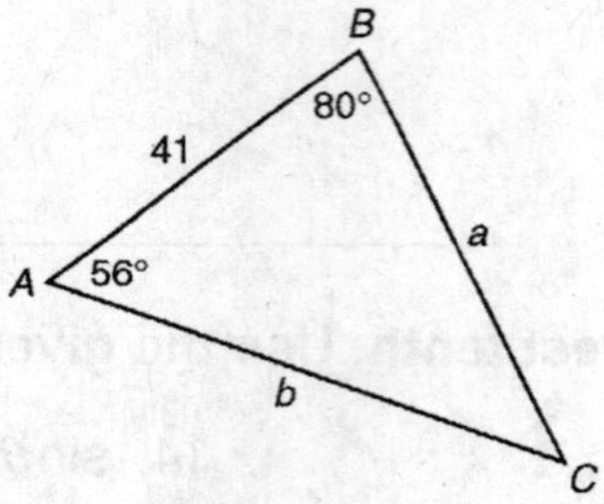

____

9.

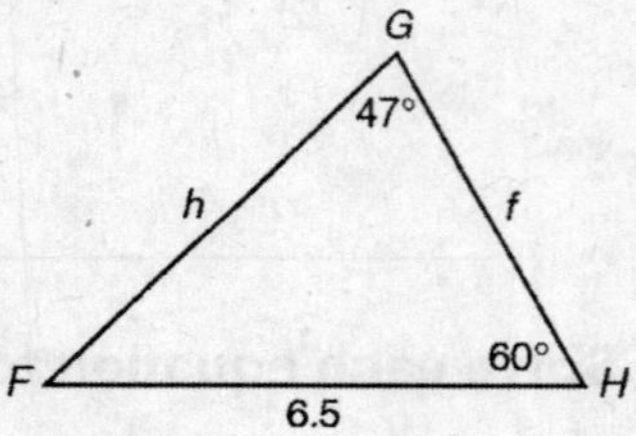

____

An artist is designing triangular mosaic tiles. Determine the number of triangles he can form from the given side and angle measures. Then solve the triangles. Round to the nearest tenth.

10. $a = 8$ cm, $b = 10$ cm, $A = 60°$

____

11. $a = 18$ cm, $b = 15$ cm, $A = 85°$

____

12. $a = 22$ cm, $b = 15$ cm, $A = 120°$

____

Solve.

13. Ann is creating a triangular frame. Two angles and the included side of the frame measure 64°, 58°, and 38 centimeters, respectively. What are the lengths of the other two sides of the frame to the nearest tenth of a centimeter?

____

Name ______________________ Date ______________ Class ______________

LESSON 10-6

Practice

The Law of Cosines

Use the given measurements to solve each triangle. Round to the nearest tenth.

1. 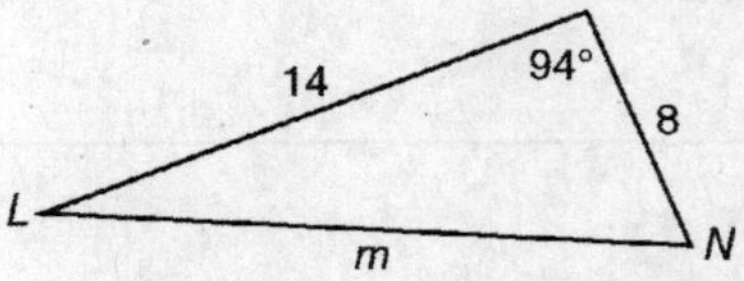

____

2. 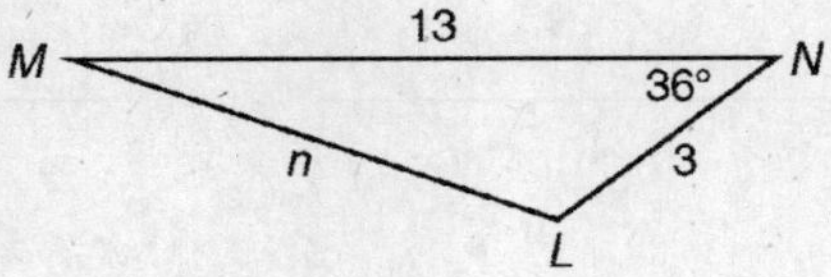

____

3. 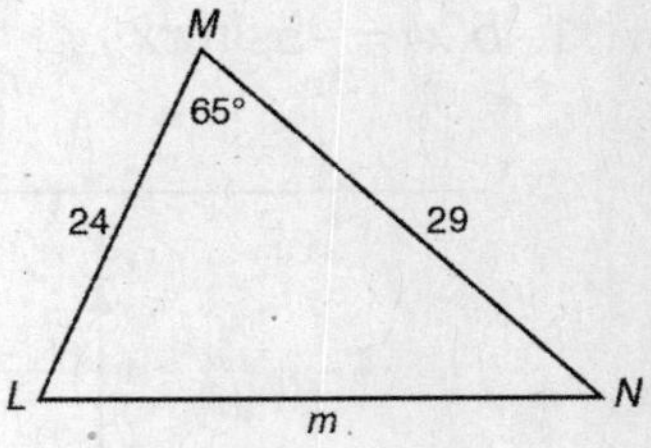

____

4. 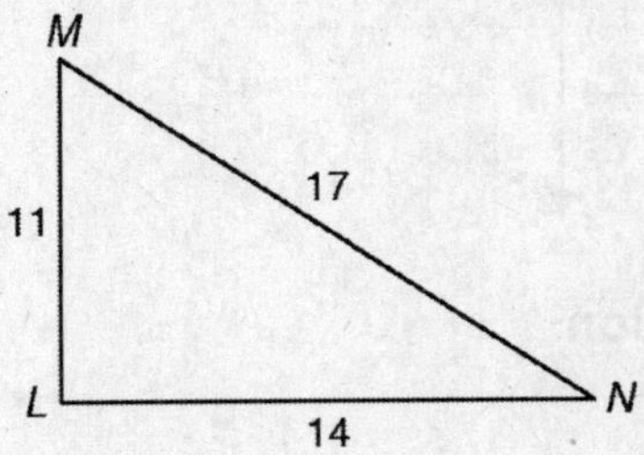

____

5. 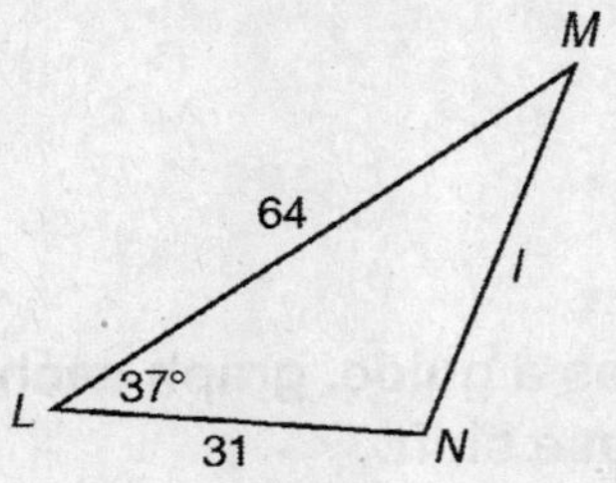

____

6. 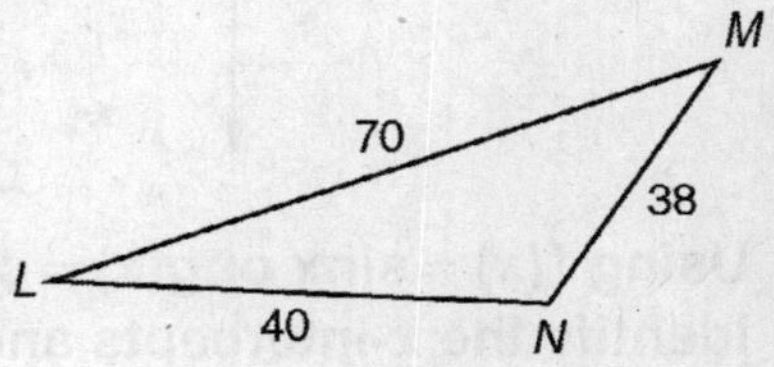

____

7. 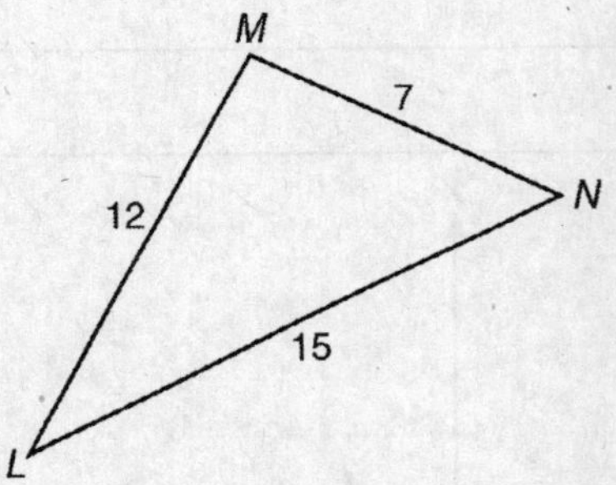

____

8. 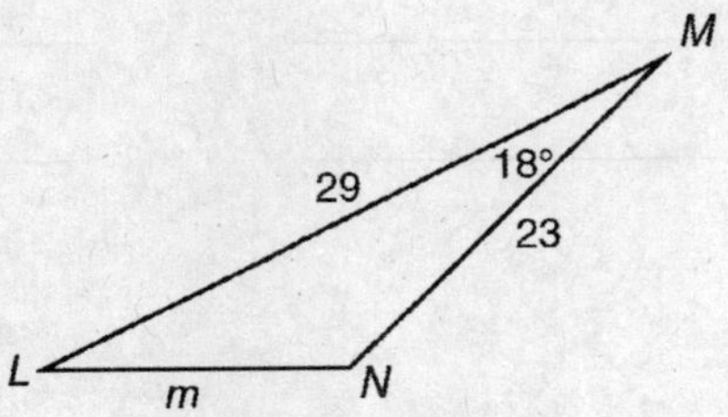

____

9. 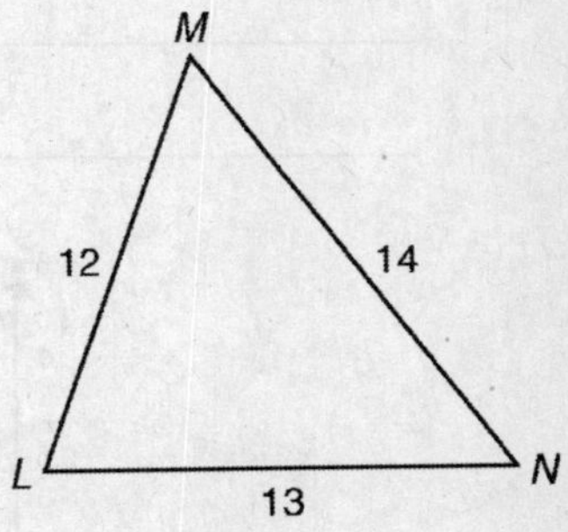

____

Solve.

10. A postal airplane leaves Island A and flies 91 miles to Island B. It drops off and picks up mail and flies 63 miles to Island C. After unloading and loading mail, the plane returns to Island A at an average rate of 300 miles per hour. How long does it take the pilot to travel from Island C to Island A?

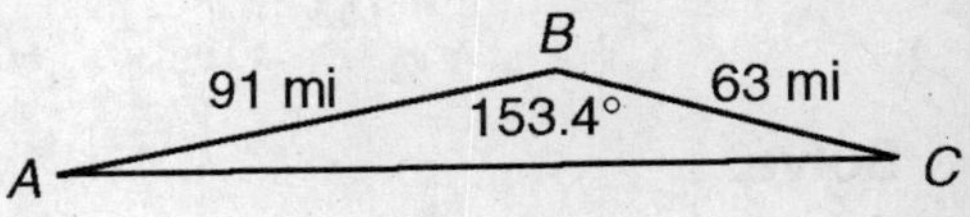

____

11. A statue is erected on a triangular marble base. The lengths of the sides of the triangle are 12 feet, 16 feet, and 18 feet. What is the area of the region at the base of the statue? ______________________

Name ______________________ Date ______________ Class ______________

LESSON 11-1

Practice

Graphs of Sine and Cosine

Using $f(x) = \sin x$ or $g(x) = \cos x$ as a guide, graph each function. Identify the amplitude and period.

1. $b(x) = -5\sin \pi x$

2. $k(x) = 3\cos 2\pi x$

________________________ ________________________

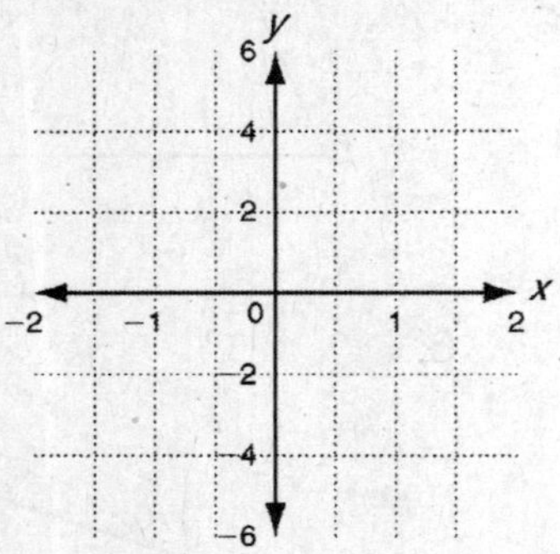

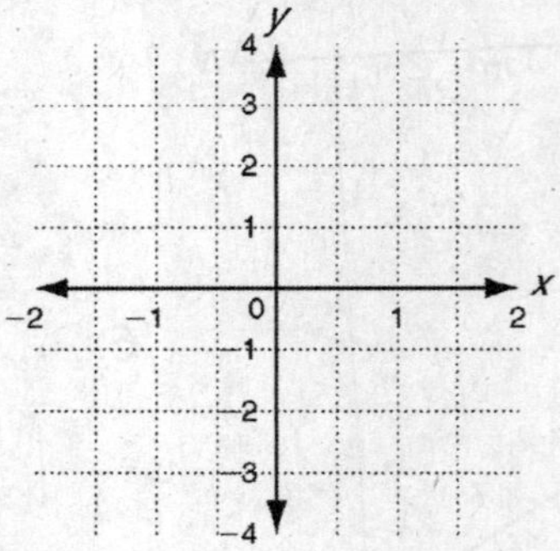

Using $f(x) = \sin x$ or $g(x) = \cos x$ as a guide, graph each function. Identify the *x*-intercepts and phase shift.

3. $h(x) = \sin\left(x + \dfrac{\pi}{4}\right)$

4. $h(x) = \cos\left(x - \dfrac{\pi}{4}\right)$

________________________ ________________________

________________________ ________________________

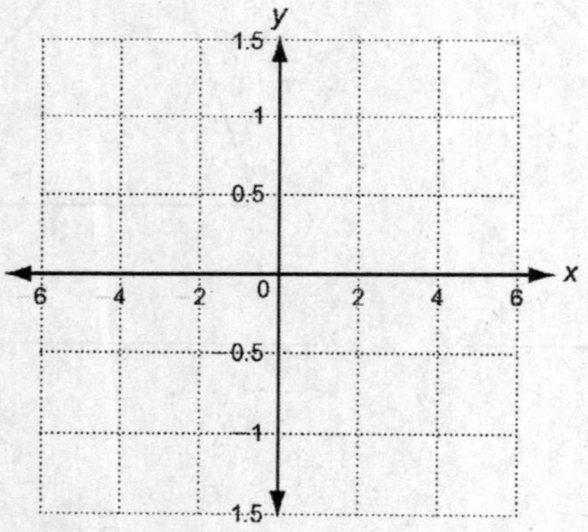

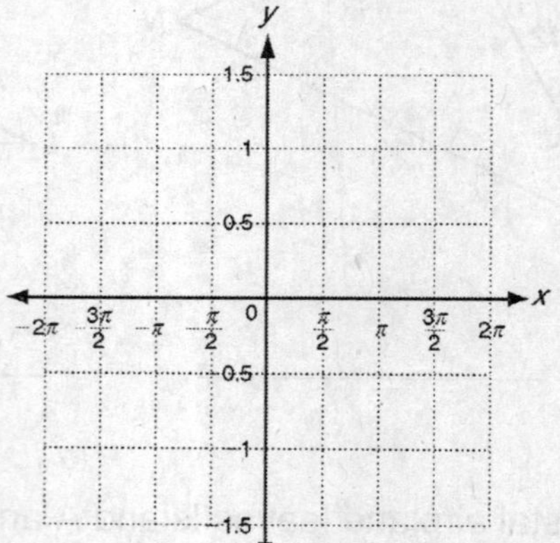

Solve.

5. a. Use a sine function to graph a sound wave with a period of 0.002 second and an amplitude of 2 centimeters.

   b. Find the frequency in hertz for this sound wave.

____

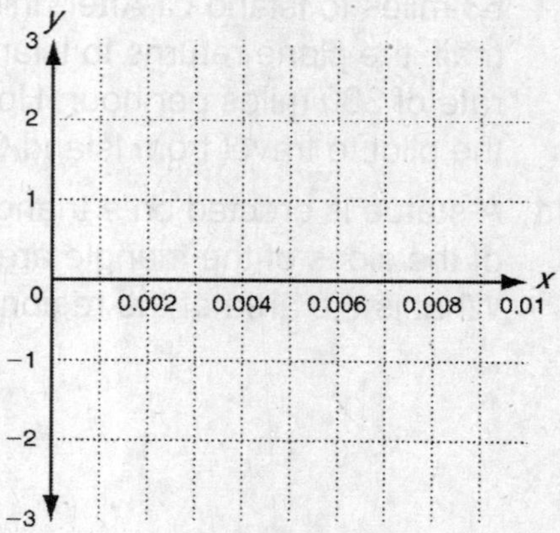

Name ______________________ Date ______________ Class ______________

LESSON 11-2

Practice

Graphs of Other Trigonometric Functions

Using $f(x) = \tan x$ and $f(x) = \cot x$ as a guide, graph each function. Identify the period, x-intercepts, and asymptotes.

1. $g(x) = 2\tan\dfrac{\pi x}{2}$

2. $t(x) = \dfrac{3}{4}\cot(x)$

______________________ ______________________

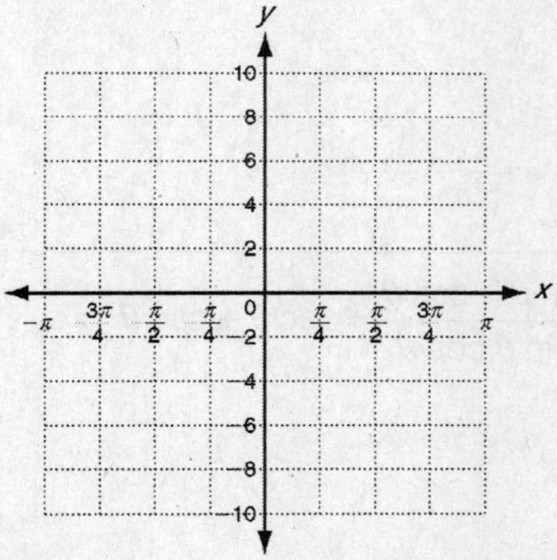

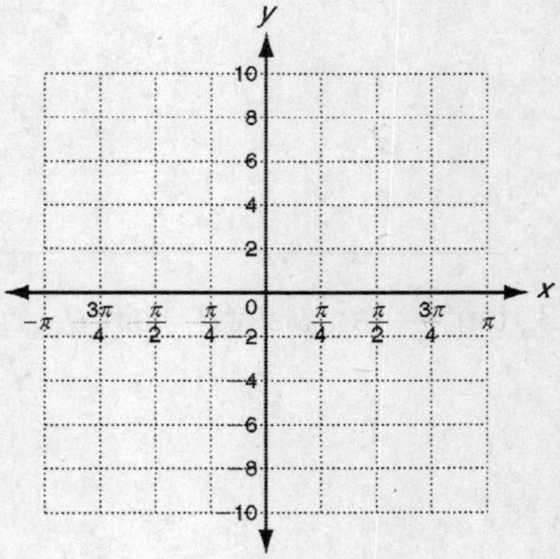

Using $f(x) = \cos x$ or $f(x) = \sin x$ as a guide, graph each function. Identify the period and asymptotes.

3. $k(x) = \sec\dfrac{x}{2}$

4. $q(x) = \dfrac{1}{2}\csc(2x)$

______________________ ______________________

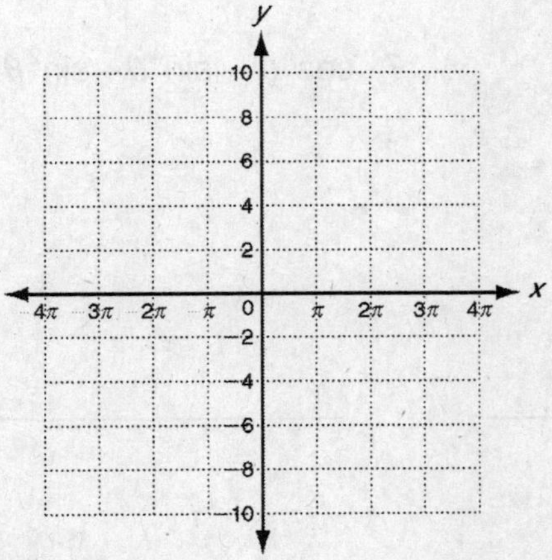

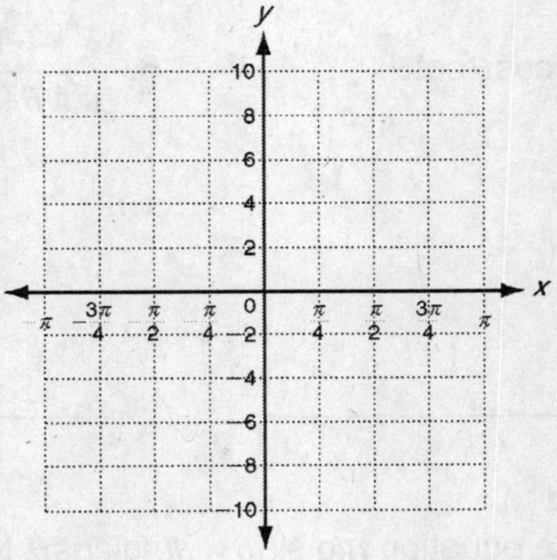

Solve.

5. The rotating light on a lighthouse is 400 feet from a cliff and completes one full rotation every 10 seconds. The equation representing the distance, a, in feet that the center of the circle of light is from the lighthouse is $a(t) = 400\sec\left(\dfrac{\pi t}{5}\right)$.

   a. What is the period of $a(t)$? ______________________

   b. Find the value of the function at $t = 10$. ______________________

Name ______________________ Date ______________ Class ______________

LESSON 11-3

Practice

Fundamental Trigonometric Identities

Prove each trigonometric identity.

1. $\sin^2\theta + \sin^2\theta \cot^2\theta = 1$

2. $\cot^2\theta \cos^2\theta = \cot^2\theta - \cos^2\theta$

3. $\tan^2\theta - \tan^2\theta \sin^2\theta = \sin^2\theta$

4. $\dfrac{\sin\theta + \cos\theta}{\sin\theta\cos\theta} = \sec\theta + \csc\theta$

Rewrite each expression in terms of cos*θ*. Then simplify.

5. $2\sin\theta \cos\theta \cot\theta$

6. $\dfrac{1 + \cot\theta}{\cot\theta\,(\sin\theta + \cos\theta)}$

7. $\cos^4\theta - \sin^4\theta + \sin^2\theta$

Solve.

8. Use the equation $mg\sin\theta = \mu mg\cos\theta$ to determine the angle at which a waxed wood block on an inclined plane of wet snow begins to slide. Assume $\mu = 0.17$.

Name ______________________ Date ____________ Class ____________

LESSON 11-4

Practice

Sum and Difference Identities

Find the exact value of each expression.

1. $\cos 120°$ ______
2. $\sin 315°$ ______
3. $\tan 255°$ ______
4. $\tan\dfrac{7\pi}{6}$ ______
5. $\sin\dfrac{\pi}{12}$ ______
6. $\cos\dfrac{3\pi}{4}$ ______

Prove each identity.

7. $\sin\left(x - \dfrac{3\pi}{2}\right) = \cos x$
8. $\cos\left(x - \dfrac{\pi}{2}\right) = \sin x$

Find each value if $\cos A = \dfrac{12}{13}$ with $0° \le A \le 90°$ and if $\sin B = \dfrac{8}{17}$ with $90° \le B \le 180°$.

9. $\sin(A + B)$ ______
10. $\cos(A + B)$ ______
11. $\tan(A + B)$ ______
12. $\sin(A - B)$ ______
13. $\cos(A - B)$ ______
14. $\tan(A - B)$ ______

Solve.

15. Find the coordinates, to the nearest hundredth, of the vertices of triangle *ABC* with *A*(1, 0), *B*(10, 0), and *C*(2, 6) after a 60° rotation about the origin.
    a. Write the matrices for the rotation and for the points. ______
    b. Find the matrix product. ______
    c. Write the coordinates. ______
16. A hill rises from the horizontal at a 15° angle. The road leading straight up the hill is 800 meters long. How much higher is the top of the hill than the base of the hill? ______

Name ________________________ Date ______________ Class ______________

LESSON 11-5

Practice

Double-Angle and Half-Angle Identities

Find sin 2*θ*, cos 2*θ*, and tan 2*θ* for each.

1. $\cos\theta = -\frac{12}{13}$ for $\pi < \theta < \frac{3\pi}{2}$

2. $\sin\theta = \frac{\sqrt{6}}{10}$ for $0 < \theta < \frac{\pi}{2}$

________________________ ________________________

3. $\sin\theta = -\frac{2}{3}$ for $\frac{3\pi}{2} < \theta < 2\pi$

4. $\tan\theta = -\frac{5}{6}$ for $\frac{\pi}{2} < \theta < \pi$

________________________ ________________________

Prove each identity.

5. $2\cos^2\theta = \cos 2\theta + 1$

6. $\tan\theta = \frac{1-\cos 2\theta}{\sin 2\theta}$

____

Use half-angle identities to find the exact value of each trigonometric expression.

7. $\tan 22.5°$

8. $\cos\frac{7\pi}{12}$

9. $\sin\frac{11\pi}{12}$

________________ ________________ ________________

Find $\sin\frac{\theta}{2}$, $\cos\frac{\theta}{2}$, and $\tan\frac{\theta}{2}$ for each.

10. $\cos\theta = \frac{3}{5}$ and $270° < \theta < 360°$

11. $\sin\theta = -\frac{\sqrt{5}}{3}$ and $180° < \theta < 270°$

________________________ ________________________

Solve.

12. A water-park slide covers 100 feet of horizontal space and is 36 feet high.

a. Write a trigonometric relation in terms of *θ*, the angle that the slide makes with the water surface. ________________

b. A new replacement slide will create an angle with the water surface that measures twice that of the original slide. The new slide will use the same horizontal space as the old slide. Write an expression that can be evaluated to find the height of the new slide. ________________

c. What is the height of the new slide to the nearest foot? ________________

Name ______________________ Date ______________ Class ______________

LESSON 11-6

Practice

Solving Trigonometric Equations

Find all of the solutions of each equation.

1. $4\tan\theta = 5\tan\theta + \sqrt{3}$

2. $\sqrt{2} - 2\sin\theta = 0$

3. $7\cos\theta - 1 = 9\cos\theta$

4. $2\tan\theta + \sqrt{3} = 5\tan\theta$

Solve each equation for the given domain.

5. $\tan^2\theta - 2\tan\theta = -1$ for $0° \le \theta \le 360°$

6. $2\sin^2\theta = 1$ for $0° \le \theta \le 360°$

7. $4\cos^2\theta = 3\cos\theta$ for $90° \le \theta \le 180°$

8. $2\sqrt{3}\cos^2\theta - \cos\theta = 2\sqrt{3}$ for $\pi \le \theta \le 2\pi$

9. $3\tan^2\theta = 2\tan\theta + 1$ for $0° \le \theta \le 90°$

10. $5\tan^2\theta = 2\tan\theta + 6$ for $180° \le \theta \le 360°$

Use trigonometric identities to solve each equation for the given domain.

11. $\sin\theta + \sin 2\theta = 0$ for $0° \le \theta \le 360°$

12. $\cos^2\theta = \sin^2\theta$ for $0° \le \theta \le 360°$

13. $\dfrac{\cos 2\theta}{\sin^2\theta} = 0$ for $0° \le \theta \le 360°$

14. $\cos 2\theta = \dfrac{1}{2}\sin\theta$ for $0° \le \theta \le 90°$

Solve.

15. The height of the water at a pier on a certain day can be modeled by $h(t) = 4.8\sin\dfrac{\pi}{6}(t + 3.5) + 9$, where h is the height in feet and t is the time in hours after midnight. When is the height of the water 6 feet?

Name ______________________ Date ______________ Class ______________

LESSON 12-1

Practice

Introduction to Conic Sections

Graph each equation on a graphing calculator. Identify each conic section. Then describe the center and intercepts.

1. $5x^2 + 5y^2 = 45$

2. $x^2 + 25y^2 = 25$

________________________ ________________________

3. $4x^2 + 4y^2 = 64$

4. $49x^2 + 4y^2 = 196$

________________________ ________________________

Graph each equation on a graphing calculator. Identify each conic section. Then describe the vertices and the direction that the graph opens.

5. $y = x^2 - 3$

6. $y^2 = x^2 + 4$

________________________ ________________________

7. $x^2 - y^2 = 1$

8. $y^2 = x + 4$

________________________ ________________________

9. $x^2 = y + 2$

10. $x = y^2 + 3$

________________________ ________________________

Find the center and radius of a circle that has a diameter with the given endpoints.

11. (–10, 5) and (–5, 17)

12. (8, 1) and (–4, 10)

13. (–7, 12) and (11, –68)

________________________ ________________________

Solve.

14. The orbit of an asteroid is modeled by the equation $9x^2 + 36y^2 = 144$.

a. Identify the conic section. ________________________

b. Identify the *x*- and *y*-intercepts of the orbit.

____

c. Suppose each unit of the coordinate plane represents 40 million miles. What is the maximum width of the asteroid's orbit?

____

Name ______________________ Date ______________ Class ______________

LESSON 12-2

Practice

Circles

Write the equation of each circle.

1. Center (8, 9) and radius $r = 10$

2. Center (–1, 5) and containing the point (23, –2)

3. Center (2, 2) and containing the point (–1, 6)

4. Center (3, –5) and containing the point (–7, 11)

5. Center (–3, 0) and radius $r = 6$

6. Center (6, –1) and radius $r = 8$

7. Center (–3, –4) and containing the point (3, 4)

8. Center (5, –5) and containing the point (1, –2)

Write the equation of the line that is tangent to each circle at the given point.

9. $x^2 + y^2 = 169$; (12, 5)

10. $(x - 2)^2 + (y - 1)^2 = 25$; (6, –2)

11. $(x - 7)^2 + (y + 3)^2 = 625$; (0, –21)

12. $(x + 3)^2 + (y + 6)^2 = 144$; (–3, 6)

Solve.

13. A rock concert is located at the point (–1, 1). The music can be heard up to 4 miles away. Use the equation of a circle to find the locations that are affected. Assume each unit of the coordinate plane represents 1 mile.

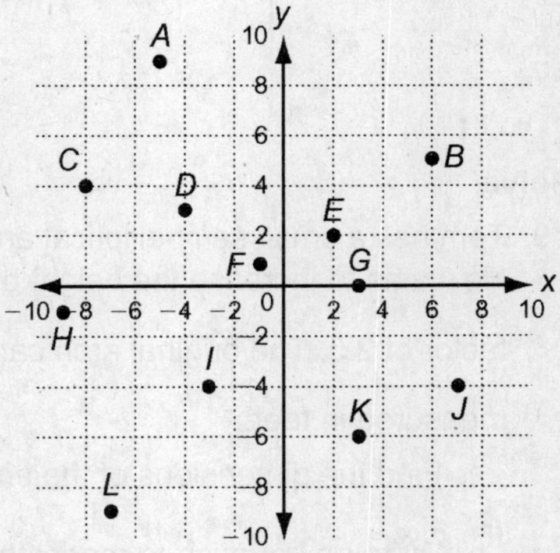

Name ______________________ Date ______________ Class ______________

LESSON 12-3

Practice

Ellipses

Find the constant sum of an ellipse with the given foci and point on the ellipse.

1. $F_1(40, 0)$, $F_2(-40, 0)$, $P(0, -9)$

____

2. $F_1(0, -20)$, $F_2(0, 20)$, $P(15, 0)$

____

Write an equation in standard form for each ellipse with center (0, 0).

3. Vertex (15, 0), focus (9, 0)

____

4. Co-vertex (0, –21), focus (–75, 0)

____

5. Co-vertex (–20, 0), focus (0, 48)

____

6. Vertex (61, 0), focus (60, 0)

____

Graph each ellipse.

7. $\dfrac{(x+3)^2}{9} + \dfrac{(y-2)^2}{16} = 11$

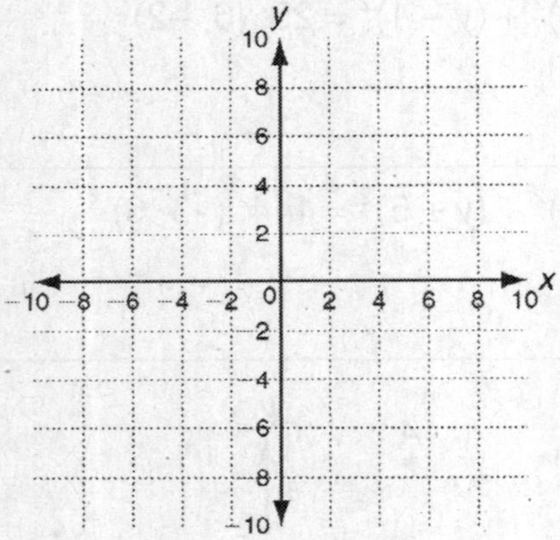

8. $\dfrac{(x-4)^2}{36} + \dfrac{(y-1)^2}{25} = 1$

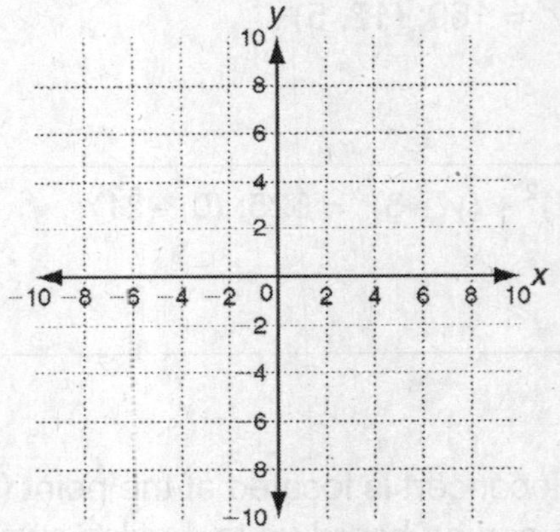

Solve.

9. Tom has a small semi-elliptical arch in his garden that he wants to enlarge. He wants to increase the height by a factor of 3 and increase the width by a factor of 2.5. The original arch can be modeled by the equation $\dfrac{y^2}{6.25} + \dfrac{x^2}{4} = 1$, measured in feet.

a. Find the dimensions of the enlarged arch. _______________

b. Write an equation to model the enlarged arch. _______________

Name ______________________ Date ______________ Class ______________

LESSON 12-4

Practice

Hyperbolas

Find the constant difference for a hyperbola with the given foci and point on the hyperbola.

1. $F_1(0, 11)$, $F_2(0, -11)$, $P(0, 7)$ ______________________

2. $F_1(-9, 0)$, $F_2(9, 0)$, $P(-8, 0)$ ______________________

Write an equation in standard form for each hyperbola with center (0, 0).

3. Co-vertex (–16, 0), focus (0, –20) ______________________

4. Vertex (24, 0), focus (–25, 0) ______________________

5. Vertex (0, –17), co-vertex (1, 0) ______________________

6. Vertex (30, 0), focus (–40, 0) ______________________

Find the vertices, co-vertices, and asymptotes of each hyperbola, and then graph.

7. $\dfrac{x^2}{196} - \dfrac{y^2}{49} = 1$ ______________________

8. $\dfrac{(y-4)^2}{36} - \dfrac{x^2}{81} = 1$ ______________________

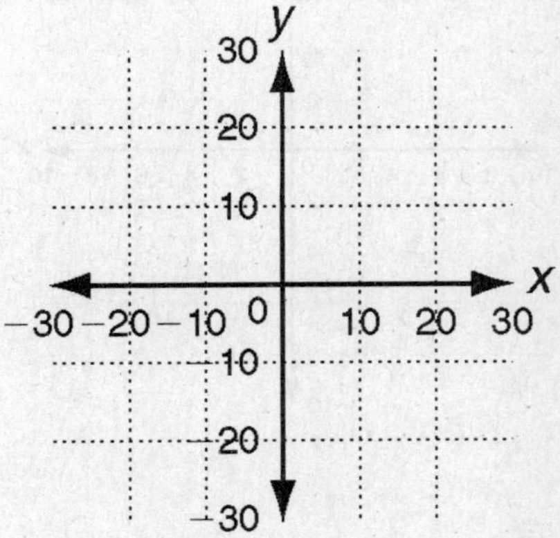

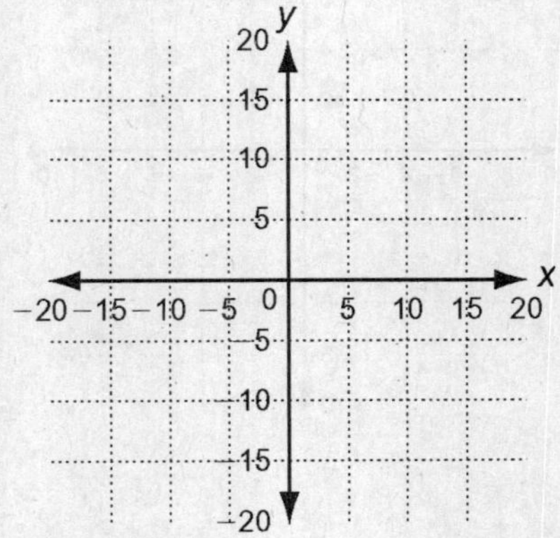

Solve.

9. A comet's path as it approaches the sun is modeled by one branch of the hyperbola $\dfrac{y^2}{1122} - \dfrac{x^2}{39{,}355} = 1$, where the sun is at the corresponding focus. Each unit of the coordinate plane represents one million miles. How close does the comet come to the sun? ______________________

Name ______________________ Date ____________ Class ____________

LESSON 12-5

Practice

Parabolas

Use the Distance Formula to find the equation of a parabola with the given focus and directrix.

1. $F(6, 0)$, $x = -3$ ______________________

2. $F(1, 0)$, $x = -4$ ______________________

Write the equation in standard form for each parabola.

3. Vertex (0, 0), directrix $y = -2$ ______________________

4. Vertex (0, 0), focus (9, 0) ______________________

5. Focus (–6, 0), directrix $x = 6$ ______________________

6. Vertex (0, 0), focus (0, –3) ______________________

Find the vertex, value of *p*, axis of symmetry, focus, and directrix of each parabola. Then graph.

7. $x - 1 = -\frac{1}{12}y^2$ ______________________

8. $y + 2 = \frac{1}{4}(x - 1)^2$ ______________________

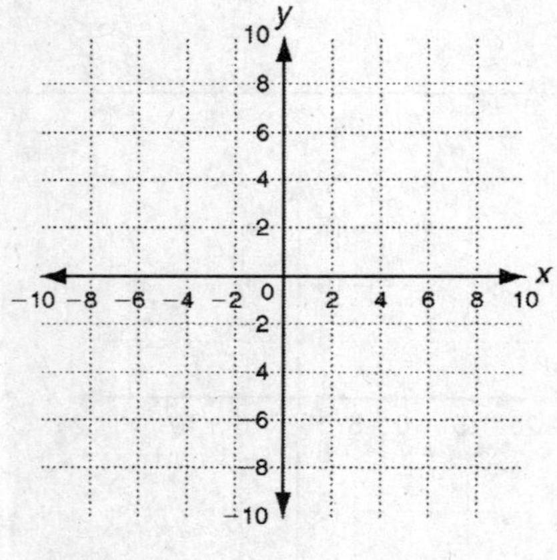

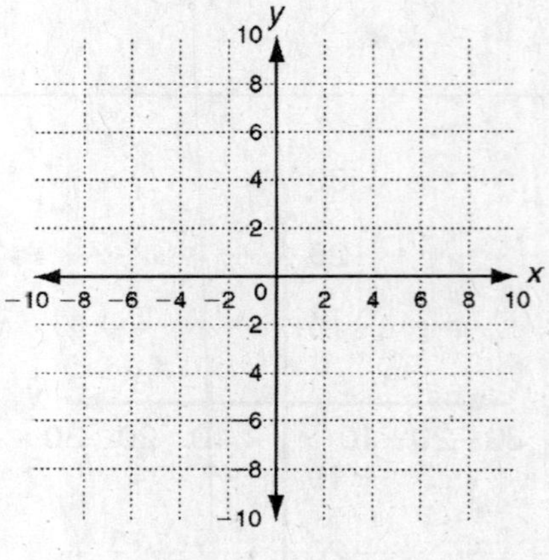

Solve.

9. A spotlight has parabolic cross sections.

   a. Write an equation for a cross section of the spotlight if the bulb is 6 inches from the vertex and the vertex is placed at the origin. ______________________

   b. If the spotlight has a diameter of 36 inches at its opening, find the depth of the spotlight if the bulb is 6 inches from the vertex. ______________________

Name ______________________ Date ______________ Class ______________

LESSON 12-6

Practice

Identifying Conic Sections

Identify the conic section that each equation represents.

1. $x - 1 = \frac{1}{4}(y - 8)^2$

2. $\frac{(y+7)^2}{6^2} + \frac{(x-9)^2}{1^2} = 1$

3. $(x - 9)^2 + (y + 1)^2 = 3^2$

4. $y + 5 = -(x - 9)^2$

5. $\frac{(y+4)^2}{4^2} - \frac{(x-4)^2}{3^2} = 1$

6. $\frac{(x-2)^2}{6^2} + \frac{(y+8)^2}{4^2} = 1$

7. $y^2 + 8x + 2y + 57 = 0$

8. $x^2 + y^2 - 4x + 4y - 17 = 0$

9. $x^2 - 9y^2 + 2x + 18y - 17 = 0$

10. $x^2 + 4y^2 - 2x - 16y + 1 = 0$

Find the standard form of each equation by completing the square. Then identify and graph each conic.

11. $x^2 - 16y^2 + 4x + 96y - 124 = 0$

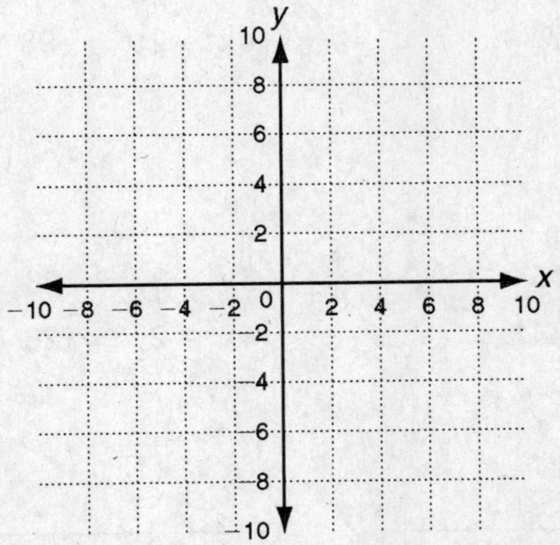

12. $x^2 + 4y^2 = 16$

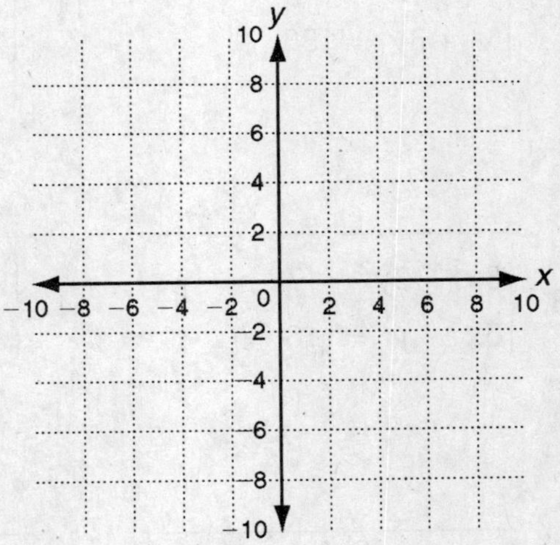

Solve.

13. A train takes a path around the town that can be modeled by the equation $x^2 + 28x + 16y = 348$. The town lies at the focus.

a. Write the equation in standard form.

b. If the measurement is in miles, how close does the train come to the town?

Name ______________________ Date ____________ Class ____________

LESSON 12-7

Practice

Solving Nonlinear Systems

Solve each system of equations by graphing.

1. $\begin{cases} 4x + y = 24 \\ x = \frac{1}{16}y^2 \end{cases}$

2. $\begin{cases} y - 4 = \frac{1}{4}x^2 \\ x + 2y = 12 \end{cases}$

3. $\begin{cases} 9y - 6x = 0 \\ \frac{x^2}{45} + \frac{y^2}{5} = 1 \end{cases}$

Solve each system of equations by using the substitution method.

4. $\begin{cases} x^2 + y^2 = 101 \\ 10x + y = 0 \end{cases}$

5. $\begin{cases} 3y = 4x \\ x^2 - y^2 = -63 \end{cases}$

6. $\begin{cases} 8y = x + 5 \\ x + 5 = \frac{1}{2}y^2 \end{cases}$

7. $\begin{cases} x^2 + y^2 = 34 \\ 3x - 3y = 6 \end{cases}$

8. $\begin{cases} x^2 + y^2 = 5 \\ y + 3 = \frac{1}{2}x^2 \end{cases}$

9. $\begin{cases} x^2 + y^2 = 109 \\ x - 7 = \frac{1}{3}y^2 \end{cases}$

Solve each system of equations by using the elimination method.

10. $\begin{cases} 2x^2 + y^2 = 86 \\ x^2 + 3y^2 = 133 \end{cases}$

11. $\begin{cases} 4x^2 + y^2 = 13 \\ 2x^2 - y^2 = -7 \end{cases}$

12. $\begin{cases} 3x^2 + 2y^2 = 350 \\ 4x^2 - 2y^2 = -98 \end{cases}$

13. $\begin{cases} 8x^2 - 3y^2 = 173 \\ 5x^2 - y^2 = 116 \end{cases}$

14. $\begin{cases} 2x^2 - 3y^2 = 15 \\ 3x^2 - 2y^2 = 341 \end{cases}$

15. $\begin{cases} 5x^2 - 3y^2 = 128 \\ 4x^2 - 2y^2 = 128 \end{cases}$

Solve.

16. The shape of a state park can be modeled by a circle with the equation $x^2 + y^2 = 1600$. A stretch of highway near the park is modeled by the equation $y = \frac{1}{40}(x - 40)^2$. At what points does a car on the highway enter or exit the park?

Name ______________________ Date ______________ Class ______________

LESSON 1-1

Problem Solving

Exploring Transformations

Harry is working on a budget for a concert. The graph shows the total cost of renting the hall. A cleaning fee of $40 for each rental is included in the graph. Use the graph for Exercises 1–6.

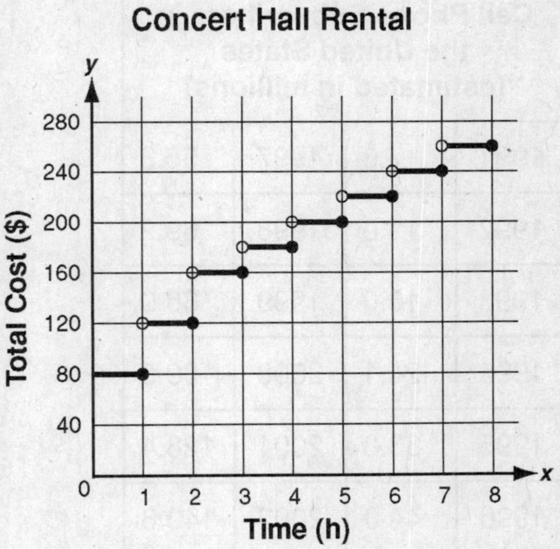

1. What is the cost of renting the hall for 2 hours? for 3 hours? for 6 hours? for 7 hours?

____

2. What is the rate per hour not including the cleaning fee if Harry rents the hall for up to 3 hours?

____

3. What is the rate per hour after the first 3 hours?

____

4. Describe the effect on the graph if the cleaning fee were changed to $25.

____

5. The managers decide that the minimum time for which the hall can be rented is 3 hours. Describe the effect this change would have on the graph above. How would the range change?

____

____

____

6. The Art Center gives Harry a graph showing its charges. This graph is the same shape as the graph above, but every point has been translated up 10 units. What would be the effect on Harry's budget if he chose to have the concert at the Art Center?

____

____

Choose the letter for the best answer.

7. Martha's profits from her bagel store last year were $0.35 per dozen bagels sold. This year her profits decreased 10%. What kind of transformation does this represent?

A vertical compression

B vertical stretch

C horizontal compression

D horizontal stretch

8. Shana drew the graph for a quadratic function. Then she did a horizontal stretch of the curve. Which transformation did she perform?

F $(x, y) \rightarrow (x, ay); |a| > 1$

G $(x, y) \rightarrow (bx, y); 0 < |b| < 1$

H $(x, y) \rightarrow (x, ay); 0 < |a| < 1$

J $(x, y) \rightarrow (bx, y); |b| > 1$

Name ______________________ Date ______________ Class ______________

LESSON 1-2

Problem Solving

Introduction to Parent Functions

Katy and Peter are writing a paper about the history and use of cell phones. They make a graph of the data in the table. They want to determine the parent function for the graph.

Cell Phone Subscribers in the United States (estimated in millions)			
1991	7.6	1997	55.3
1992	11.0	1998	69.2
1993	16.0	1999	86.0
1994	24.1	2000	109.5
1995	33.8	2001	128.4
1996	44.0	2002	140.8

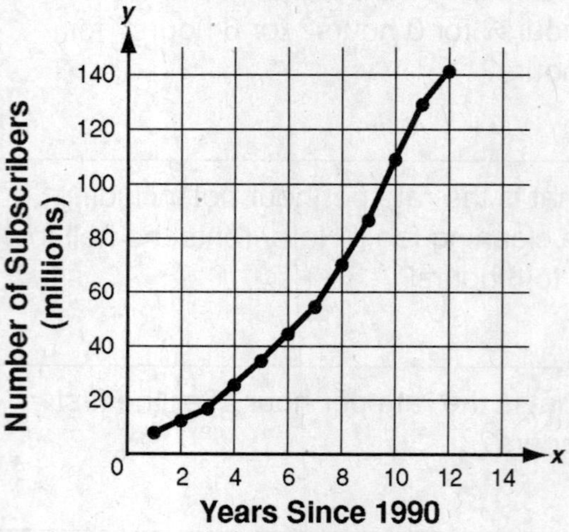

1. Peter wants to compare the graph to the function $f(x) = 7x + 2$. How would the graph of $f(x) = 7x + 2$ compare to its parent function $f(x) = x$?

____

2. What is the value $f(x) = 7x + 2$ for 1996, when $x = 6$? Does that point fit the graph? Try some other values of x for the function $f(x) = 7x + 2$. How well do the results fit the range of the graph?

____

3. Katy wants to compare the graph to the function $f(x) = x^2 + 5$. How would the graph of $f(x) = x^2 + 5$ compare to its parent function $f(x) = x^2$?

____

4. Find the value of $f(x) = x^2 + 5$ for 1996, when $x = 6$? Does that point fit the graph? Try some other values of x for the function $f(x) = x^2 + 5$. How well do the results fit the range of the graph?

____

5. Which parent function and transformation best models these data?

____

Name ______________________ Date ______________ Class ______________

LESSON 1-3

Problem Solving

Transforming Linear Functions

The students in Ms. Hari's English class are planning to print a booklet of their creative writings. Use the table of publishing prices.

Publishing Prices		
	Text Only	**Color Graphic**
Per page	\$0.55	\$1.25
Cover	\$2.25	\$3.50

1. The students decide to print a booklet containing black and white text only. Write a function, $C(p)$, to show the cost of printing a booklet of p pages with a cover that also has text only.

____

2. Julie wants the booklet cover to have a color graphic. Write a new function, $J(p)$, to show this cost for a booklet of p pages.

____

3. What is the slope of each function? What does the slope tell you about the relationship of the lines?

____

4. What is the y-intercept of each function? What is represented by the y-intercept?

____

5. Describe the transformation that has been applied to the graph by the decision to change the cover.

____

6. Oscar suggests that the booklet have 30 pages, one for each person in the class. What is the cost of printing 50 booklets, using the function $J(p)$?

____

Choose the letter for the best answer.

7. Lee writes a function for the cost of p pages, all in color, with a plain text cover. What transformation does this apply to the graph of $C(p)$?

   A Horizontal stretch

   B Horizontal compression

   C Vertical stretch

   D Vertical compression

8. Tina finds a printer who will print text pages at \$0.25 a page, with a color cover for \$2.00. Using this printer, what is the cost of 50 booklets of 30 pages each?

   A \$950

   B \$725

   C \$600

   D \$475

Name ______________________ Date ______________ Class ______________

LESSON 1-4

Problem Solving

Curve Fitting with Linear Models

As a science project, Shelley is studying the relationship of car mileage (miles per gallon) and speed (miles per hour). The table shows the data Shelley gathered using her family's hybrid vehicle.

Speed (miles per hour)	30	40	50	60	70
Mileage (miles per gallon)	34.0	33.5	31.5	29.0	27.5

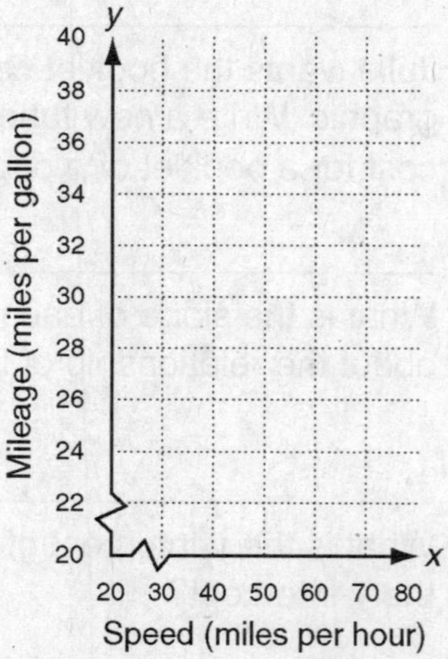

1. Make a scatter plot of the data. Identify the correlation.

____

2. Sketch a line of best fit on the graph.
3. Use two points on the line to find the slope.

____

4. Use the point-slope form to write an equation that models the data.

____

5. Use a graphing calculator to plot the data. Find the value of the correlation coefficient *r*.

____

6. What does the value of *r* tell you about the data?

____

7. What equation do you find with the calculator for the line of best fit?

____

Use the equation you wrote in Exercise 3. Choose the letter for the best answer.

8. Predict the mileage for a speed of 55 miles per hour.
   A 30
   B 34
   C 39
   D 46

9. Predict the speed if the mileage is 28 miles per gallon.
   A 32
   B 35
   C 67
   D 75

Name ______________________ Date ______________ Class ______________

LESSON 2-1

Problem Solving

Using Transformations to Graph Quadratic Functions

Christa and Jelani are standing at the top of the Leaning Tower of Pisa in Italy, 185 feet above the ground. Jelani wonders what the path of a dropped object would be as it falls to the ground from the top of the tower. The height of an object after *t* seconds is given by the function, $f(t) = -16t^2 + 185$.

1. Complete the table to show the height, $f(t)$, of the object for different values of t.

2. Plot the ordered pairs from the table and draw the graph to show the path of the object.

Time (t)	$f(t) = -16t^2 + 185$	$(t, f(t))$
0	$f(0) = -16(0)^2 + 185$	
1	$f(1) = -16(1)^2 + 185$	
2		
3		
4		

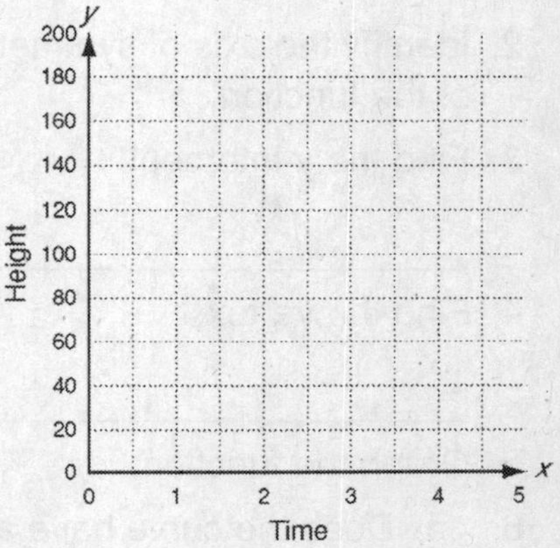

3. What is the parent function for the graph? ______________

4. What is the name for this U-shaped curve? ______________

5. Describe the transformations of the parent function into $f(t) = -16t^2 + 185$, which describes the path of an object falling from 185 feet.

____

Choose the letter for the best answer.

6. Mario dropped a wrench from the top of a sailboat mast 58 feet high. Which function describes the path of the falling wrench?

A $f(t) = 16(t - 58)^2 - 185$

B $f(t) = -16(t - 58)^2 + 185$

C $f(t) = 16t^2 - 58$

D $f(t) = -16t^2 + 58$

7. Delle wants to transform the parent function $f(t) = t^2$ into $f(t) = -4(t - 0.6)^2 + 6$. Which is NOT a step in that transformation?

A Translation 6 units up

B Translation 0.6 unit left

C Reflection across the *x*-axis

D Vertical stretch by a factor of 4

Name ______________________ Date ______________ Class ______________

LESSON 2-2

Problem Solving

Properties of Quadratic Functions in Standard Form

Kim wants to buy a used car with good gas mileage. He knows that the miles per gallon, or mileage, varies according to various factors, including the speed. He finds that highway mileage for the make and model he wants can be approximated by the function $f(s) = -0.03s^2 + 2.4s - 30$, where s is the speed in miles per hour. He wants to graph this function to estimate possible gas mileages at various speeds.

1. Determine whether the graph opens upward or downward. ______________________
2. Identify the axis of symmetry for the graph of the function. ______________________
3. Find the y-intercept.

____

4. Find the vertex.

____

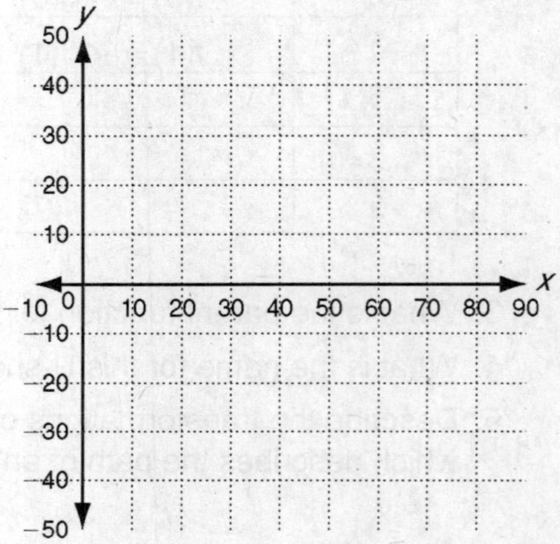

5. Graph the function.
6. a. Does the curve have a maximum or a minimum value?

____

b. What is the value of the y-coordinate at the maximum or minimum?

____

c. Explain what this point means in terms of gas mileage.

____

A ball is hit into the air from a height of 4 feet. The function $g(t) = -16t^2 + 120t + 4$ can be used to model the height of the ball where t is the time in seconds after the ball is hit. Choose the letter for the best answer.

7. About how long is the ball in the air?
   A 3.5 seconds
   B 3.75 seconds
   C 7 seconds
   D 7.5 seconds

8. What is the maximum height the ball reaches?
   A 108 feet
   B 124 feet
   C 229 feet
   D 394 feet

Name ______________________ Date ____________ Class ____________

LESSON 2-3

Problem Solving

Solving Quadratic Equations by Graphing and Factoring

Erin and her friends launch a rocket from ground level vertically into the air with an initial velocity of 80 feet per second. The height of the rocket, $h(t)$, after t seconds is given by $h(t) = -16t^2 + 80t$.

1. They want to find out how high they can expect the rocket to go and how long it will be in the air.

   a. Use the standard form $f(x) = ax^2 + bx + c$ to find values for a, b, and c. ____________

   b. Use the coordinates for the vertex of the path of the rocket to find t, the number of seconds the rocket will be in the air before it starts its downward path. ____________

   c. Substitute the value for t in the given function to find the maximum height of the rocket. How high can they expect their rocket to go? ____________

   d. Megan points out that the rocket will have a height of zero again when it returns to the ground. How long will the rocket stay in the air? ____________

2. Megan gets ready to launch the same rocket from a platform 21 feet above the ground with the same initial velocity. How long will the rocket stay in the air this time?

   a. Write a function that represents the rocket's path for this launch. ____________

   b. Factor the corresponding equation to find the values for t when h is zero. ____________

   c. Erin says that the roots of the equation are $t = 5.25$ and $t = -20.25$ and that the rocket will stay in the air 5.5 seconds. Megan says she is wrong. Who is correct? How do you know?

   ____

   ____

Choose the letter for the best answer.

3. Which function models the path of a rocket that lands 3 seconds after launch?

   A $h(t) = -16t^2 + 32t + 48$

   B $h(t) = -16t^2 + 32t + 10.5$

   C $h(t) = -16t^2 + 40t + 48$

   D $h(t) = -16t^2 + 40t + 10.5$

4. Megan reads about a rocket whose path can be modeled by the function $h(t) = -16t^2 + 100t + 15$. Which could be the initial velocity and launch height?

   A 15 ft/s; 100 ft off the ground

   B 16 ft/s; 100 ft off the ground

   C 100 ft/s; 15 ft off the ground

   D 171 ft/s; 15 ft off the ground

Name ______________________ Date ____________ Class ____________

LESSON 2-4

Problem Solving

Completing the Square

Sean and Mason run out of gas while fishing from their boat in the bay. They set off an emergency flare with an initial vertical velocity of 30 meters per second. The height of the flare in meters can be modeled by $h(t) = -5t^2 + 30t$, where *t* represents the number of seconds after launch.

1. Sean thinks the flare should reach at least 15 meters to be seen from the shore. They want to know how long the flare will take to reach this height.

   a. Write an equation to determine how long it will take the flare to reach 15 meters. ____________

   b. Simplify the function so you can complete the square. ____________

   c. Solve the equation by completing the square. ____________

   d. Mason thinks that the flare will reach 15 meters in 5.4 seconds. Is he correct? Explain.

   ____

   e. Sean thinks the flare will reach 15 meters sooner, but then the flare will stay above 15 meters for about 5 seconds. Is he correct? Explain.

   ____

2. Sean wants to know how high the flare will reach above the surface of the water.

   a. Write the function in vertex form, factoring so the coefficient of t^2 is 1. ____________

   b. Complete the square using the vertex form of the function. ____________

   c. How high will the flare reach? ____________

Choose the letter for the best answer.

3. Use the vertex form of the function to determine how long after firing the flare it will reach its maximum height.

   A 3 s

   B 5 s

   C 9 s

   D 15 s

4. The boys fire a similar flare from the deck 5 meters above the water level. Which statement is correct?

   A The flare will reach 45 m in 3 s.

   B The flare will reach 50 m in 3 s.

   C The flare will reach 45 m in 3.5 s.

   D The flare will reach 50 m in 3.5 s.

Name ____ Date ___________________ Class __________________

LESSON 2-5

Problem Solving

Complex Numbers and Roots

At a carnival, a new attraction allows contestants to jump off a springboard onto a platform to be launched vertically into the air. The object is to ring a bell located 20 feet overhead. The distance from the bell in feet is modeled by the function $dt = 16t^2 - bt + 20$, where t is the time in seconds after leaving the platform, and b is the takeoff velocity from the platform.

1. Kate watches some of the contestants. She theorizes that if the platform launches a contestant with a takeoff velocity of at least 32 feet per second, the contestant can ring the bell.

   a. Find the zeros for the function using 32 feet per second as the takeoff velocity. ________________________

   b. Is Kate's theory valid? Explain.

   ____

2. Mirko suggests they vary the value of b and determine for which values of b the roots are real.

   a. Complete the table to show the roots for different values of b.

   b. For which values of b in the table are the roots real?

   ____

   c. What difference does it make if the roots are real?

   ____

b	Function	Roots
24	$d(t) = 16t^2 - 24t + 20$	
32	$d(t) = 16t^2 - \_\_t + 20$	
40	$d(t) = 16t^2 - \_\_t + 20$	
48	$d(t) = 16t^2 - \_\_t + 20$	

3. Using the results from the table, and the function, estimate the minimum takeoff velocity needed for a contestant to be able to ring the bell. ________________________

Choose the letter for the best answer.

4. Mirko suggests using four bells at heights of 15, 20, 25, and 30 feet from the platform. How many of the bells can a contestant reach if the takeoff velocity is 32 feet per second?

   A 3 C 1

   B 2 D 0

5. At what height must a bell be placed for a contestant to reach it with a takeoff velocity of 48 feet per second?

   A 20 feet or less

   B 25 feet or less

   C 30 feet or less

   D 36 feet or less

Name ______________________ Date ____________ Class ____________

LESSON 2-6

Problem Solving

The Quadratic Formula

In a shot-put event, Jenna tosses her last shot from a position of about 6 feet above the ground with an initial vertical and horizontal velocity of 20 feet per second. The height of the shot is modeled by the function $h(t) = -16t^2 + 20t + 6$, where t is the time in seconds after the toss. The horizontal distance traveled after t seconds is modeled by $d(t) = 20t$.

1. Jenna wants to know the exact distance the shot travels at a velocity of 20 feet per second.

   a. Use the Quadratic Formula $t = \dfrac{-b \pm \sqrt{b^2 - 4ac}}{2a}$ to solve the height function for t. ____________

   b. Use the value for t and the distance function to find the distance her shot travels. ____________

2. Jenna is working to improve her performance. She makes a table to show how the horizontal distance varies with velocity. Complete the table.

	Velocity (ft/s)	Formula	Time (s)	Distance (ft)
a.	22	$t = \dfrac{-22 \pm \sqrt{(22)^2 - 4(-16)(6)}}{2(-16)}$		
b.	25			
c.	28			

Jenna has not reached her full potential yet. Her goal is to toss the shot from a height of 6 feet 6 inches with a vertical and horizontal velocity of 30 feet per second. Choose the letter for the best answer.

3. If she achieves her goal, how long will her shot stay in the air?

   A 1.65 s
   B 1.87 s
   C 2.07 s
   D 2.27 s

4. If she achieves her goal, what horizontal distance will the shot travel?

   A 41.4 ft
   B 56.1 ft
   C 62.1 ft
   D 68.1 ft

Name ______________________ Date ______________ Class ______________

LESSON 2-7

Problem Solving

Solving Quadratic Inequalities

The manager at Travel Tours is proposing a fall tour to Australia and New Zealand. He works out the details and finds that the profit *P* for *x* persons is $P(x) = -28x^2 + 1400x - 3496$. The owner of Travel Tours has decided that the tour will be canceled if the profit is less than \$10,000.

1. a. Write an inequality that you could use to find the number of people needed to make the tour possible. ______________

   b. Solve the related equation to find the critical values. ______________

   c. Test an *x*-value in each interval.

x-value	Evaluate	$P \geq 10{,}000$?
10	$-28(10)^2 + 1400(10) - 3496$	
30		
40		

   d. How many people will Travel Tours need to make the tour possible? ______________

2. A year later, the owner of Travel Tours decides that the Australia/New Zealand tour will have to make a profit of at least \$12,000 for the tour to be possible. What effect will this have on the range of people able to take this tour?

____

The manager plans a tour to the Fiji Islands and determines that the profit *P* for *x* persons is $P(x) = -40x^2 + 1920x - 3200$. Choose the letter for the best answer.

3. In order to make \$10,000 profit, how many people will it take for this tour to happen?

   A Between 9 and 39 people

   B Between 14 and 36 people

   C At least 22 people

   D At least 30 people

4. The owner thinks the company should make at least \$15,000 profit on the Fiji Islands tour. How many people will it take for the tour to happen?

   A Between 9 and 39 people

   B Between 13 and 35 people

   C At least 22 people

   D At least 35 people

Name ______________________ Date ______________ Class ______________

LESSON 2-8

Problem Solving

Curve Fitting with Quadratic Models

Ellen and Kelly test Ellen's new car in an empty parking lot. They mark a braking line where Ellen applies the brakes. Kelly then measures the distance from that line to the place where Ellen stops, for speeds from 5 miles per hour to 25 miles per hour.

Brake Test

Speed (mi/h)	5	10	15	20	25
Stopping Distance (ft)	7	17	30	46	65

1. Ellen wants to know the stopping distance at 60 miles per hour. She cannot drive the car at this speed in the parking lot, so they decide to try curve fitting, using the data they have collected.

   a. Can you use a quadratic function to represent the data in the table? Explain how you know.

   ____

   b. Use three points to write a system of equations to find *a*, *b*, and *c* in $f(x) = ax^2 + bx + c$. ______________

   c. Use any method to solve 3 equations with 3 variables. Find the values for *a*, *b*, and *c*. ______________

   d. Write the quadratic function that models the stopping distance of Ellen's car. ______________

   e. What is the stopping distance of Ellen's car at 60 miles per hour? ______________

The table shows the sizes and prices of decorative square patio tiles. Choose the letter for the best answer.

Patio Tiles Sale

Side Length (in.)	6	9	12	15	18
Price Each ($)	1.44	3.24	5.76	9.00	12.96

2. What quadratic function models the price of the patio tiles?

   A $P(x) = 0.4x^2$

   B $P(x) = 0.04x^2$

   C $P(x) = 0.04x^2 + 0.4x$

   D $P(x) = 0.04x^2 + x + 0.4$

3. What is the second difference constant for the data in the table?

   A 1.44

   B 1.08

   C 0.72

   D 0.36

Name ______________________________ Date ______________ Class______________

LESSON 2-9

Problem Solving

Operations with Complex Numbers

Hannah and Aoki are designing fractals. Aoki recalls that many fractals are based on the Julia Set, whose formula is $Z_{n+1} = (Z_n)^2 + c$, where *c* is a constant. Hannah suggests they make their own fractal pattern using this formula, where $c = 1$ and $Z_1 = 1 + 2i$.

1. Complete the table to show values of *n* and Z_n.

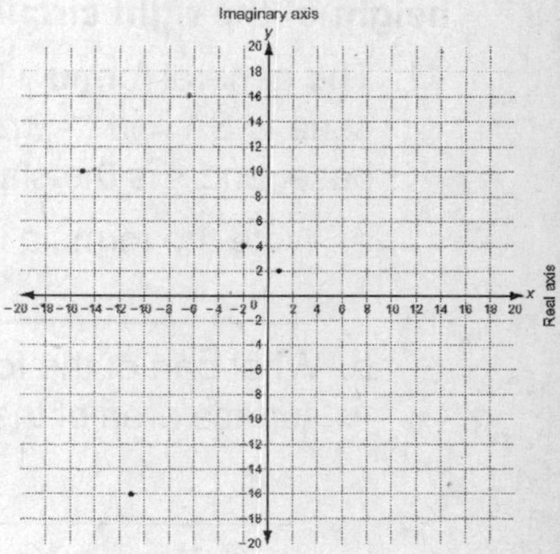

n	$Z_{n+1} = (Z_n)^2 + c$	Z_n
1	$Z_1 = 1 + 2i$	$Z_1 = 1 + 2i$
2	$Z_2 = (1 + 2i)^2 + 1$	$Z_2 =$
3	$Z_3 = (\_\_\_\_\_\_\_\_)^2 + 1$	$Z_3 =$
4	$Z_4 = (\_\_\_\_\_\_\_\_)^2 + 1$	$Z_4 =$

2. Four points are shown on the complex plane. Which point is not part of the fractal pattern they have created? Explain.

____

____

Choose the letter for the best answer.

3. Aoki creates a second pattern by changing the value of *c* to 3. What happens to Z_n as *n* increases?
   A The imaginary part is always twice the real part.
   B The real and imaginary parts become equal.
   C The real part becomes zero.
   D The imaginary part becomes zero.

4. Hannah changes the formula to $Z_{n+1} = \frac{1}{(Z_n)^2} + c$. Leaving $c = 1$ and $Z_1 = 1 + 2i$, what is the value of Z_2?
   A $0.48 - 0.16i$
   B $0.88 - 0.16i$
   C $1.2 - 0.4i$
   D $2.2 - 0.4i$

5. Aoki takes Hannah's new formula, leaves $c = 1$, and sets $Z_1 = \frac{1}{1+2i}$. What is the value of Z_3?
   A $Z_3 = -11 - 16i$
   B $Z_3 = 2 + 2i$
   C $Z_3 = 0.48 - 0.16i$
   D $Z_3 = 147.4 + i$

6. Hannah reverts to $Z_{n+1} = (Z_n)^2 + c$. She sets $Z_1 = i$ and $c = i$. Which statement is NOT true?
   A Z_n flip-flops between $(-1 + i)$ and $(-i)$.
   B The coefficient of *i* never reaches 2.
   C The imaginary part becomes zero.
   D On a graph $Z_1 - Z_3$ create a triangle.

Name ______________________ Date ______________ Class ______________

LESSON 3-1

Problem Solving

Polynomials

As part of a project to build a model castle, Julian wants to find the surface area of solid towers of various sizes, shaped like the one shown in the figure below. The diameter of the circular base is *d* inches, the height of the cylinder is *d* + 4 inches, and the slant height of the right circular cone is *d* – 0.6 inch.

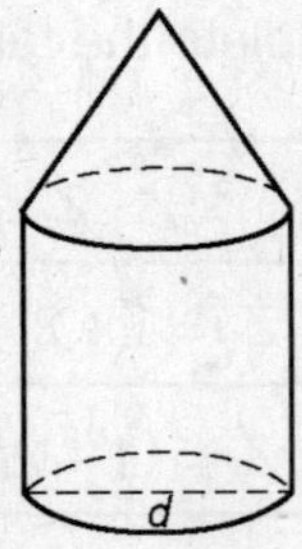

1. The general formula for the lateral surface area of a cone is $SA = \pi r^2 - \pi rs$, where *r* is the radius of the base, and *s* is the slant height of the cone.

   a. Write the formula in terms of *d*.

   ____

   b. What part of the formula will you use to find the surface area of the cone part of the model? Why?

   ____

   ____

   ____

2. The general formula for the surface area of a cylinder (with radius *r* and height *h*) is $SA = 2\pi r^2 + 2\pi rh$.

   a. Write the formula in terms of *d*. ______________________

   b. What part of the formula will you use to find the surface area of the cylinder part of the model? Why?

   ____

3. Write a general polynomial expression for the surface area of the model tower.

   ____

Choose the letter for the best answer.

4. What is the approximate surface area in square inches of a tower with a diameter of 5 inches?

   A 278 C 44
   B 196 D 38

5. What is the approximate surface area in square inches of a tower with a diameter of 10 inches?

   A 176 C 666
   B 278 D 1174

6. What is the approximate surface area in square inches of a tower where the height of the cylinder is 12 inches?

   A 931 C 445
   B 716 D 395

7. What is the approximate surface area in square inches of a tower where the slant height of the cone is 3.4 inches?

   A 103 C 158
   B 134 D 268

Name ______________________ Date ______________ Class ______________

LESSON 3-2

Problem Solving

Multiplying Polynomials

Latesha is making an open wooden toy box to hold the building blocks at her day care center. She has a square panel of cedar with side length of 24 inches. The first step is to cut out congruent squares from each corner. She needs to know what the side length of the cutout square should be in order for the finished toy box to have the greatest volume possible.

1. Draw a sketch to help solve the problem.

2. The toy box will be square and *x* inches deep. Write an expression for the side length of the finished box. ______________________

3. Write an equation to represent the volume. ______________________

4. Express the volume as the sum of monomials. ______________________

5. Latesha decides to try some possible values for *x*. She knows that *x* must be less than 12. Explain why.

____

6. Complete the table for each value of *x*. Round each volume to the nearest square inch.

***x* (in.)**	2	3	4	5	6
Volume (sq in.)					

7. Latesha decides that she will use an integer value for *x*, so that she does not have to cut fractions of an inch.

   a. What value for *x* should she choose? ______________________

   b. Explain why this is the best choice.

   ____

   c. What are the dimensions of her finished toy box?

   ____

Name ______________________ Date ______________ Class ______________

LESSON 3-3

Problem Solving

Dividing Polynomials

An art class is making pedestals in the shape of regular prisms to display sculptures in an art show. Blake is in charge of the mirrors for the tops of the pedestals. He needs to estimate the total area of the mirrored surfaces. He will use that total to help determine the amount of mirrored product to purchase.

The figures below show the shape of the bases for each of the three kinds of prisms that will be used for pedestals. Each regular polygon has a side length of *x*. Recall that, for a prism, $V = Bh$.

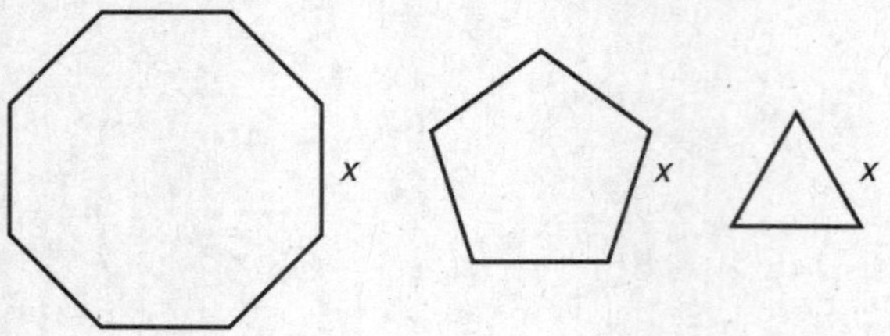

1. The triangular prism has a height of $2x + 1$ and its volume can be modeled by $V(x) = \frac{\sqrt{3}}{2}x^3 + \frac{\sqrt{3}}{4}x^2$. What is the area of the top of the pedestal?

____

Choose the letter for the best answer.

2. The volume of the pentagonal prism can be modeled by $V = 6.88x^3 - 1.72x^2$. Which expression represents the area of the top of the prism if the height is $4x - 1$?

   A $0.57x^2$
   B $1.72x^2$
   C $2.28x^2$
   D $6.88x^2$

3. The volume of the octagonal prism can be modeled by $V = 4.83x^3 - 24.15x^2$. Which expression represents the area of the top of the prism if the height is $x - 5$?

   A $48.3x^2$
   B $38.64x^2$
   C $4.83x^2$
   D $3.86x^2$

4. Which expression represents the total area that will be mirrored?

   A $A = x^2\left(\frac{\sqrt{3}}{4} + 6.55\right)$
   B $A = 6.98x$
   C $A = 12.58\,x^3 + 22.86\,x^2$
   D $A = \sqrt{6.98x}$

5. If $x = 5$, what is the total mirrored area in square units?

   A 6.98
   B 34.9
   C 69.8
   D 174.5

Name ______________________ Date ______________ Class ______________

LESSON 3-4

Problem Solving

Factoring Polynomials

Paulo is drawing plans for a set of three proportional nesting baskets, in the shape of open rectangular prisms.

1. The volume for the middle-sized basket (B) can be modeled by the function $V_B(x) = x^3 - 8x^2 + 4x + 48$. Use the graph to factor V_B.

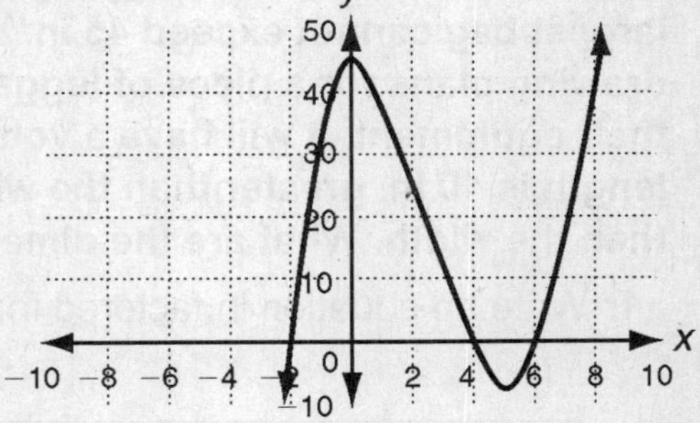

   a. What are the values of x where $V_B = 0$?

   ____

   b. Use these zeros to write the factors.

   ____

2. The volume for the largest basket (C) can be modeled by the function $V_C(x) = 2x^3 + 10x^2 + 8x$. Use the graph to factor V_C.

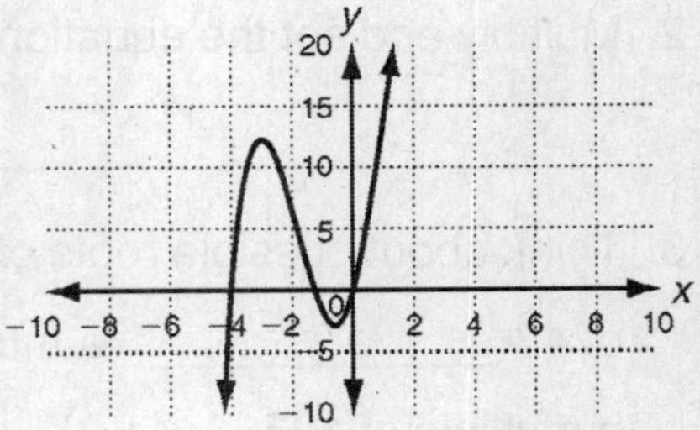

   a. What are the values of x where $V_C = 0$?

   ____

   b. Use these zeros to write the factors.

   ____

3. The volume for the smallest basket (A) can be modeled by the function $V_A(x) = x^3 - 22x^2 + 157x - 360$. Use the graph to factor V_A.

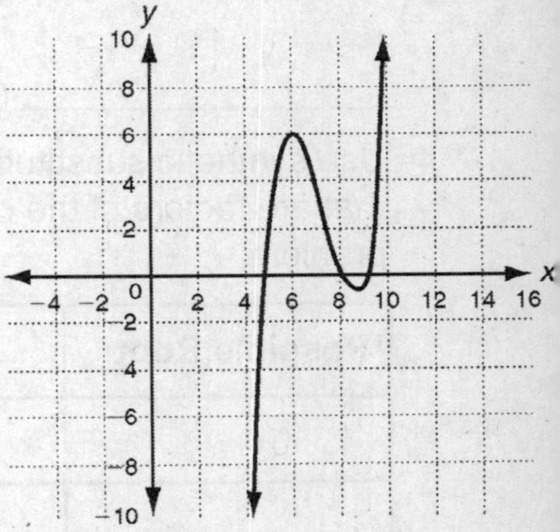

   a. What are the values of x where $V_A = 0$?

   ____

   b. Use these zeros to write the factors.

   ____

4. Complete the table. Use $x = 12$ units to find the actual dimensions and volume.

Basket	Dimensions (in terms of x)	Actual Dimensions	Volume
A			
B			
C			

5. Are the actual dimensions of the three baskets proportional? Explain.

____

6. Are the volumes of the three baskets proportional? Explain.

____

Name ______________________ Date ______________ Class______________

LESSON 3-5

Problem Solving

Finding Real Roots of Polynomial Equations

Most airlines have rules concerning the size of checked baggage. The rules for Budget Airline are such that the dimensions of the largest bag cannot exceed 45 in. by 55 in. by 62 in. A designer is drawing plans for a piece of luggage that athletes can use to carry their equipment. It will have a volume of 76,725 cubic inches. The length is 10 in. greater than the width and the depth is 14 in. less than the width. What are the dimensions of this piece of luggage?

1. Write an equation in factored form to model the volume of the piece of luggage.

____

2. Multiply and set the equation equal to zero.

____

3. Think about possible roots of the equation. Could a root be a multiple of 4? ____________ a multiple of 5? ____________ a multiple of 10? ____________. How do you know?

____

4. Use synthetic substitution to test possible roots. Choose positive integers that are factors of the constant term and reasonable in the context of the problem.

Possible Root	**1 −4 −140 −76,725**

____

Choose the letter for the best answer.

5. Which equation represents the factored polynomial?
   A $(w + 55)(w^2 + 25w + 1550) = 0$
   B $(w - 35)(w^2 + 60w + 1405) = 0$
   C $(w - 45)(w^2 + 41w + 1705) = 0$
   D $(w - 4)(w^2 - 140w + 76,725) = 0$

6. Which could be the dimensions of this piece of luggage?
   A 31 in. by 45 in. by 55 in.
   B 45 in. by 55 in. by 55 in.
   C 45 in. by 45 in. by 55 in.
   D 45 in. by 55 in. by 62 in.

Name ______________________ Date ______________ Class ______________

LESSON 3-6

Problem Solving

Fundamental Theorem of Algebra

A company that makes accessories for cars needs a container like that shown at the right to hold touch-up paint. The hemispherical top will be fitted with a brush applicator. The cylindrical part of the container should be 4 inches tall. The volume of the entire container is $\frac{13}{12}\pi$ cubic inches. Find the value of x, the radius of the hemisphere.

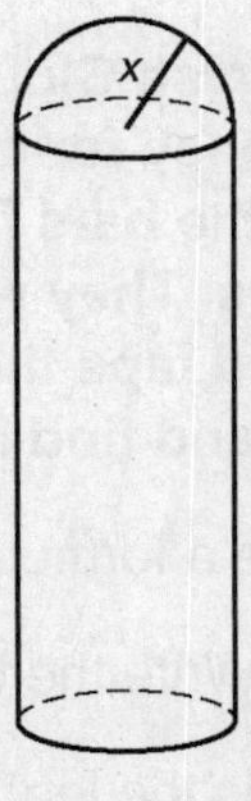

1. a. Write a formula for the volume of the cylindrical part of the container.

   ____

   b. Write a formula for the volume of the hemispherical part of the container.

   ____

2. Write an equation to represent the total volume of the container.

   ____

3. Write the equation in standard form.

   ____

4. Graph the equation with a graphing calculator. Hint: Use a window with x-values from –8 to 5 with a scale of 1, and y-values from –20 to 250 with a scale of 30 to see the general shape of the graph. Sketch the graph. Then focus on the area of the positive root by using a window of –8 to 3 on the x-axis and –20 to 20 on the y-axis. Use Trace to help you find a possible positive root.

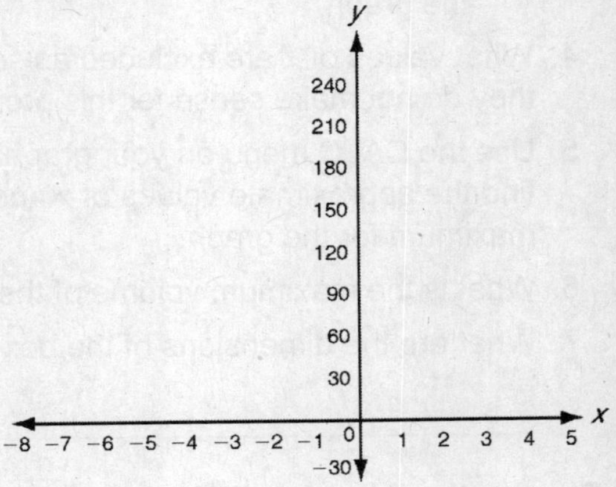

5. Verify the root using synthetic substitution. What is the positive root?

   ____

6. Use the Quadratic Formula to find approximate values for the other two roots. Explain why these two roots cannot also be solutions to the problem.

   ____

7. What is the value of x, the radius of the hemisphere, for this paint container? ______________

Name ______________________ Date ____________ Class ____________

LESSON 3-7

Problem Solving

Investigating Graphs of Polynomial Functions

The Spanish Club members are baking and selling fruit bars to raise money for a trip. They are going to make open boxes to display the bars from sheets of cardboard that are 11 inches by 17 inches. They will cut a square from each corner and fold up the sides and tape them. Find the maximum value for the volume of the box and find its dimensions.

1. Write a formula to represent the volume of the box. ____________

2. a. Write the equation in standard form. ____________

   b. Is the leading coefficient positive or negative? ____________

   c. Is the degree of the polynomial even or odd? ____________

   d. Describe the end behavior of the graph.

   ____

3. Use a graphing calculator to graph the equation. Hint: Try a window from –10 to 10 on the *x*-axis, with a scale of 1, and from –500 to 500 on the *y*-axis, with a scale of 100.

   a. How many turning points does the graph have? ____________

   b. Estimate the local maxima and minima from the graph. ____________

4. What values of *x* are excluded as solutions because they do not make sense for this problem? ____________

5. Use the CALC menu on your graphing calculator to find the approximate values of *x* and *y* at the local maximum for the graph. ____________

6. What is the maximum volume of the box? ____________

7. What are the dimensions of the box to the nearest tenth of an inch?

   ____

Choose the letter for the best answer.

8. Arturo is going to build a dog run using one side of his house and 100 feet of fencing. His design has an area that can be modeled by $A(x) = 100x - 7x^2$. What is the maximum area he can enclose?

   A 357 ft^2

   B 204 ft^2

   C 100 ft^2

   D 70 ft^2

9. In order to eliminate some choices on a standardized test, Ruth identifies which of these functions could NOT have a local maximum.

   A $F(x) = -7x^2 + 5x + 2$

   B $F(x) = -7x^3 + 5x - 11$

   C $F(x) = 7x^3 - 5x^2 - 2$

   D $F(x) = 7x^2 - 3x - 18$

Name ______________________ Date ______________ Class ______________

LESSON 3-8

Problem Solving

Transforming Polynomial Functions

A traffic engineer determines that the number of cars passing through a certain intersection each week can be modeled by $C(x) = 0.02x^3 + 0.4x^2 + 0.2x + 35$, where x is the number of weeks since the survey began. A new road has just opened that affects the traffic at that intersection. Let $N(x) = C(x) + 200$.

1. Find the rule for $N(x)$.

____

2. What transformation of $C(x)$ is represented by $N(x)$?

____

3. On the graph of $C(x)$, sketch the graph for $N(x)$.

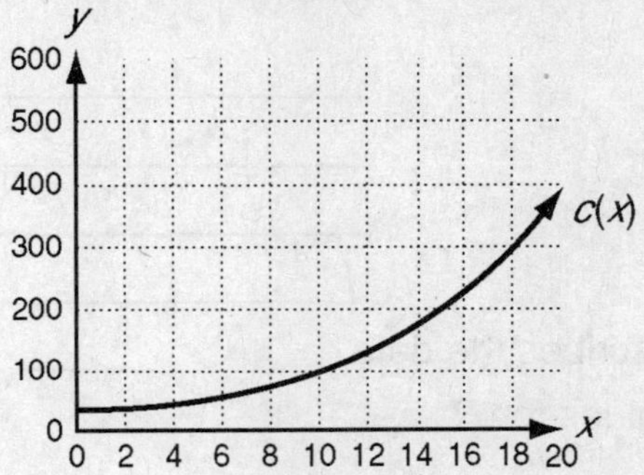

4. Use a graphing calculator to graph $N(x)$. Use a window from 0 to 20 with a scale of 1 on the x-axis and from 0 to 500 with a scale of 1 on the y-axis. Compare it to your sketch. Explain why only the values in Quadrant 1 are considered for this problem.

____

5. Explain the meaning of the transformation of $C(x)$ into $N(x)$ in terms of the weekly number of cars passing through the intersection.

____

6. Emergency roadwork temporarily closes off most of the traffic to this intersection. Write a function $R(x)$ that could model the effect on $C(x)$ Explain how the graph of $C(x)$ might be transformed into $R(x)$.

____

7. Describe the transformation $2C(x)$ by writing the new rule and explaining the change in the context of the problem.

____

Name ________________________ Date ______________ Class ______________

LESSON 3-9

Problem Solving

Curve Fitting with Polynomial Models

Carla has been making a "wild scape" in her backyard. The table shows the number of birds visiting her feeder at the same hour on the first day of each month since she began her project. Use a polynomial model to make a reasonable estimate of the number of birds there might be in July.

Birds at Feeder from 7:00 to 8:00 A.M.					
Jan	Feb	Mar	Apr	May	Jun
3	8	18	36	65	108

1. Use finite differences to determine the degree of the polynomial that best fits the data.
   a. First differences ______________
   b. Second differences ______________
   c. Third differences ______________
   d. Fourth differences ______________
   e. Which degree polynomial best describes the data? ______________
2. Use your graphing calculator to find values for R^2.
   a. For LinReg, R^2= ______________.
   b. For QuadReg, R^2= ______________.
   c. For CubicReg, R^2= ______________.
3. Write the polynomial model for this data. ______________
4. Use your polynomial model to make a reasonable estimate of the number of birds there might be in July. ______________

The table below shows the number of travel insurance policies sold by a travel agency over a six-year period. Choose the letter for the best answer.

Year	2001	2002	2003	2004	2005	2006
Policies Sold	73	126	163	185	192	184

5. Which function best models the data?
   A $f(x) \approx -0.926x^2 - 6.88x + 6.3$
   B $f(x) \approx -7.59x^2 + 75.27x + 5.5$
   C $f(x) \approx 0.05x^3 + 8.06x^2 + 76.74x + 4.3$
   D $f(x) \approx -0.02x^3 + 0.34x^2 - 9.47x + 2.8$

6. Use the polynomial model to estimate the number of policies that may be sold in 2008.
   A About 150
   B About 140
   C About 130
   D About 120

Name ______________________ Date ______________ Class ______________

LESSON 4-1

Problem Solving

Exponential Functions, Growth, and Decay

Justin drove his pickup truck about 22,000 miles in 2004. He read that in 1988 the average residential vehicle traveled about 10,200 miles, which increased by about 2.9% per year through 2004.

1. Write a function for the average mileage, $m(t)$, as a function of t, the time in years since 1988. ______________

2. Assume that the 2.9% increase is valid through 2008 and use your function to complete the table to show the average annual miles driven.

Year	1988	1992	1996	2000	2004	2008
t	0	4				
m (t)	10,200					

3. Did Justin drive more or fewer miles than the average residential vehicle driver in 2004? by how much (to the nearest 100 miles)?

____

4. Later Justin read that the annual mileage for light trucks increased by 7.8% per year from 1988 to 2004.
   a. Write a function for the average miles driven for a light truck, $n(t)$, as a function of t, the time in years since 1988. He assumes that the average number of miles driven in 1988 was 10,200. ______________
   b. Graph the function. Then use your graph to estimate the average number of miles driven (to the nearest 1000) for a light truck in 2004.

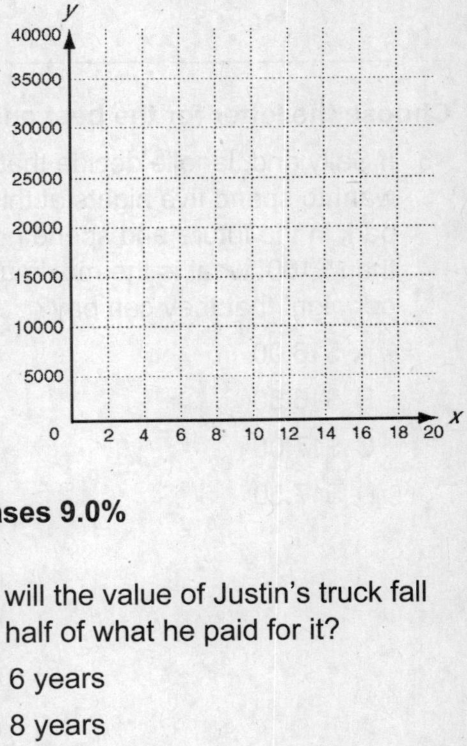

   ____
   c. Did Justin drive more or fewer miles than the average light truck driver in 2004? by how much?

____

Justin bought his truck new for $32,000. Its value decreases 9.0% each year. Choose the letter for the best answer.

5. Which function represents the yearly value of Justin's truck?
   A $f(t) = 32{,}000(1 + 0.9)^t$
   B $f(t) = 32{,}000(1 - 0.9)^t$
   C $f(t) = 32{,}000(1 + 0.09)^t$
   D $f(t) = 32{,}000(1 - 0.09)^t$

6. When will the value of Justin's truck fall below half of what he paid for it?
   F In 6 years
   G In 8 years
   H In 10 years
   J In 12 years

Name ______________________ Date ______________ Class ______________

LESSON 4-2

Problem Solving

Inverses of Relations and Functions

Sally and Janelle pay a total of $47.96 to camp for three nights at a state park. This includes a one-time park entrance fee of $5 and 9% sales tax. They paid $12 per night to stay for three nights last year, and the one-time park entrance fee was $5.

1. By how much per night has the price changed since last year?
   a. Write an equation for the total price, *p*, as a function of the price per night, *n*. ______________
   b. Find the inverse function that models the price per night as a function of the total price. ______________
   c. Evaluate the inverse function to find *n*, the price per night. ______________
   d. By how much has the price per night changed since last year? ______________
2. Sally is thinking about whether they want to stay at the park next year. Assume that the entrance fee and the sales tax rate will not change.
   a. If the price per night does not increase from this year's price, how much will it cost to stay for five nights next year?

   ____

   b. If the park management quotes them a price of $87.20 for five nights next year, what is the increase in the price per night?

   ____

Choose the letter for the best answer.

3. If Sally and Janelle decide that they want to spend five nights at this same park in the future and spend no more than $100, what is the maximum price per night that they can pay?
   A $16.00
   B $16.50
   C $17.00
   D $17.50
4. If the price of a camping vacation can be expressed as a function of the number of nights, what does the inverse function represent?
   F Number of nights as a function of the price per night
   G Number of nights as a function of the price of the vacation
   H Price of the vacation as a function of the price per night
   J Price of the vacation as a function of the number of nights

Name ______________________ Date ____________ Class ____________

LESSON 4-3

Problem Solving

Logarithmic Functions

The acidity of rainwater varies from location to location. Acidity is measured in pH and is given by the function $pH = -\log[H^+]$, where $[H^+]$ represents the hydrogen ion concentration in moles per liter. The table gives the $[H^+]$ of rainwater in different locations.

Hydrogen Ion Concentration of Rainwater	
Location	$[H^+]$ (moles per liter)
Central California	0.0000032
Eastern Texas	0.0000192
Eastern Ohio	0.0000629

1. Find the acidity of rainwater in eastern Ohio.
   a. Substitute the hydrogen ion concentration for rainwater in eastern Ohio in the function for pH.

   ____

   b. Evaluate the function. What is the acidity of rainwater in eastern Ohio to the nearest tenth of a unit?

   ____

2. Find how the acidity of rainwater in central California compares to the acidity of rainwater in eastern Ohio.
   a. Write a function for the acidity of rainwater in central California. ________________________
   b. Evaluate the function. What is the acidity of rainwater in central California to the nearest tenth of a unit? ________________________
   c. Compare the pH of rainwater in the two locations. Is the pH of rainwater in eastern Ohio greater than or less than that in central California? By how much? ________________________

Choose the letter for the best answer.

3. What is the pH of rainwater in eastern Texas?

   A pH = 3.7 C pH = 4.4

   B pH = 4.0 D pH = 4.7

4. Nick makes his own vegetable juice. It has a hydrogen ion concentration of 5.9×10^{-6} moles per liter. What is the pH of his vegetable juice?

   F pH = 4.9 H pH = 5.1

   G pH = 5.0 J pH = 5.2

5. What is the pH of a sample of irrigation water with a hydrogen ion concentration of 8.3×10^{-7} moles per liter?

   A pH = 6.1 C pH = 6.3

   B pH = 6.2 D pH = 6.4

6. What is the pH of a shampoo sample with a hydrogen ion concentration of 1.7×10^{-8} moles per liter?

   F pH = 7.4 H pH = 7.8

   G pH = 7.6 J pH = 8.0

Name ______________________ Date ______________ Class ______________

LESSON 4-4

Problem Solving

Properties of Logarithms

Trina and Willow are researching information on earthquakes. One of the largest earthquakes in the United States, centered at San Francisco, occurred in 1906 and registered 7.8 on the Richter scale. The Richter magnitude of an earthquake, *M*, is related to the energy released in ergs, *E*, by the formula $M = \frac{2}{3}\log\left(\frac{E}{10^{11.8}}\right)$.

1. Find the amount of energy released by the earthquake in 1906.

   a. Substitute 7.8 for magnitude, *M*, in the equation. ______________________

   b. Solve for the value of log *E*. ______________________

   c. Willow says that *E* is equal to 10 to the power of the value of log *E*. Is she correct? What property or definition can be used to find the value of *E*? Explain.

   ____

   d. Trina says the energy of the 1906 earthquake was 3.16×10^{23} ergs. Willow says the energy was $10^{23.5}$ ergs. Who is correct? How do you know?

   ____

Choose the letter for the best answer.

2. An earthquake in 1811 in Missouri measured 8.1 on the Richter scale. About how many times as much energy was released by this earthquake as by the California earthquake of 1906?

   A 2.8

   B 3.0

   C 3.6

   D 5.7

3. Another large earthquake in California measured 7.9 on the Richter scale. Which statement is true?

   F 0.1 times as much energy was released by the larger earthquake.

   G The difference in energy released is 1.31×10^{23} ergs.

   H The energy released by the second earthquake was 3.26×10^{23} ergs.

   J The total energy released by the two earthquakes is equal to the energy released by an 8.0 earthquake.

4. Larry wrote the following: $\log 10^{0.0038} = 3.8 \times 10^{-3}$. Which property of logarithms did he use?

   A Product Property

   B Quotient Property

   C Inverse Property

   D Power Property

5. Vijay wants to change $\log_5 7$ to base 10. Which expression should he use?

   F $\dfrac{\log_{10} 7}{\log_{10} 5}$　　H $\dfrac{\log_{10} 7}{\log_5 5}$

   G $\dfrac{\log_{10} 5}{\log_{10} 7}$　　J $\dfrac{\log_7 5}{\log_{10} 7}$

Name ______________________ Date ______________ Class______________

LESSON 4-5

Problem Solving

Exponential and Logarithmic Equations and Inequalities

While John and Cody play their favorite video game, John drinks 4 cups of coffee and a cola, and Cody drinks 2 cups of brewed tea and a cup of iced tea. John recalls reading that up to 300 mg of caffeine is considered a moderate level of consumption per day. The rate at which caffeine is eliminated from the bloodstream is about 15% per hour.

Caffeine Content of Some Beverages

Beverage	Caffeine (mg per serving)
Brewed coffee	103
Brewed tea	36
Iced tea	30
Cola	25

1. John wants to know how long it will take for the caffeine in his bloodstream to drop to a moderate level.

   a. How much caffeine did John consume?

   ____

   b. Write an equation showing the amount of caffeine in the bloodstream as a function of time. ______________________

   c. How long, to the nearest tenth of an hour, will it take for the caffeine in John's system to reach a moderate level? ______________________

2. a. Cody thinks that it will take at least 8 hours for the level of caffeine in John's system to drop to the same level of caffeine that Cody consumed. Explain how he can use his graphing calculator to prove that.

   ____

   b. What equations did Cody enter into his calculator?

   ____

   c. Sketch the resulting graph.

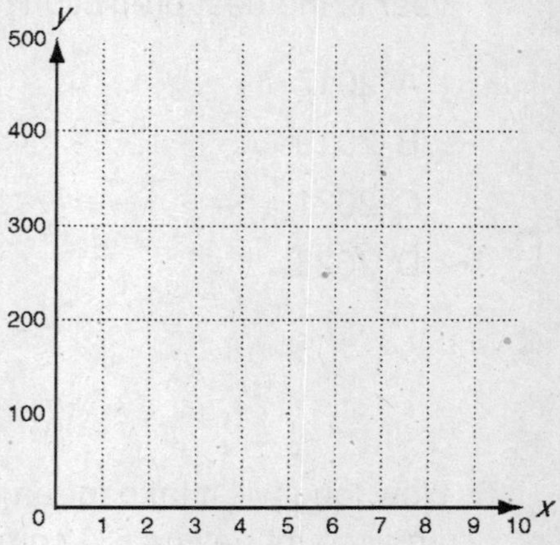

Choose the letter for the best answer.

3. About how long would it take for the level of caffeine in Cody's system to drop by a factor of 2?

   A 0.2 hour

   B 1.6 hours

   C 2.7 hours

   D 4.3 hours

4. If John drank 6 cups of coffee and a cola, about how long would it take for the level of caffeine in his system to drop to a moderate level?

   F 0.5 hour

   G 1.6 hours

   H 4.7 hours

   J 5.3 hours

Name ______________________ Date ______________ Class ______________

LESSON 4-6

Problem Solving

The Natural Base, e

Irene reads that the 2004 census of whooping cranes tallied 213 birds at one wildlife refuge in Texas. This number exceeded the 2003 record by 19. If the population of whooping cranes can be modeled using the exponential growth function $P_t = P_0 e^{kt}$, the population, P_t, at time t can be found, where P_0 is the initial population and k is the growth factor. Predict the population of whooping cranes over the next few years.

1. What was the size of the population of whooping cranes in 2003? ______________

2. Use the population figures for 2003 and 2004 to find the growth factor, k.

____

3. Complete the table to predict the population of whooping cranes through 2010.

Year	2006	2007	2008	2009	2010
t	3				
Population, P_t					

Choose the letter for the best answer.

4. Irene wants to know when the population of whooping cranes will exceed 1000. Using the 2003 population as P_0, which year is the best prediction?

   A 2017

   B 2019

   C 2021

   D 2023

5. Irene wonders how the 2010 whooping crane population would change if the growth factor doubled. Which statement is true?

   F The population would increase by a factor of e^2.

   G The population would increase by a factor of $e^{0.0934}$.

   H The population would increase by a factor of $e^{(0.0934)(7)}$.

   J The population would increase by a factor of $7e^2$.

6. How long will it take for an investment in an account paying 6% compounded continuously to double?

   A 10.2 years

   B 10.8 years

   C 11.6 years

   D 12.4 years

7. Darlene has a sample of a fossil that has 33% of its original carbon-14. Carbon-14 has a half-life of 5730 years. The decay constant for carbon-14 is 1.2×10^{-4}. Find the age of the fossil.

   F About 7820 years

   G About 8450 years

   H About 8980 years

   J About 9240 years

Name ______________________ Date ______________ Class ______________

LESSON 4-7

Problem Solving

Transforming Exponential and Logarithmic Functions

Alex is studying a new species of hybrid plant. The average height of the plant can be modeled by the function $h(t) = 2 \ln (t + 1.25)$, where h is the height in feet and t is the number of weeks after planting.

1. Alex graphs the function to see the rate an average plant grows.

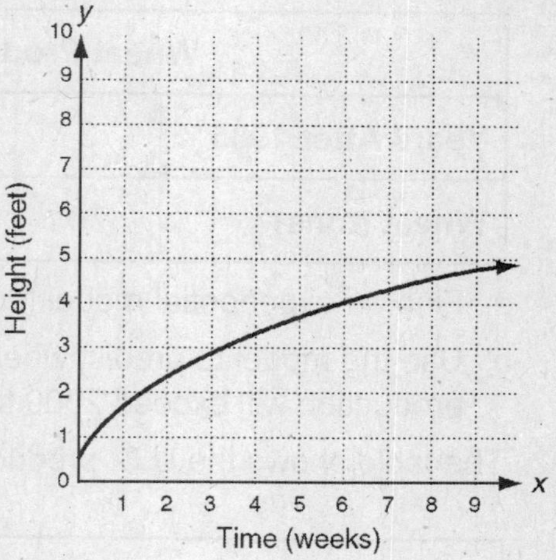

   a. About how tall can he expect the plant to be after 3 weeks?

   ____

   b. What is the y-intercept? What does it tell Alex about the plant?

   ____

2. Alex plants seeds and finds that the height is now modeled by the parent function.

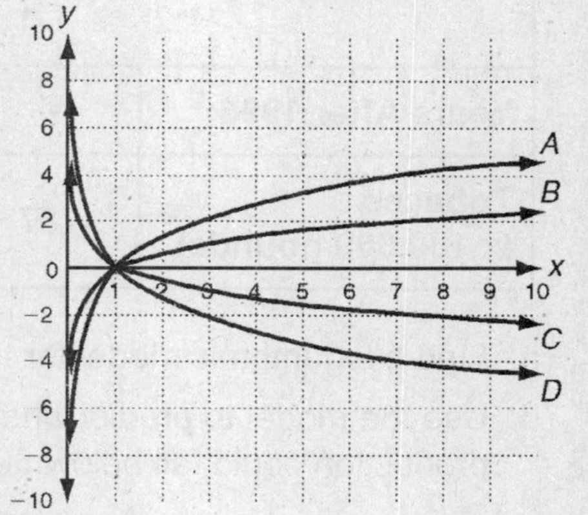

   a. Give the parent function $g(t)$. ______________

   b. Describe how the function $h(t)$ is transformed from the parent function.

   ____

   c. Choose the letter of the graph that represents the parent function.

   ____

Alex experiments with different fertilizers and finds that he can change the growth curve of the hybrid plant. Choose the letter for the best answer.

3. Alex finds that the height of the plants can now be modeled by the function $f(t) = 1.5 \ln (t + 1) + 0.4$. Which statement describes the transformation from the parent function?

   A Translation 0.4 unit up and 1 unit left; vertical stretch by 1.5

   B Translation 1 unit up and 0.4 unit right; vertical stretch by 1.5

   C Translation 0.4 unit down and 1 unit left; horizontal stretch by 1.5

   D Translation 1 unit down and 0.4 unit right; horizontal stretch by 1.5

4. Alex looks at the graph of the growth of his plants after trying a different fertilizer. The graph is transformed from the parent function by a vertical compression by a factor of 0.5 and a translation 1 unit right. Which function describes this transformation?

   F $k(t) = 2 \ln (t + 1)$

   G $k(t) = 2 \ln (t - 1)$

   H $k(t) = 0.5 \ln (t - 1)$

   J $k(t) = 0.5 \ln (t + 1)$

Name ______________________ Date ______________ Class ______________

LESSON 4-8

Problem Solving

Curve Fitting with Exponential and Logarithmic Models

Solve.

1. A small group of farmers joined together to grow and sell wheat in 1985. The table shows how their production of wheat increased over 20 years.

Wheat Produced by Growers Co-op						
Years After 1985	3	6	10	13	16	20
Wheat (tons)	70	105	150	210	340	580

a. Find an exponential model for the data. ______________

b. Use the model to predict when their wheat production will exceed 2000 tons. ______________

2. The table shows the U.S. production of tobacco from 1997 to 2002.

Tobacco Production						
Years After 1996	1	2	3	4	5	6
Tobacco (× 100,000 pounds)	1787	1480	1293	1053	992	890

a. Find a logarithmic model for the data. ______________

b. Use the model to predict when tobacco production could fall below 50,000,000 pounds. ______________

Robert recently discovered a forgotten student loan bill. The amount due after 10 years is now $10,819.33. He found some old statements and determined that after 7 years the bill was $8831.80 and after 5 years he owed $7714.03. Choose the letter for the best answer.

3. Which function models the data?

A $S(x) = 5000(1.07)^x$

B $S(x) = 1.07(5000)^x$

C $S(x) = 5500(1.07)^x$

D $S(x) = 1.07(5500)^x$

4. How much did Robert borrow initially?

F $5750

G $5500

H $5250

J $5000

5. Robert is planning to pay the loan in full next year. How much will he owe then?

A $12,092.14

B $11,925.07

C $11,869.33

D $11,576.69

6. What is the interest rate on Robert's student loan?

F 7%

G 6%

H 5%

J 4%

Name ______________________ Date ____________ Class ____________

LESSON 5-1

Problem Solving

Variation Functions

Last semester 5 of Mr. Dewayne's students built a 7-foot sailboat in 195 working hours. The time, *t*, that it takes for a group of students to build a sailboat varies inversely as the number of students. Mr. Dewayne uses this data to plan activities for next semester.

1. How many working hours would it take 12 students to build the same kind of sailboat?

   a. Write an equation relating the time required to the number of students working. ____________

   b. Find the constant k. ____________

   c. Explain the meaning of k in terms of student hours.

   ____

   d. Solve the equation to answer the question. ____________

2. How many students would be needed to build a 7-foot sailboat in 75 working hours? ____________

Choose the letter for the best answer.

3. Which equation represents the number of hours it would take 15 students to build a 7-foot sailboat?

   A $\frac{195}{5} = \frac{t}{15}$

   B $\frac{t}{195} = \frac{15}{5}$

   C $(195)(5) = 15t$

   D $195t = (5)(15)$

4. How many students must Mr. Dewayne get to participate in order to build a 7-foot sailboat in 65 hours?

   A 14 students

   B 15 students

   C 16 students

   D 17 students

5. Penny sells hot dogs from a cart at the beach. Her daily income, s, varies directly as the number of hot dogs, h, that she sells, and $s = \$255.50$ when $h = 73$. Find h when $s = \$304.50$.

   A 81

   B 83

   C 85

   D 87

6. The cost, c, of hiring a contractor to build a patio varies jointly as the area, A, in square feet, of the patio and the price, p, per square foot of the patio tiles; and $c = \$2832$ when $A = 80\text{ ft}^2$ and $p = \$2.95$. Find p when $c = \$4368$ and $A = 112\text{ ft}^2$.

   A \$2.95

   B \$3.25

   C \$3.45

   D \$3.60

Name ______________________ Date ____________ Class ____________

LESSON 5-2

Problem Solving

Multiplying and Dividing Rational Expressions

Anders designs a running field that consists of three concentric tracks as shown in the diagram.

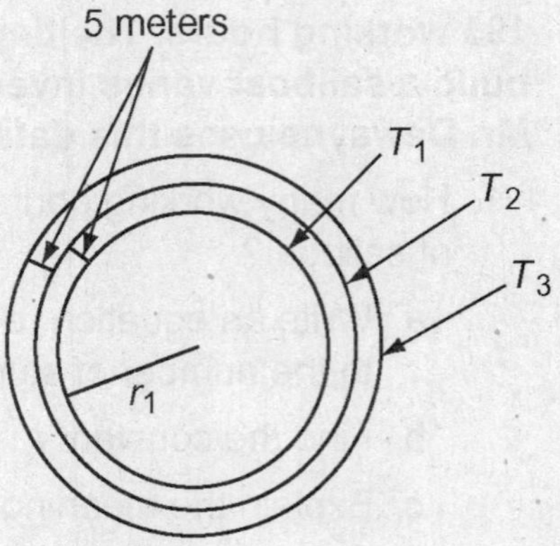

1. How do the lengths of each track compare?

   a. Write an equation for the length of the inner track, T_1, in terms of radius, r_1.

   ____

   b. Write an equation for the length of the middle track, T_2, in terms of radius r_1.

   ____

   c. Then write a rational expression for the ratio of the length of track T_2 to the length of track T_1 in terms of radius r_1.

   ____

2. Mari writes the expression $\frac{(r_1+10)(r_1-5)}{r_1^2-25}$ for the ratio of the length of the outer track, T_3, to that of the middle track, T_2. Anders thinks that is the wrong expression. Simplify Mari's expression to determine if she is correct. Explain.

   ____

   ____

3. Anders sets the radius of the inner track, T_1, at 70 meters.

   a. How many times longer is the middle track, T_2, than the inner track, T_1? ______________________

   b. How many times longer is the outer track, T_3, than the middle track, T_2? ______________________

   c. How many times longer is the outer track, T_3, than the inner track, T_1? ______________________

Choose the letter for the best answer.

4. How many times as large is the area enclosed by the outer track, T_3, than the area enclosed by the inner track, T_1?

   A $\left(\frac{10}{r_1}\right)$

   B $\left(\frac{10}{r_1}\right)^2$

   C $\left(\frac{r_1+10}{r_1}\right)$

   D $\left(\frac{r_1+10}{r_1}\right)^2$

5. What is the ratio of the area between the inner track and the outer track to the area enclosed by the inner track?

   A $20\left(\frac{r_1+5}{r_1^2}\right)$

   B $\frac{(r_1+10)^2-1}{r_1^2}$

   C $\pi\left(\frac{r_1+10}{r_1}\right)^2$

   D $\pi\left(\frac{10}{r_1}\right)^2$

Name ______________________ Date ____________ Class ____________

LESSON 5-3

Problem Solving

Adding and Subtracting Rational Expressions

Vicki and Lorena motor downstream at about 6 knots (nautical miles per hour) in their boat. The return trip is against the current, and they can motor at only about 3 knots.

1. Vicki wants to find the average speed for the entire trip.

   a. Write an expression for the time it takes to travel downstream plus the time it takes for the return trip if the distance in each direction is *d*. ______________________

   b. What is the total distance they travel downstream and upstream in terms of *d*? ______________________

   c. Write an expression for their average speed using the expressions for the total time and the total distance. ______________________

   d. Vicki says that the average speed is 4 knots. Lorena says that the average speed is 4.5 knots. Explain who is correct and why.

   ____

2. If they delay the return trip until the current changes direction, they can motor back at 4 knots. What is the average speed for the entire trip under these conditions?

   ____

Zak runs at an average speed of 7.0 miles per hour during the first half of a race and an average speed of 5.5 miles per hour during the second half of the race. Choose the letter for the best answer.

3. Which expression gives Zak's average speed for the entire race?

   A $\frac{(7+5.5)}{2}$

   B $\frac{12.5(7+5.5)d}{2}$

   C $\frac{(38.5)d}{(7+5.5)}$

   D $\frac{2(38.5)d}{(7+5.5)d}$

4. If Zak runs the race in 1.25 hours, what is the length of the race in miles?

   A 3.85

   B 6.25

   C 7.7

   D 12.5

5. In a later race, Zak increased his average speed during the second half of the race to 6.0 miles per hour. What is his average speed for this race in miles per hour?

   A 6.42

   B 6.46

   C 6.52

   D 6.56

6. It took Zak 1.6 hours to run this later race. What is the length of this race in miles?

   A 5.17

   B 7.28

   C 9.55

   D 10.34

Name ____________________ Date ______________ Class______________

LESSON 5-4

Problem Solving

Rational Functions

Members of a high school cheerleading squad plan a trip to support their robotics team at a regional competition. The trip will cost $70 per person plus a $420 deposit for the bus.

1. Find the total cost of the trip per cheerleader.

   a. Write a function that represents the total cost of the trip per cheerleader.

   ____

   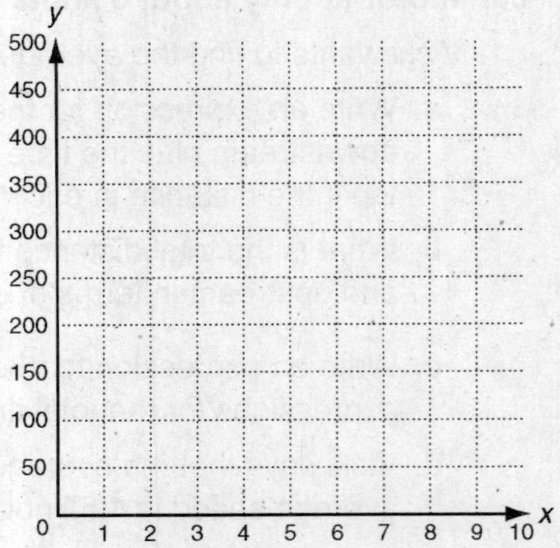

   b. Graph the function on your graphing calculator. Sketch a graph to represent the function.

   c. Use your graph to determine the cost per person if

   5 cheerleaders go on the trip. ______________

   7 cheerleaders go on the trip. ______________

   10 cheerleaders go on the trip. ______________

   d. What is the horizontal asymptote of the function? What does it mean in terms of the cost per person of the trip?

   ____

2. Stanton invites the cheerleaders to support the school's dive team at their next competition. The trip will cost $145 per person plus a $1000 deposit.

   a. Write a function to represent the cost of the trip per person. ______________

   b. What is the cost per person if

   5 cheerleaders go on the trip? ______________

   7 cheerleaders go on the trip? ______________

   10 cheerleaders go on the trip? ______________

   c. What is the increased cost for each of 10 cheerleaders to go with the dive team rather than to go with the robotics team? ______________

Choose the letter for the best answer.

3. The deposit for the bus on the robotics trip increases to $550. By how much does the cost per person increase if 10 cheerleaders go on the trip?

   A $13

   B $37

   C $83

   D $112

4. There are 15 cheerleaders signed up to go to the competition with the dive team. What is the cost per person to the nearest dollar?

   A $76

   B $103

   C $212

   D $304

Name ________________________ Date ______________ Class______________

LESSON 5-5

Problem Solving

Solving Rational Equations and Inequalities

Norton and Jessie have a lawn service business. Sometimes they work by themselves, and sometimes they work together. They want to know if it is worthwhile to work together on some jobs.

1. Norton can mow a large lawn in about 4.0 hours. When Norton and Jesse work together, they can mow the same lawn in about 2.5 hours. Jesse wants to know how long it would take her to mow the lawn if she worked by herself.

   a. Write an expression for Jessie's rate, using *j* for the number of hours she would take to mow the lawn by herself. ________________

   b. Write an equation to show the amount of work completed when they work together. ________________

   c. How long would it take Jessie to mow the lawn by herself? ________________

2. Jessie can weed a garden in about 30 minutes. When Norton helps her, they can weed the same garden in about 20 minutes. Norton wants to know how long it would take him to weed the garden if he worked by himself.

   a. Write an expression for Norton's rate, using *n* for the number of hours he would take to weed the garden by himself. ________________

   b. Write an equation to show the amount of work completed when they work together. ________________

   c. How long would it take Norton to weed the garden by himself? ________________

Choose the letter for the best answer.

3. Norton can edge a large lawn in about 3.0 hours. Jessie can edge a similar lawn in about 2.5 hours. Which equation could be used to find the time it would take them to edge that lawn if they worked together?

   A $\frac{1}{3} - \frac{1}{2.5} = \frac{1}{t}$

   B $\frac{1}{3} - \frac{1}{2.5} = t$

   C $\frac{1}{3} + \frac{1}{2.5} = \frac{1}{t}$

   D $\frac{1}{3} + \frac{1}{2.5} = t$

4. When Jessie helps Norton trim trees, they cut Norton's time to trim trees in half. What can be said about the time it would take Jessie to do the job alone?

   A Jessie would take the same amount of time as Norton.

   B Jessie would take half the time that Norton takes.

   C Jessie would take twice the time that Norton takes.

   D There is not enough information.

Name ______________________ Date ______________ Class ______________

LESSON 5-6

Problem Solving

Radical Expressions and Rational Exponents

Louise is building a guitar-like instrument. It has small metal bars, called frets, positioned across its neck so that it can produce notes of a specific scale on each string. The distance a fret should be placed from the bridge is related to a string's root note length by the function $d(n) = r\left(2^{-\frac{n}{12}}\right)$, where r is the length of the root note string and n is the number of notes higher than that string's root note. Louise wants to know where to place frets to produce different notes on a 50-cm string.

1. Find the distance from the bridge for a fret that produces a note exactly one octave (12 notes) higher than the root note.
   a. Substitute values for r and n in the given function. ______________
   b. How far from the bridge should the fret be placed? ______________
   c. What fraction of the string length is the distance of this fret from the bridge? ______________
2. Complete the table to find the distance from the bridge, for frets that produce every other note of an entire scale on this string.

Notes Higher than the Root Note	2	4	6	8	10	12
Distance of Fret from Bridge (cm)						

Choose the letter for the best answer.

3. Rafael made a ceramic cube in art class. The cube has a volume of 336 cm^3. What is the side length of the cube to the nearest centimeter?
   A 7
   B 12
   C 18
   D 56

4. Yolanda has an exercise ball with a volume of 7234 in.^{3}. Find the radius of the exercise ball to the nearest inch.
   A 24
   B 21
   C 19
   D 12

5. Which formula could you use to find the area of one side of a cube if the volume were given?
   A $A = V^{\frac{3}{2}}$
   C $A = V^{\frac{2}{3}}$
   B $A = V^{-\frac{3}{2}}$
   D $A = V^{-\frac{2}{3}}$

6. A party tent in the shape of a hemisphere has a volume of 14,130 m^3. What is the area of the ground that the tent covers in square meters?
   A 653.1
   C 1121.5
   B 706.5
   D 1256.0

Name ______________________ Date ______________ Class ______________

LESSON 5-7

Problem Solving

Radical Functions

On Earth the distance, *d*, in kilometers, that one can see to the horizon is a function of altitude, *a*, in meters, and can be found using the function $d(a) = 3.56\sqrt{a}$. To find the corresponding distance to the horizon on Mars, the function must be stretched horizontally by a factor of about $\frac{9}{5}$.

1. a. Write the function that corresponds to the given transformation.

   ____

   b. Use a graphing calculator to graph the function and the parent function. Sketch both curves on the coordinate plane.

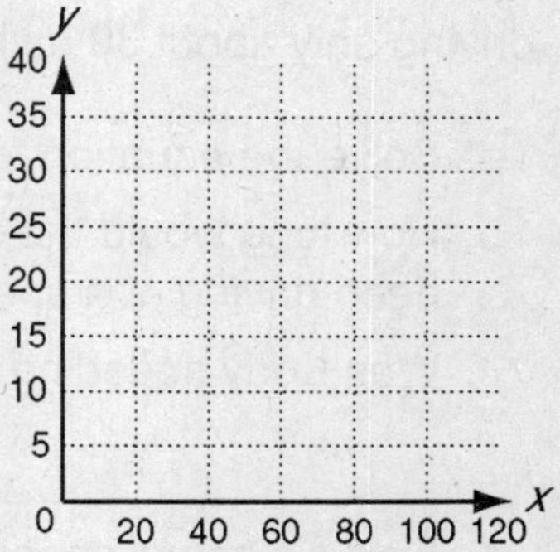

   c. Use your graph to determine the approximate distance to the horizon from an altitude of 100 meters:

   on Earth ______________________

   on Mars ______________________

Choose the letter for the best answer.

2. Which equation represents the radius of a sphere as a function of the volume of the sphere?

   A $r = \sqrt[3]{\frac{3\pi}{4V}}$ C $r = \sqrt[3]{\frac{4V}{3\pi}}$

   B $r = \sqrt[3]{\frac{3V}{4\pi}}$ D $r = \sqrt[3]{\frac{4\pi}{3V}}$

3. Alice graphed a function that is found only in the first quadrant. Which function could she have used?

   A $f(x) = \sqrt{x+2}$ C $f(x) = \sqrt{x} + 2$

   B $f(x) = -\sqrt{x}$ D $f(x) = \sqrt{x-2}$

4. Harry made a symmetrical design by graphing four functions, one in each quadrant. The graph of which function is in the third quadrant?

   A $f(x) = 4\sqrt{x}$ C $f(x) = -4\sqrt{x}$

   B $f(x) = 4\sqrt{-x}$ D $f(x) = -4\sqrt{-x}$

5. The side length of a cube can be represented by $s = \sqrt{\frac{T}{6}}$, where T is the surface area of the cube. What transformation is shown by $s = \sqrt{\frac{T}{3}}$?

   A Horizontal compression by a factor of 0.5

   B Horizontal stretch by a factor of 2

   C Vertical compression by a factor of 0.5

   D Vertical stretch by a factor of 2

6. The hypotenuse of a right isosceles triangle can be written $H = \sqrt{2x^2}$, where x is the length of one of the legs. Which function models the hypotenuse when the legs are lengthened by a factor of 2?

   A $H = \sqrt{2x^2} + 2$ C $H = \sqrt{4x^2}$

   B $H = \sqrt{2x^2} + 4$ D $H = \sqrt{8x^2}$

Name ______________________ Date ____________ Class ____________

LESSON 5-8

Problem Solving

Solving Radical Equations and Inequalities

The formula $s = \sqrt{30fd}$ can be used to estimate the speed, *s*, in miles per hour that a car is traveling when it goes into a skid, where *f* is the coefficient of friction and *d* is the length of the skid marks in feet.

1. How does the speed vary as the length of the skid marks? ____________

2. Kody skids to a stop on a street with a speed limit of 35 mi/h. His skid marks measure 52 ft, and the coefficient of friction is 0.7. Kody says that he was driving only about 30 mi/h. Kody wants to prove that he was not speeding.

   a. Solve the equation for *d* in terms of *s*. ____________

   b. How long would the skid marks be if he had been driving at a speed of 35 mi/h? ____________

   c. Was Kody speeding or not? Explain how you know.

   ____

   d. Find his actual speed. ____________

3. Ashley skids to a stop on a street with a speed limit of 15 mi/h to avoid a dog who runs into the street about 20 ft ahead of her. Ashley claims to have been going less than 15 mi/h. The coefficient of friction is 0.7.

   a. If Ashley were driving the speed limit, by what distance would she have missed the dog?

   ____

   b. If Ashley were driving less than 10 mi/h, by what distance would she have missed the dog?

   ____

Choose the letter for the best answer.

4. Barney was driving at 25 mi/h. A car pulls out 30 ft ahead of him. Which statement is true?

   A Barney hits the car.

   B Barney stops less than a foot from the car.

   C Barney misses the car by 3 ft.

   D Barney's skid marks measure 23 ft.

5. On a busy highway with a speed limit of 70 mi/h, a truck ahead of Verna jack-knifes across the road. Verna skids to a stop 10 ft short of the truck. Her skid marks measure 260 ft. Was Verna speeding?

   A Yes; her speed was 73.9 mi/h.

   B Yes; her speed was 75.3 mi/h.

   C No; her speed was 70 mi/h.

   D No; her speed was only 63 mi/h.

Name ____________________ Date ____________ Class ____________

LESSON 6-1

Problem Solving

Multiple Representations of Functions

Yvonne opened a new video game store. The table shows a record of her sales for the first five weeks. To break even, she needs to sell at least $12,500 worth of merchandise each week. She assumes the sales trend will continue and wants to know what to expect over the next weeks.

Weekly Store Sales	
Week	**Sales ($)**
1	8470
2	8920
3	9360
4	9790
5	10,210

1. Graph the data using weeks as the independent variable and sales as the dependent variable.

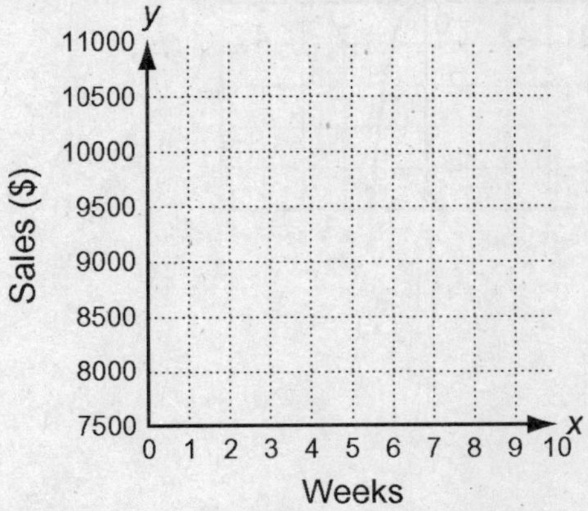

2. Yvonne thinks she can model her sales data using a quadratic function. Is she correct? How do you know?

____

3. Use a graphing calculator to perform the appropriate regression on the data. Write the equation that models the data. ____________

4. What sales can Yvonne expect in week 6? ____________

5. When will her sales exceed $11,000 per week? ____________

6. When will she break even? ____________

7. When will sales be twice the sales of week 1? ____________

Choose the letter for the best answer.

8. Which equation represents a steady increase of $420 per week in sales from week 5 on?

A $y = -420x + 10{,}210$

B $y = 420x + 10{,}210$

C $y = -5x^2 + 420x + 10{,}210$

D $y = -420x^2 + 10{,}210x$

9. During which week will Yvonne break even if the sales pattern changes and sales in week 6 and week 7 are $10,640 and $11,080, respectively?

F Week 9

G Week 10

H Week 11

J Week 12

Name ______________________ Date ____________ Class ____________

LESSON 6-2

Problem Solving

Comparing Functions

Sketch the graph of the function.

1. The quadratic function passes through points (–2, 0) and (2, 0). Find the point that represents the vertex.

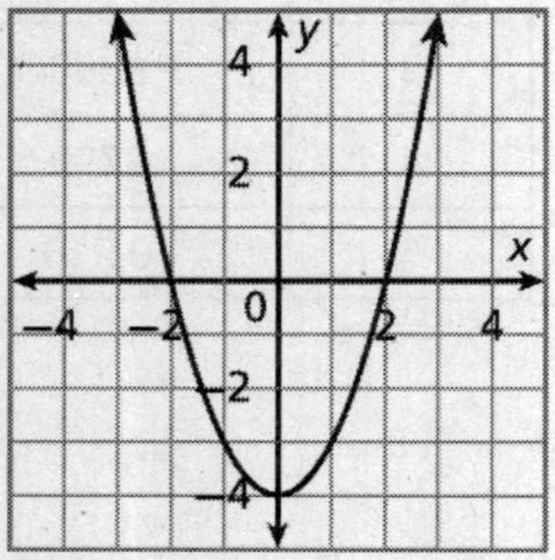

Solution:
Step 1: Plot the zeros.
Step 2: Find the vertex.
$(x + 2)(x - 2) = x^2 - 4$
vertex: (0, -4)
Step3: Sketch the graph.

2. The cubic function passes through points (–2, 16), (–1, 2), (1, –2), and (2, –16). Find the point that represents the zero.

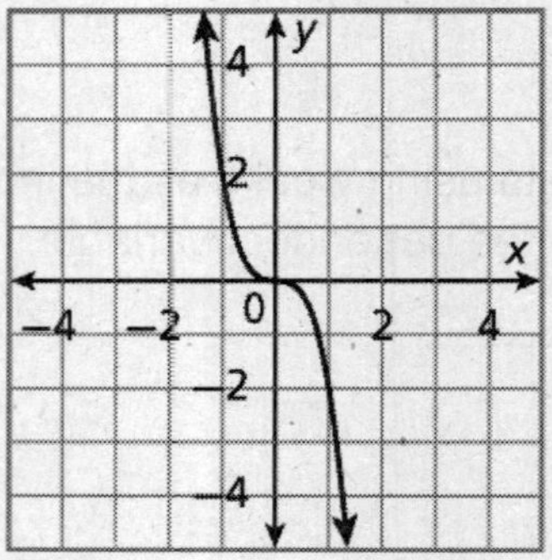

_______________________________ _______________________________

Determine which function matches the graph shown.

3.

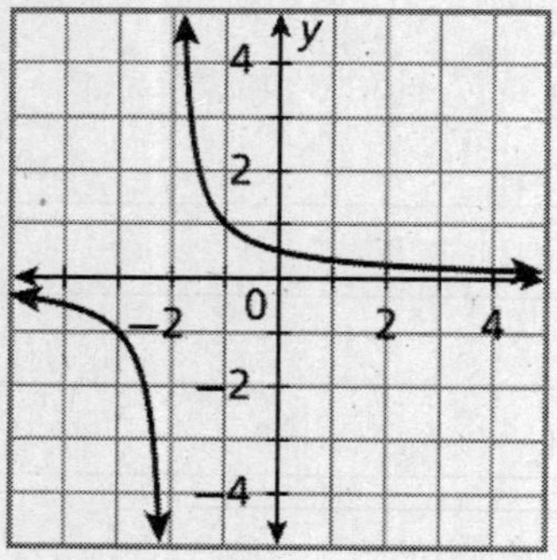

A $y = \ln x$

B $y = \log x$

C $y = \dfrac{1}{x+2}$

4.

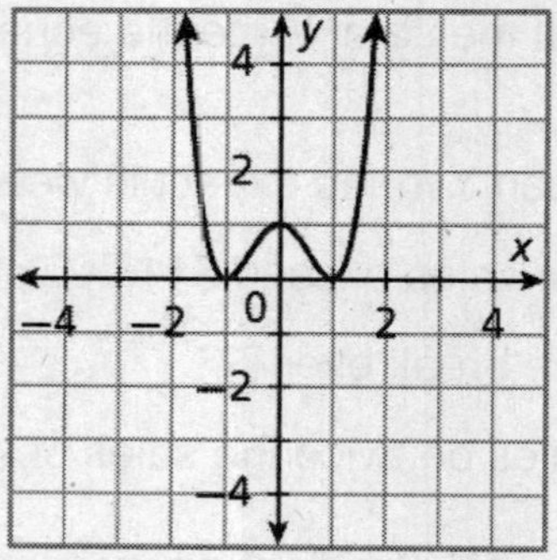

F $y = x^2 + 1$

G $y = x^2 - 2x + 1$

H $y = x^4 - 2x^2 + 1$

Name ______________________ Date ______________ Class ______________

LESSON 6-3

Problem Solving

Piecewise Functions

Roscoe earns $9.50 per hour at the woodcrafts store for up to 40 hours per week. For each hour over 40 hours he earns $13.00 per hour. Company policy limits his hours to no more than 60 per week. Roscoe wants to know how much he can earn in a week.

1. Complete the table to show his earnings for 30, 40, 50, and 60 hours per week.

Hours per Week (t)	Roscoe's Earnings, $E(t)$				
	Hours ≤ 40 ($9.50 per h)		Hours > 40 ($13.00 per h)		Total Earnings
30	30	$285	0	$0	$285
40					
50					
60					

2. Graph earnings as a function of hours worked, using the data from the table. Roscoe thinks the points lie in a straight line. Is he correct?

____

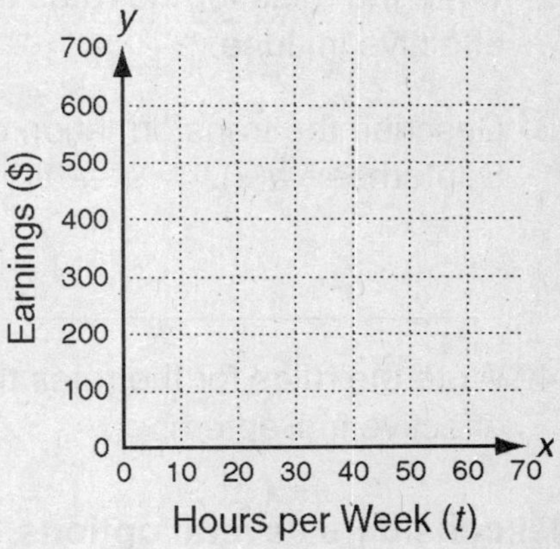

3. Draw line segments to join the points, including the point that represents earnings for 0 hours worked. Describe the graph in terms of line segments and the slope of each segment. Explain the meaning of the slope in terms of rate of pay.

____

____

4. Use the slope and a point on each line segment to write a piecewise function for earnings $E(t)$ as a function of hours worked (t). _______________________________

Choose the letter for the best answer.

5. How much will Roscoe earn if he works 56.5 hours in one week?

   A $594.50

   B $610.00

   C $625.50

   D $734.50

6. Roscoe earned $471 last week. How many hours did he work?

   F 45

   G 47

   H 49

   J 51

Name ______________________ Date ______________ Class______________

LESSON 6-4

Problem Solving

Transforming Functions

In March, Mei researches the sports clubs in her area. One club charges different rates according to the number of hours of use per month. The rate scale is modeled by the piecewise function below, where *x* is the number of hours of use.

$$f(x) = \begin{cases} 5x + 105 & \text{if } 0 \le x < 12 \\ 165 & \text{if } 12 \le x \le 20 \\ 7(x-20) + 165 & \text{if } x > 20 \end{cases}$$

Mei learns that all rates will increase by 10% in June. In September the club is planning to add a $5 monthly energy fee.

1. Describe the transformation of the fees in March, $f(x)$, to the fees in June, $g(x)$.

 ____

2. Write the rules for the rates that will be effective in June. ______________________

3. Describe the transformation of the fees in June, $g(x)$, to the fees in September, $h(x)$.

 ____

4. Write the rules for the rates that will be effective in September. ______________________

Mei considers several options. Choose the letter for the best answer.

5. How much will she pay if she joins and uses the club for 10 hours in March?

 A $95.00

 B $110.00

 C $155.00

 D $165.00

6. How much will she pay if she joins and uses the club for 10 hours in July?

 F $115.50

 G $165.50

 H $170.50

 J $175.50

7. How much will she pay if she joins and uses the club between 12 and 20 hours in August?

 A $215.50

 B $181.50

 C $165.00

 D $155.50

8. How much will she pay if she joins and uses the club for 25 hours in October?

 F $192.50

 G $208.00

 H $215.50

 J $225.00

Name ______________________ Date ____________ Class ____________

LESSON 6-5

Problem Solving

Operations with Functions

Andy is buying a new laptop computer. The store is offering a 15% discount on the model he wants. Andy also has a certificate from the manufacturer good for $120 off his next computer purchase. Andy wants to know whether he will pay less if the certificate amount is deducted before or after the discount is applied.

1. Write a function, D, to represent the price of the computer after the discount is applied. Use p to represent the original price. ______________
2. Write a function, R, to represent the price after the certificate amount is deducted. ______________
3. Find the composite function $R(D(p))$ and then describe what it means in terms of the final price of the computer.

____

4. Find the composite function $D(R(p))$ and then describe what it means in terms of the final price of the computer.

____

5. Will Andy pay less if the certificate amount is deducted before or after the discount is applied? Explain.

____

Emily has a coupon from her favorite store for $5 off any item this month. A sales tax of 8% is applied after the value of a coupon or discount is deducted. Let p represent the original price, $t(p)$ the price after tax, and $d(p)$ the price after the value of a coupon or discount is deducted. Choose the letter for the best answer.

6. Which function describes the final price of an item with price, p?
   A $td(p)$ C $d(t(p))$
   B $dt(p)$ D $t(d(p))$

7. Emily picks out a backpack with a price tag of p. Which expression gives the amount that Emily will pay?
   F $1.08(p - 5)$ H $0.92(p - 5)$
   G $(p - 5) + 0.08$ J $1.08p - 5$

8. If Emily uses her coupon to buy a pair of jeans that has been marked down to $50, what will she pay?
   A $41.40
   B $45.00
   C $48.60
   D $49.00

9. A month later Emily buys a jacket on sale at 30% off. Which expression gives the amount that she pays after tax?
   F $(p - 0.3) + 1.08$
   G $1.08(0.7p)$
   H $0.7p + 1.08p$
   J $0.92(p - 0.3)$

Name ______________________ Date ____________ Class ____________

LESSON 6-6

Problem Solving

Functions and Their Inverses

A juice drink manufacturer is designing an advertisement for a national sports event on its cans. The lateral surface area of the cans is given by the function $L(h) = 2.5\pi h$, where h is the height of the can. The total surface area of the can is given by the function $T(h) = 2.5\pi(h + 1.25)$.

1. The graphic designer needs to know how the height of the can varies as a function of the lateral surface area.

   a. Find the inverse, $h(L)$, of the function $L(h)$.

   ____

   b. Explain the meaning of the inverse function.

   ____

   c. If the lateral surface area of one can is 35.34 in^2, what is the height of this can? ____________

Choose the letter for the best answer.

2. The manufacturer produces cans in different sizes. The height of one can is 5.5 in. The designer is planning to use only half the lateral surface area of this can. What is this area?

   A 8.8 in^2

   B 11.0 in^2

   C 21.6 in^2

   D 43.2 in^2

4. The total surface area of one size of can is 45.16 in^2. What is the height of this can?

   A 3.5 in.

   B 4.5 in.

   C 5.5 in.

   D 6.5 in.

3. The designer is studying the possibility of using the total surface area of each can. Which function gives height, $h(T)$, as a function of total surface area, T?

   F $h(T) = \dfrac{T}{2.5\pi} - 1.25$

   G $h(T) = \dfrac{T}{2.5\pi} + 1.25$

   H $h(T) = (2.5\pi)(T - 1.25)$

   J $h(T) = (2.5\pi)(T + 1.25)$

5. The designer updates an old advertisement that covers the lateral surface area, L, of a can to create a new advertisement that covers the total surface area, T, of the can. Which function gives this area?

   F $T = (2.5\pi)(L + 1.25)$

   G $T = (2.5\pi)(L - 1.25)$

   H $T = L - 2.5\pi(1.25)$

   J $T = L + 2.5\pi(1.25)$

Name ______________________ Date ______________ Class ______________

LESSON 6-7

Problem Solving

Modeling Real-World Data

The table shows the population of Lincoln Valley over the last 7 years. The town council is developing long-range plans and is considering how the population might grow in the future if the current trend continues.

Lincoln Valley Population 2000–2006							
Year	1	2	3	4	5	6	7
Population	1049	1137	1229	1326	1434	1542	1662

1. What is the independent variable? What is the dependent variable? Assign x or y to each variable.

____

2. Make a scatter plot of the data. Do the data form a linear pattern? For this to be true, explain what must be true about finite differences.

____

3. Use the table of data.

   a. Find the first differences.

   ____

   b. Find the second differences.

   ____

   c. Find the third differences.

   ____

   d. Find the ratios between y-values.

   ____

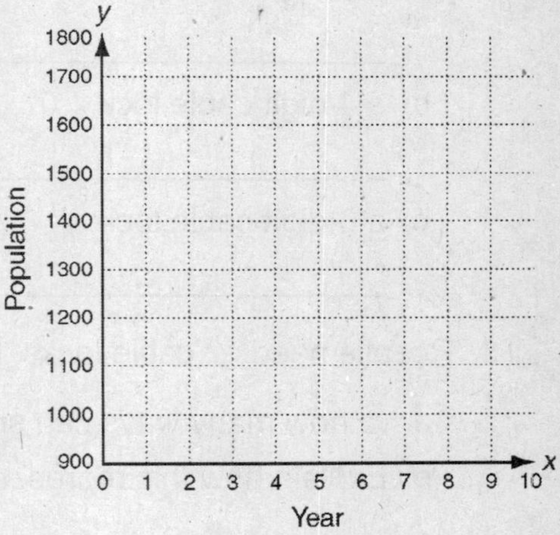

4. What kind of function will best describe the data? Justify your conclusion.

____

Choose the letter for the best answer.

5. Which function best models the given data?

   A $y = 101.9x + 932.1$

   B $y = 3.1x^2 + 77.0x + 969.6$

   C $y = 996.6x^{0.233}$

   D $y = 974.9(1.08)^x$

6. Predict the population of Lincoln Valley in 2012.

   F 2270

   G 2450

   H 2650

   J 2860

Name ________________ Date ____________ Class ____________

LESSON 7-1

Problem Solving

Permutations and Combinations

Rosalie is looking at locks. The label *combination lock* confuses her. She wonders about the number of possible permutations or combinations a lock can have.

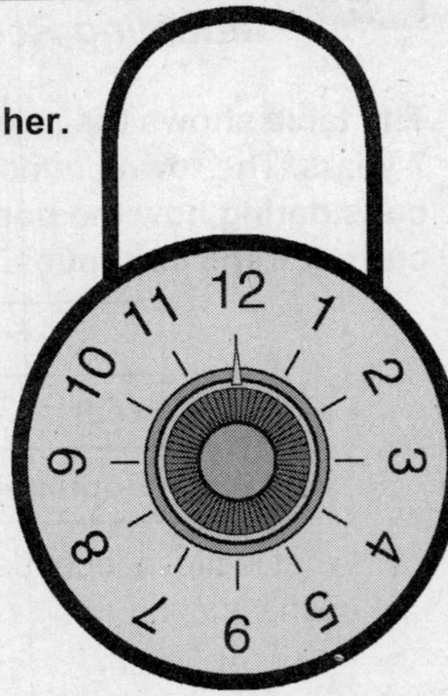

1. She looks at one circular lock with 12 positions. To open it she turns the dial clockwise to a first position, then counterclockwise to a second position, then clockwise to a third position

   a. Write an expression for the number of 3-position codes that are possible, if no position is repeated.

   ____

   b. Explain how this represents a combination or a permutation.

   ____

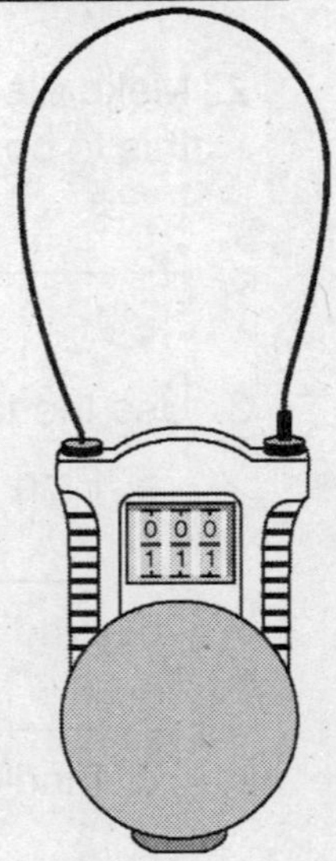

2. Rosalie looks at cable locks. Each position can be set from 0 to 9. How many different codes are possible for each lock if no digits are repeated in each code?

   a. a 3-digit cable lock

   ____

   b. a 4-digit cable lock

   ____

   c. a 6-digit cable lock

   ____

3. Rosalie needs 2 cable locks, but there are 13 types of locks to choose from.

   a. In how many ways can she choose 2 different locks? ____________

   b. Explain how this represents a permutation or a combination.

   ____

4. Explain why you think Rosalie might be confused by the label *combination lock.*

   ____

Rosalie wants to lock her bicycle near the library. There are 7 slots still open in the bike rack. Choose the letter for the best answer.

5. Rosalie arrives at the same time as 2 other cyclists. In how many ways can they arrange their bikes in the open slots?

   A 7
   B 35
   C 210
   D 343

6. Suppose Rosalie arrived just ahead of the 2 other cyclists and selected a slot. In how many ways can the others arrange their bikes in the open slots?

   F 2
   G 15
   H 24
   J 30

Name ______________________ Date ______________ Class ______________

LESSON 7-2

Problem Solving

Theoretical and Experimental Probability

As part of a grant to improve bus routes to and from school, Hogan and Jane gather traffic flow statistics for one intersection. They make a table to show their findings for between 7:45 A.M. and 8:00 A.M. on a Monday morning.

Traffic Direction	Number of Vehicles
Straight through	282
Turn north	94
Turn south	188

1. Analyze the statistics.

   a. Write and evaluate an expression for $P(N)$, the probability that a vehicle will turn north.

   ____

   b. Write and evaluate an expression for the probability that a vehicle will turn north or go straight through the intersection.

   ____

   c. Write and evaluate an expression for the probability that a vehicle will not turn north.

   ____

2. The police department gathers statistics on Tuesday. Officers count a total of 608 vehicles, of which 380 go straight through the intersection, 76 turn north, and the rest turn south.

   a. What is the probability that a vehicle will turn north? ______________

   b. What is the probability that a vehicle will turn north or go straight through the intersection? ______________

   c. What is the probability that a vehicle will not turn north? ______________

3. Does this represent theoretical or experimental probability? Explain.

____

Math Assessment Survey				
Activity	**Group Projects**	**Keep a Journal**	**Multiple Choice**	**Word Problems**
Student Response	57	18	35	10

A teacher surveys students on how they would prefer to have work assessed in math class. Choose the letter for the best answer.

4. What is the probability that a randomly chosen student prefers assessment through a group project?

   A $\frac{1}{12}$ C $\frac{19}{40}$

   B $\frac{53}{120}$ D $\frac{21}{40}$

5. Which expression gives the probability that a randomly chosen student will not want multiple-choice questions?

   F $\frac{7}{24}$ H $1-\frac{7}{24}$

   G $1+\frac{7}{24}$ J $35-\frac{7}{24}$

Name ______________________ Date ____________ Class ______________

LESSON 7-3

Problem Solving

Independent and Dependent Events

The table shows student participation in different sports at a high school. Suppose a student is selected at random.

Sports Participation by Grade

	Track	Volleyball	Basketball	Tennis	No Sport
Grade 9	12	18	15	9	66
Grade 10	6	20	12	2	95
Grade 11	15	11	8	5	61
Grade 12	7	6	10	12	50

1. What is the probability that a student is in grade 10 and runs track?
   a. Find the probability that a student is in grade 10, *P*(10). ____________
   b. Find the probability that a student runs track, given that the student is in grade 10, *P*(*Tr* | 10), ____________
   c. Find *P* (10 and *Tr*) = *P*(10) · P(*Tr* | 10). ____________
2. What is the probability that a student is in grade 12 and runs track or plays tennis?
   a. Find the probability that a student is in grade 12, *P*(12). ____________
   b. Find the probability that a student runs track or plays tennis, given that the student is in grade 12, *P*(*Tr* or *Te* | 12). ____________
   c. Find *P*(12 or (*Tr* or *Te*)). ____________
3. During a fire drill, the students are waiting in the parking lot. What is the probability that one student is in grade 12 and runs track or plays tennis, and the student standing next to her is in grade 10 and runs track?
   a. Find the probability for the first student. ____________
   b. Find the probability for the second student. ____________
   c. Find the probability for the event occurring. ____________
   d. Are these events independent or dependent? Explain.

____

Samantha is 1 of 17 students in a class of 85 who have decided to pursue a business degree. Each week, a student in the class is randomly selected to tutor younger students. Choose the letter for the best answer.

4. What is the probability of drawing a business student one week, replacing the name, and drawing the same name the next week?

   A 3.4 C 0.04

   B 0.2 D 0.002

5. What is the probability of drawing Samantha's name one week, not replacing her name, and drawing the name of another business student the next week?

   F $\frac{1}{85} \cdot \frac{16}{84}$ H $\frac{17}{85} \cdot \frac{16}{84}$

   G $\frac{1}{85} \cdot \frac{17}{84}$ J $\frac{17}{85} \cdot \frac{17}{84}$

Name ______________________________ Date ______________ Class ______________

LESSON 7-4

Problem Solving

Two-Way Tables

1. The table shows the number of students who would drive to school if the school provided parking spaces. Make a table of joint relative frequencies and marginal relative frequencies.

	Grades 9-10	Grades 11-12
Always	32	122
Sometimes	58	44
Never	24	120

	Grades 9-10	Grades 11-12	Total
Always	32/400 = 0.080	32/400 = 0.305	0.080 + 0.305 = 0.385
Sometimes	58/400 = 0.145	32/400 = 0.110	0.145 + 0.110 = 0.255
Never	32/400 = 0.060	32/400 = 0.300	0.060 + 0.300 = 0.360
Total	0.080 + 0.145 + 0.060 = 0.285	0.305 + 0.110 + 0.300 = 0.715	1

2. Gerry collected data and made a table of marginal relative frequencies on the number of students who participate in chorus and the number who participate in band.

		Chorus		
		Yes	**No**	**Total**
Band	**Yes**	0.38	0.29	0.67
	No	0.09	0.24	0.33
	Total	0.47	0.53	1.0

a. If you are given that a student is in chorus, what is the probability that the student also is in band? Round your answer to the nearest hundredth.

____

b. If you are given that a student is not in band, what is the probability that the student is in chorus? Round your answer to the nearest hundredth.

____

Select the best answer.

3. What is the probability if a student is not in chorus, then that student is in band?

A 0.29 C 055

B 038

4. What is the probability that if a student is not in band, then that student is not in chorus?

F 0.09 H 0.73

G 0.33

Name ______________________ Date ______________ Class ______________

LESSON 7-5

Problem Solving

Compound Events

Of 100 students surveyed, 44 are male and 54 are in favor of a change to a 9-period, 4-day school week. Of those in favor, 20 are female. One student is picked at random from those surveyed.

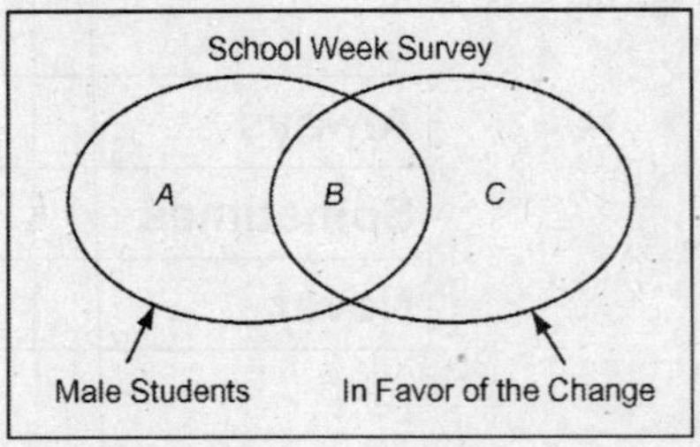

1. What is the probability that the student is male or favors the change? Use the Venn diagram.
   a. What is represented by the total of $A + B$?

   ____

   b. What is represented by the total of $B + C$?

   ____

   c. How many of those in favor of the change are male? ______________
   d. Find the values for A, B, and C and label the diagram.
   e. Write and evaluate an expression for the probability that the student is male or favors the change. ______________
2. What is the probability that the student is female or opposes the change?
   a. How many students are female? ______________
   b. How many students oppose the change? ______________
   c. If you draw a Venn diagram to show females and those opposed to the change, what is the meaning and value of the overlapping area?

   ____

   d. Write and evaluate an expression for the probability that the student is female or opposes the change. ______________
3. Of the students surveyed, 27 plan to start their own businesses. Of those, 18 are in favor of the change to the school week. Write and evaluate an expression for the probability that a student selected at random plans to start his or her own business or favors the change.

   ____

Sean asks each student to cast a vote for the type of class he or she would prefer. Of the students, 55% voted for online classes, 30% voted for projects, and 15% voted for following the textbook. Choose the letter for the best answer.

4. Which description best describes Sean's experiment?

   A Simple events

   B Compound events

   C Mutually exclusive events

   D Inclusive events

5. What is the probability that a randomly selected student voted for online classes or projects?

   F $\frac{33}{200}$

   G $\frac{7}{10}$

   H $\frac{1}{4}$

   J $\frac{17}{20}$

Name ______________________ Date ______________ Class ______________

LESSON 8-1

Problem Solving

Measures of Central Tendency and Variation

Each week, Damien records the miles per gallon for his car, to the nearest whole number. Over a period of 10 weeks, the data are 18, 17, 19, 18, 18, 25, 29, 30, 26, 19. He wants to arrange and summarize his data so that he can analyze it.

1. Make a box-and-whisker plot of his data.
   a. Order the data from least to greatest. ______________________
   b. Identify the minimum, maximum, median, first quartile, and third quartile.

   ____

   c. Use the number line to make a box-and-whisker plot of the data. Find and label the interquartile range.

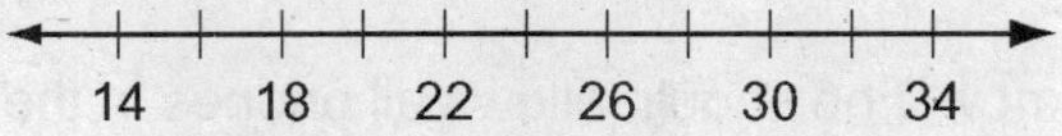

   d. Explain what the interquartile range represents in terms of the car's miles per gallon.

   ____

2. Find the standard deviation for the data.
   a. Write an equation and solve to find the mean. ______________________
   b. Complete the table to show the difference between the mean and each data value, and the square of that difference.

Data Value, *x*	18	17	19	18	18	25	29	30	26	19
$x - \bar{x}$										
$(x - \bar{x})^2$										

   c. Explain how to use the data from the table to find the standard deviation.

   ____

   d. What is the standard deviation for the data? ______________________
   e. Explain what the standard deviation represents in terms of the car's miles per gallon.

   ____

3. Damien thinks that the standard deviation is a more reliable measure of dispersion than the interquartile range. Is he correct? Explain.

____

____

____

Name ______________________ Date ______________ Class ______________

LESSON 8-2

Problem Solving

Data Gathering

100 students out of 1100 at a school were surveyed. The results are recorded in each problem below. For Exercises 1–4, predict the number of students in the population that would answer similarly.

1. 82 students said they would take a study hall or resource period if it were offered. **Solution:** 82 x 11 = 902 902 students

2. 12 students said they were members of the after-school music program. _____ x _____ = 132 ______________

3. 94 students said they used the Internet for their homework. ______________

4. 32 students said they drove to school. ______________

5. The principal wanted to know if he should allow cell phones in the classroom. He surveyed the students in Algebra 2 class. Decide whether the sampling method could result in a biased sample. Explain your reasoning.

____

6. A discount store chain wants to know how often families in a certain area would shop regularly at a discount store. Their representative surveys 100 people at a mall in the same area. Are his results likely to be representative of the population? Explain.

____

Select the best answer.

7. The director of the Glee Club would like to know if her Booster Club parents would do a fundraiser. Which sampling method is most likely to yield an accurate prediction of the population?

   A Survey every 3rd Booster Club parent who comes to a fundraiser meeting.

   B Survey every 10th Booster Club parent who comes to a fundraiser meeting.

   C Survey only the parents who respond to a letter from the director.

8. The principal of the school would like to determine if the cafeteria should sell snacks during non-lunch hour periods. Which sampling method is most likely to yield an accurate prediction of the population?

   F Survey every 20th student who enters the cafeteria during lunch hour.

   G Survey 50 random students each from the 9th, 10th, 11th, and 12th grades.

   H Survey the first 25 students that walk into the school.

Name ______________________ Date ______________ Class ______________

LESSON 8-3

Problem Solving

Surveys, Experiments, and Observational Studies

Explain whether each situation is an experiment or an observational study.

1. A teacher plays music during all tests given in a one-month period and compares the class grades with a similar class that does not have music played during tests.

   Solution: The teacher applies a treatment (playing music during tests) to some of the individuals (the class). This situation is an example of an experiment.

2. A real estate developer records the listing and selling prices of all homes in one area to determine the difference in the listing price and the selling price.

   Does the real estate developer control the individuals or apply a treatment? ______________

   Is the situation an experiment or an observational study? ______________

The study described below is a randomized controlled experiment. Describe the treatment, the treatment group, and the control group.

3. At a seed farm, 50 randomly chosen seeds were treated to temperatures above 100°F, and 50 other randomly chosen seeds were left at normal temperatures. At the end of the growing season, the heated group sprouted 20% faster than the non-heated group.

   ____

   ____

4. An engineer recruits 40 volunteers, and randomly assigns them to two groups. One group fills their cars with gasoline with an additive. The other group fills their cars with plain gasoline. The group that uses the additive sees a 5% decrease in fuel efficiency.

   ____

   ____

Choose the method that would be least biased.

5. An ice cream company wants to test whether the quality of ingredients it uses affects the taste of the product.

   A randomized comparative experiment

   B observational study

   C survey

6. An auto manufacturer wants to measure the fuel efficiency of a new hybrid car.

   F randomized comparative experiment

   G observational study

   H survey

Name ______________________ Date ______________ Class ______________

LESSON 8-4

Problem Solving

Significance of Experimental Results

Martin and Leandra are conducting a science experiment. They predict that frozen newspaper is stronger than ice. For the experiment, they made sheets of ice and sheets of frozen newspaper. They then placed weights on the sheets and recorded when the sheets collapsed. Their results are shown below.

Material	Trial 1	Trial 2	Trial 3	Trial 4	Trial 5
Ice	25 lb	22 lb	27 lb	26 lb	21 lb
Newspaper	35 lb	37 lb	30 lb	31 lb	40 lb

1. What are the median weights?

   Solution: Arrange each data set in order from least to greatest, and choose the middle value. ice: 25 lb, newspaper: 35 lb

2. What are the minimum weights? ______________

3. What are the maximum weights? ______________

4. Compare the results. Is there enough evidence to reject the null hypothesis?

   ____

   ____

   ____

   ____

Select the best answer.

5. If $\mu = 112$, $\bar{x} = 110$, $\sigma = 4$, and $n = 4$, what is z?

   A −2 C 1

   B −1

6. If $\mu = 50$, $\bar{x} = 60$, $\sigma = 1$, and $n = 25$, what is z?

   F 1 H 50

   G 25

7. If $\mu = 120$, $z = 4$, $\sigma = 12$, and $n = 9$, what is $\bar{x}$?

   A 136 C 81

   B 104

8. If $z = -1$, $\bar{x} = 19$, $\sigma = 15$, and $n = 25$, what is μ?

   F 16 H 25

   G 22

Name ______________________ Date ____________ Class ____________

LESSON 8-5

Problem Solving

Sampling Distributions

Interpret the margin of error.

1. An airline company polls passengers to find out which services they could cut to lower the cost of tickets. 56% of passengers said they could do without free drinks. 44% of passengers said they could do without in-flight movies. The margin of error for the poll was ±7%. Does the poll clearly predict the outcome of the voting?

   Solution: No; 56% ± 7% = 49% to 63%. 44% ± 7% = 37% to 51%. The intervals overlap, so the poll does not clearly indicate the outcome of the voting.

2. A circus wants to add a new act to the show. It polls a group of regular circus-goers. 48% said they would like to see a lion tamer. 52% said they would like to see more clowns. The margin of error for the poll was ±1%. Does the poll clearly indicate the majority's preference?

   ____

   ____

   ____

   ____

3. A school polled the students to see which new class they would prefer. 47% said East Asian History. 53% said Southern African Studies. The margin of error for the poll is ±3%. Does the poll clearly indicate the majority's preference?

   ____

   ____

   ____

4. The school's cafeteria polled students to find out what new meal they would prefer. 42% of the students said they would prefer fish. 58% of the students said they would prefer veggie burgers. The margin of error for the poll is ±5%. Does the poll clearly indicate the majority's preference?

   ____

   ____

   ____

Classify the sample.

5. A group of participants are chosen at random from a list.

   A self-selected sample

   B simple random sample

   C stratified sample

6. Participants are divided into groups, then chosen at random from those groups.

   F self-selected sample

   G simple random sample

   H stratified sample

7. Every sixth person is chosen from a list.

   A self-selected sample

   B simple random sample

   C systematic sample

8. Volunteers call a toll–free number to answer a survey.

   F self-selected sample

   G simple random sample

   H stratified sample

Name ______________________ Date ______________ Class ______________

LESSON 8-6

Problem Solving

Binomial Distributions

Sales records for the snack machines show that 1 out of every 6 students buys a bag of trail mix. There are 5 students waiting to use the machines. Melanie uses the formula for binomial probability, $P(r) = {}_nC_r p^r q^{n-r}$, to determine the number of students expected to buy trail mix.

1. What is the probability of exactly 3 students buying a bag of trail mix?
   a. What is the probability of each student buying a bag of trail mix? ______________
   b. Define each variable used in the formula and give its value.

   ____

   c. Write the binomial formula using these values. ______________
   d. Solve the equation to give the probability of exactly 3 students buying a bag of trail mix. ______________
2. What is the probability of at least 1 student buying a bag of trail mix?
   a. Describe a method to solve involving the sum of probabilities.

   ____

   b. Describe a method to solve that uses the formula $P(E) + P(\text{not } E) = 1$.

   ____

   c. Use either method to determine the probability of at least 1 student buying a bag of trail mix. ______________
3. After school, 4 students line up to buy snacks from the machine. What is the probability that they will all buy a bag of trail mix? ______________

Sports drinks are purchased by 3 out of 4 students using the snack machines. There are 3 students at the machines now. Choose the letter for the best answer.

4. Which expression gives the probability of exactly 2 students buying an energy drink?

   A $P(2) = {}_3C_2\left(\frac{3}{4}\right)^2\left(\frac{1}{4}\right)^1$

   B $P(2) = {}_4C_3\left(\frac{2}{3}\right)^2\left(\frac{1}{3}\right)^1$

   C $P(3) = {}_3C_2\left(\frac{3}{4}\right)^1\left(\frac{1}{4}\right)^2$

   D $P(3) = {}_4C_3\left(\frac{2}{3}\right)^1\left(\frac{1}{3}\right)^2$

5. What is the probability that at least 2 of the students will buy an energy drink?

   F 42%

   G 50%

   H 75%

   J 84%

Name ______________________ Date ______________ Class ______________

LESSON 8-7

Problem Solving

Fitting to a Normal Distribution

The scores on a test are normally distributed with a mean of 70 and a standard deviation of 6. Use the table below to answer the questions.

z	−2.5	−2	−1.5	−1	−0.5	0	0.5	1	1.5	2	2.5
Area	0.01	0.02	0.07	0.16	0.31	0.5	0.69	0.84	0.93	0.98	0.99

1. a. Estimate the probability that a randomly selected student scored less than 76.

   Solution: $z = \frac{76-70}{6} = \frac{6}{6} = 1$ 0.84

   b. Estimate the probability that a randomly selected student scored less than 79.

   $z = \frac{\_\_\_ - 70}{6} = \frac{\_\_\_}{6} = \_\_\_$ ______________

   c. Estimate the probability that a randomly selected student scored greater than 82. ______________

   d. Estimate the probability that a randomly selected student scored greater than 55. ______________

   e. Estimate the probability that a randomly selected student scored between 64 and 76. ______________

   f. Estimate the probability that a randomly selected student scored between 67 and 79. ______________

A student is analyzing a set of normally distributed data, but the data provided is incomplete. The student knows that the mean of the data is 120. The student also knows that 84% of the data are less than 130.

2. What is the standard deviation for this data?

   A −10

   B 10

   C 120

3. Use the table of z-scores above to determine which statement about this data is true.

   F About 90% of the values are greater than 140.

   G About 50% of the values are greater than 130.

   H About 68% of the values are between 110 and 130.

Name ______________________ Date ______________ Class______________

LESSON 8-8

Problem Solving

Analyzing Decisions

A game of chance is being played with a spinner divided into 8 equal sections as shown.

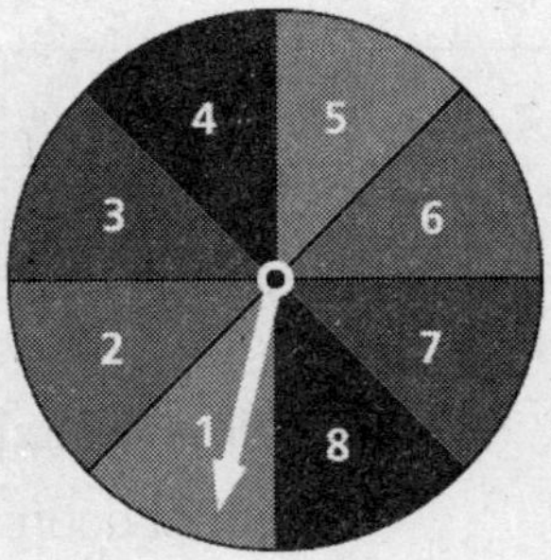

1. What is the expected value of a spin of the spinner?

   Solution: (1/8)(1) + (1/8)(2) + (1/8)(3) + (1/8)(4) + (1/8)(5) + (1/8)(6) + (1/8)(7) + (1/8)(8) = 0.125+ 0.25 + 0.375 + 0.5 + 0.625 + 0.75 + 0.875 + 1 = ____4.5____

2. If the game assigns a value of two points to a spin of 1, 2, or 3, four points to a spin of 4, 5, or 6, and eight points to a spin of 7 or 8, what is the expected value of a spin of the spinner for this game?

   (3/8)(2) + (3/8)(4) + (2/8)(__) = 0.75 + ___ + ___ = ____

   ____

3. A charity organization is having a raffle as part of its annual fundraising drive. The top prize is worth $1,000 and the probability of winning is 0.5%. The second prize is worth $100 and the probability of winning is 5%. Find the expected value of a raffle ticket.

   ____

4. In a carnival game, a bail is hidden under one of three shells. A player pays $2 per guess. After each guess, the shells are mixed up again. The prize for guessing the right shell is $3. What is the expected value for playing this game once? Explain what this means for the player.

   ____

5. Marilyn is buying a new GPS, and is deciding whether to buy a 1-year warranty. The warranty costs $40, and covers all repairs. If she does not get the warranty, there is a 10% chance she will have to replace the GPS for $100 within the first year, and a 15% chance that she will need a repair costing $50. Should she buy the warranty? Explain.

   ____

   ____

Choose the letter for the best answer.

6. Matt and Jenny are playing a game with a six-sided number cube labeled 1–6. If the cube lands on the numbers 1 through 4, they get 3 points. If the cube lands on any other number, they get 6 points. What is the expected value of rolling the number cube?

   A 3 points C 6 points

   B 4 points

7. Which of the following has the highest expected value?

   F number cube with sides 1, 3, 5, 7, 9, 11

   G number cube with sides 2, 4, 6, 8, 10, 12

   H spinner divided into 5 equal sections labeled 2, 4, 6, 8,

Name ______________________ Date ______________ Class ______________

LESSON 9-1

Problem Solving

Introduction to Sequences

Tina is working on some home improvement projects involving repeated tasks. She wants to analyze her work patterns.

1. Tina is hammering nails into wallboard. With the first hit, a nail goes in 13.5 millimeters; with the second, it goes in an additional 9 mm; with the third, it goes in an additional 6 mm; and with the fourth it goes in 4 mm further. Suppose this pattern continues. Predict how far the nail would go in with the seventh hit.

   a. Complete the table to find first differences, second differences, and ratios.

Distance	13.5mm	9mm	6mm	4mm
Ratios	$\frac{2}{3}$			
First Differences	–4.5			
Second Differences				

   b. How do you know whether the rule for the sequence of distances that the nail goes in is linear, quadratic, or exponential? ________________

   c. Write a possible rule for a_n , the *n*th term in the sequence. ________________

   d. If this pattern continues, how far would the nail go in with the seventh hit? ________________

2. Tina builds a fence for her neighbor. It takes her 10 minutes to pound the first fence post into the ground. The neighbor predicts that Tina should improve her time on each successive fence post according to the rule $a_n = F - 2(n - 1)$, where F is the time for the first fence post, and a_n is the time it takes to pound in the *n*th post.

   a. Use the rule to find the time it should take Tina to pound each of the first 4 fence posts into the ground. ________________

   b. If the rule that describes Tina's time on each successive post is $a_n = F - 1.\ 5^{n-1}$, how long will it take her to pound the fourth fence post into the ground? ________________

The label on Pete's blue jeans states that, when washed, the jeans will lose 5% of their color. Choose the letter for the best answer.

3. Which rule describes the percent of color left in the blue jeans after *n* washings?

   A $a_n = 100\ (0.05)^n$

   B $a_n = 100\ (0.95)^n$

   C $a_n = 100\ (0.95)^n$

   D $a_n = 100\ (0.05)^n$

4. How much of the original color will be left after 8 washings?

   F 66%

   G 60%

   H 40%

   J 34%

Name ______________________ Date ______________ Class ______________

LESSON 9-2

Problem Solving

Series and Summation Notation

Todd joins a fitness club. During the first week of training, his biceps increase by 4 millimeters. The trainer says Todd can expect his biceps to continue to increase each week, but only by about 90% of the increase of the week before.

1. Todd wants to know how much his biceps will increase in 8 weeks.

   a. Write a rule for the *k*th term in the sequence that represents the amount of muscle increase each week. ______________

   b. Write the summation notation using $\sum$ for the first 8 terms. ______________

   c. Expand the series and evaluate to find the amount by which Todd's biceps will increase in 8 weeks. ______________

2. Todd thinks that, if he works out extra hard each week, his biceps should increase by at least an additional half-millimeter each week. If this is true, how much will his biceps increase after 8 weeks? ______________

   a. Write a rule for the *k*th term in the sequence that represents the minimum amount of muscle increase each week. ______________

   b. Use summation notation to represent the minimum total amount of muscle increase after 8 weeks. ______________

   c. What is the minimum increase in size in Todd's biceps after 8 weeks? ______________

   d. At this rate, how many weeks would it take to reach or exceed the total muscle increase predicted by the trainer? ______________

Rodrigo puts his change into a bowl each evening. On Monday he puts 2 quarters in the bowl and decides to try and increase the amount each evening by at least 10 cents over the evening before. Choose the letter for the best answer.

3. Which series represents the minimum amount in the bowl Saturday morning?

   A $\sum_{k=1}^{5} 0.1(0.5)^{k-1}$

   B $\sum_{k=1}^{5} 0.5(0.1)^{k-1}$

   C $\sum_{k=1}^{5} 0.5 + 0.1(k-1)$

   D $\sum_{k=1}^{5} 0.1 + 0.5(k-1)$

4. What is the minimum amount in the bowl the following Monday morning?

   F \$3.50

   G \$5.60

   H \$6.80

   J \$7.60

Name ______________________ Date ______________ Class ______________

LESSON 9-3

Problem Solving

Arithmetic Sequences and Series

Violet has the book and the assignment for her literature class. Counting today, Monday, as day 1, she sees that she must read through page 385 by day 12, and through page 665 by day 20.

1. If Violet reads an equal number of pages each day, how many pages will she have read by this Friday?

   a. First write a rule for the *n*th term of an arithmetic sequence that represents the number of pages, a_n, that she will have read after *n* days. ______________

   b. Explain how to find the common difference by using the rule with the given data.

   ____

   c. What is the common difference, and what does it mean in terms of Violet's assignment?

   ____

   d. How many pages must Violet read today, Monday? Explain how you know this.

   ____

   e. Use the rule to find the number of pages Violet will have read by Friday. ______________

2. Violet looks at the table of contents in her book. She sees that each of the first 6 chapters is 2 pages longer than the preceding chapter, with the first chapter having 10 pages.

   a. How many pages are in the sixth chapter? Write a rule for the number of pages, a_n, in chapter *n*. Then solve for $n = 6$. ______________

   b. How pages are in the first 6 chapters? Use the formula for the sum of the first *n* terms of an arithmetic sequence. ______________

Choose the letter for the best answer.

3. Violet reads the first 385 pages by day 6. Which expression gives the minimum pages she must read each day to finish 665 pages by day 20?

   A $6\left(\dfrac{665+385}{2}\right)$

   B $\dfrac{665-385}{6}$

   C $14\left(\dfrac{665+385}{2}\right)$

   D $\dfrac{665-385}{14}$

4. Page 385 of Violet's book is 15 pages before the end of a 40-page chapter. If chapter 1 contains 10 pages, which chapter contains page 385?

   F Chapter 15

   G Chapter 16

   H Chapter 19

   J Chapter 25

Name ______________________ Date ______________ Class ______________

LESSON 9-4

Problem Solving

Geometric Sequences and Series

Crystal works at a tree nursery during the summer. She wonders why the lower branches of one particular type of tree drop off. The nurseryman explains that each layer of branches absorbs about 10% of the sunlight and lets the rest through to the next layer. If a layer receives less than 25% of the sunlight, those branches will drop off.

1. Crystal counts 7 distinct healthy layers on one tree. She wants to know how many more layers the tree will grow before starting to lose layers of branches.

   a. Write the rule for the *n*th term, a_n, of a geometric sequence. ______________

   b. If a_n represents the percent of sunlight reaching layer *n*, what is the value of a_1? How do you know?

   ____

   c. What is the value of *r*? What does it represent?

   ____

   d. Write the rule to find the percent of sunlight reaching layer 7. Solve for a_7. ______________

   e. About how many layers of branches will this tree have before a bottom layer drops off? ______________

2. The nurseryman points to a denser type of tree and states that only about 75% of sunlight gets through to each lower layer, but that a layer of this type of tree needs only about 15% of the original sunlight to survive.

   a. What percent of sunlight gets through to layer 7 of this tree? ______________

   b. How many layers of branches could this type of tree support? ______________

Jackson usually runs 8 laps around the football field and consistently completes the first lap in 3 minutes. During one practice session, his coach notes that it takes him 15% longer to complete each lap than the previous lap. Choose the letter for the best answer.

3. How long does it take Jackson to complete the eighth lap?

   A 5.25 min

   B 6.03 min

   C 6.93 min

   D 7.98 min

4. How long does it take Jackson to complete all 8 laps?

   F 9.18 min

   G 20.39 min

   H 41.18 min

   J 61.18 min

Name ______________________ Date ______________ Class ______________

LESSON 9-5

Problem Solving

Mathematical Induction and Infinite Geometric Series

Diego drops a ball from different heights. He determines that after each bounce the ball rises to 80% of its previous height. He wants to find out how the total vertical distance that the ball falls before it comes to rest varies with the height from which it is dropped.

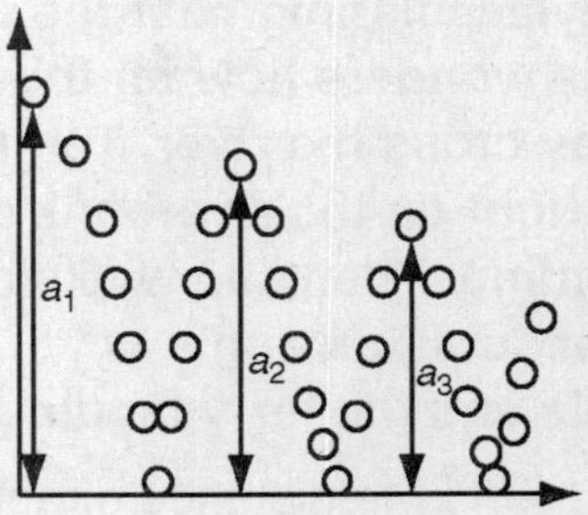

1. Diego drops the ball from a height of 8 feet and calculates the total vertical distance that the ball falls.

   a. Find the total vertical distance that the ball has fallen by the third bounce, $a_1 + a_2 + a_3$.

   ____

   b. Is this a converging or diverging series? How do you know?

   ____

   c. Write a rule and solve for the total vertical distance that the ball falls. ______________

2. Next Diego drops the ball from a height of 6 feet. What is the total vertical distance that the ball falls from this initial height? ______________

3. Complete the table.

Drop Height (ft)	Total Vertical Distance (ft)
12	
8	
6	
3	
1	

4. Write an equation to show the relationship between the drop height and the total vertical distance that the ball travels.

____

Kali notices that each year after the first year, a particular plant in her backyard adds only about 25% of the previous year's new growth to its height. The first year's growth from a seed was 3 feet. Choose the letter for the best answer.

5. Which statement describes the plant's ultimate height?
   A Its height will converge to 4 ft.
   B Its height will converge to 4.5 ft.
   C Its height will converge to 12 ft.
   D Its height will not converge.

6. In which year will new growth be less than 0.1 ft?
   F First year
   G Second year
   H Third year
   J Fourth year

Name ______________________________ Date ______________ Class ______________

LESSON 10-1

Problem Solving

Right-Angle Trigonometry

Kayla is fishing near the ferry landing near her home. She wonders how far the ferries actually travel when they cross the river. To find out, she puts a fishing pole upright on the riverbank directly across from the ferry landing. Then she walks down the bank 180 yards and measures an angle of 75° between the lines to her fishing pole and the ferry landing on the opposite bank.

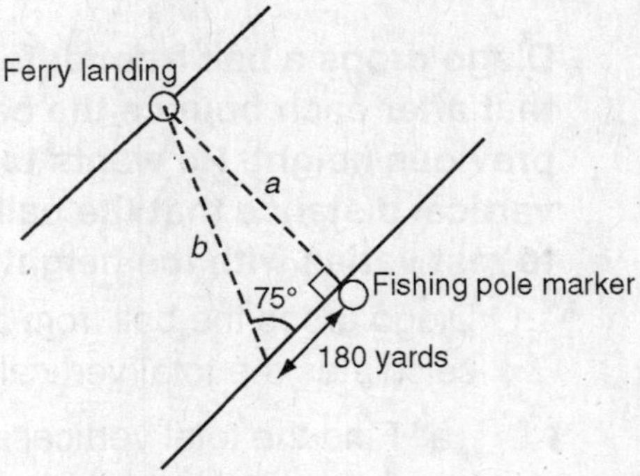

1. Find the distance directly across the river.
   a. On the diagram, name the side of the triangle that represents the distance Kayla wants to determine. ______________
   b. Write a trigonometric function that relates the known distance and angle to the required distance. ______________
   c. Find the distance to the nearest yard directly across the river. ______________
2. Kayla walks another 200 yards down the riverbank. At this point the ferries seem to come straight at her at an angle of 60° to the line to her fishing pole. If the boats travel along this line to compensate for the current, how far do they travel?
   a. How far is she from her fishing pole now? ______________
   b. Write the trigonometric function that relates this distance and angle to the required distance, *c*. ______________
   c. What is the distance that the ferries travel if they travel along this line? ______________

At a hot-air balloon festival, Luis watches a hot-air balloon rise from a distance of 200 yards. Choose the letter for the best answer.

3. From Luis's position, the balloon seems to hover at an angle of elevation of 50°. Which trigonometric function gives the height of the balloon, *h*?

   A 200 sin 50°

   B 200 tan 50°

   C $\frac{200}{\cos 50°}$

   D $\frac{200}{\cot 50°}$

4. After a short while, the balloon seems to hover at an angle of 75°. How high is it off the ground now?

   F 193 yd

   G 207 yd

   H 746 yd

   J 773 yd

Olivia has a pool slide that makes an angle of 25° with the water. The top of the slide stands 4.5 feet above the surface of the water. Choose the letter for the best answer.

5. How far out into the pool will the slide reach?

   A 2.1 ft

   B 5.0 ft

   C 7.6 ft

   D 9.7 ft

6. The slide makes a straight line into the water. How long is the slide?

   F 5.0 ft

   G 7.6 ft

   H 9.7 ft

   J 10.6 ft

Name ______________________ Date ______________ Class ______________

LESSON 10-2

Problem Solving

Angles of Rotation

Isabelle and Karl agreed to meet at the rotating restaurant at the top of a tower in the town center. The restaurant makes one full rotation each hour.

1. Isabelle waits for Karl, who arrives 30 minutes later. Through how many degrees does the restaurant rotate between the time that Isabelle arrives and the time that Karl arrives? ________

2. Since the restaurant is busy, they don't get menus for another ten minutes. How much farther has the restaurant rotated? ________

3. By the time they are served dinner, the restaurant has rotated to an angle 30° short of its orientation when Isabelle arrived.

   a. Write an expression for the length of time that Isabelle has been there. ________

   b. How long has she been there? ________

   c. How long has Karl been there? ________

   d. How far has the restaurant rotated since Karl arrived? ________

4. When their bill comes, it includes a note that the restaurant has rotated 840° since Isabelle arrived.

   a. How long has it been since they were served dinner? ________

   b. How many rotations has the restaurant made since Isabelle arrived? ________

   c. How far is the restaurant from its orientation when Karl arrived? ________

5. On their way out, they stop and look at a map. A museum is located at a point northeast of the tower with coordinates (3, 2).

   a. Write the trigonometric function for the angle that the line from the tower to the museum makes with a line due north from the tower. ________

   b. Isabelle says that the museum is exactly 4 kilometers from the tower. How much farther north is the museum than the tower? ________

An advertisement on a kiosk near the bus stop rotates through 765° while Aaron waits for his bus. Choose the letter for the best answer.

6. What is the difference in the orientation of the advertisement between when Aaron arrived at the bus stop and when the bus came?

   A 45°

   B 90°

   C 315°

   D 405°

7. If the advertisement rotates at a rate of one rotation every 10 minutes, how long does Aaron wait for his bus?

   F Less than 2 min

   G Between 2 min and 10 min

   H Between 10 min and 20 min

   J More than 20 min

Name ______________________ Date ______________ Class ______________

LESSON 10-3

Problem Solving

The Unit Circle

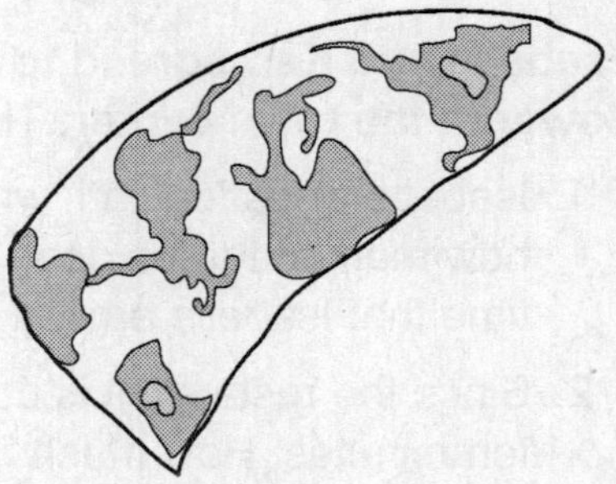

Gabe is spending two weeks on an archaeological dig. He finds a fragment of a circular plate that his leader thinks may be valuable. The arc length of the fragment is about $\frac{1}{6}$ the circumference of the original complete plate and measures 1.65 inches.

1. A similar plate found earlier has a diameter of 3.14 inches. Could Gabe's fragment match this plate?
   a. Write an expression for the radius, *r*, of the earlier plate. ______
   b. What is the measure, in radians, of a central angle, θ, that intercepts an arc that is $\frac{1}{6}$ the length of the circumference of a circle? ______
   c. Write an expression for the arc length, *S*, intercepted by this central angle. ______
   d. How long would the arc length of a fragment be if it were $\frac{1}{6}$ the circumference of the plate? ______
   e. Could Gabe's plate be a matching plate? Explain.

   ____

   ____

2. Toby finds another fragment of arc length 2.48 inches. What fraction of the outer edge of Gabe's plate would it be if this fragment were part of Gabe's plate? ______

The diameter of a merry-go-round at the playground is 12 feet. Elijah stands on the edge and his sister pushes him around. Choose the letter for the best answer

3. How far does Elijah travel if he moves through an angle of $\frac{5\pi}{4}$ radians?

   A 12.0 ft
   B 15.1 ft
   C 23.6 ft
   D 47.1 ft

4. Through what angle does Elijah move if he travels a distance of 80 feet around the circumference?

   F $\frac{40}{3}\pi$ radians
   G $\frac{80}{3}$ radians
   H $\frac{40}{3}$ radians
   J $\frac{20}{3}$ radians

Virgil sets his boat on a 1000-yard course keeping a constant distance from a rocky outcrop. Choose the letter for the best answer.

5. If Virgil keeps a distance of 200 yards, through what angle does he travel?

   A 5π radians
   B 5 radians
   C 10 radians
   D 10π radians

6. If Virgil keeps a distance of 500 yards, what fraction of the circumference of a circle does he cover?

   F $\frac{1}{\pi}$
   G $\frac{\pi}{3}$
   H $\frac{3}{4\pi}$
   J $\frac{3\pi}{4}$

Name ______________________ Date ____________ Class __________

LESSON 10-4

Problem Solving

Inverses of Trigonometric Functions

Rafe is concerned that some recently constructed buildings in his town do not comply with code restrictions. New buildings are limited to a maximum of 40 feet in height.

1. When working with angles of elevation from his eye level, Rafe realizes that he must allow for his own height, 5 feet 9 inches, in his calculations. Explain how he can do this.

____

2. On the building plans, the height of the new bank is 33 feet. Rafe calculates what the angle of elevation should be from 100 feet away if the bank is 33 feet tall.

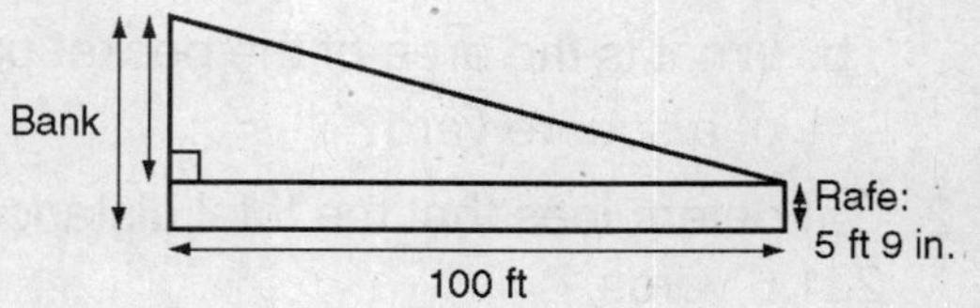

a. Label the diagram to show the height of the bank that Rafe will use in his calculations. Mark the angle of elevation.

b. Write a trigonometric function for the assumed angle of elevation, *θ*.

____

c. To the nearest tenth of a degree, what is the assumed angle of elevation?

____

d. Using a clinometer, Rafe measures the angle of elevation to be 14.2°. Does the bank comply with the building code? Explain.

____

3. On the plans, the height of the new inn is 39 feet. Rafe finds the angle of elevation and compares it to what he measures.

a. Predict the angle of elevation of the highest point on this building from a distance of 100 feet and allowing for Rafe's height. ____________

b. Predict the angle of elevation of the highest point on a building that is 40 feet tall, allowing for Rafe's height. ____________

c. If Rafe measures an angle of elevation of 19.0°, how does the height of the inn compare to its declared height of 39 feet? Explain.

____

____

4. Carrie says the angle of elevation of the top of the flagpole at school is 55.9° from a distance of 20 feet away and allowing for her height of 5 feet 6 inches.

a. Write and evaluate an expression for the height of the flagpole to the nearest tenth of a foot. ____________

b. What should be the angle of elevation if Rafe measures it from a distance of 50 feet away? Write and evaluate an expression.

____

Name ________________________ Date ______________ Class______________

LESSON 10-5

Problem Solving

The Law of Sines

In the middle of town, State and Elm streets meet at an angle of 40°. A triangular pocket park between the streets stretches 100 yards along State Street and 53.2 yards along Elm Street. Hoa and Cat walk around the pocket park every day at lunchtime.

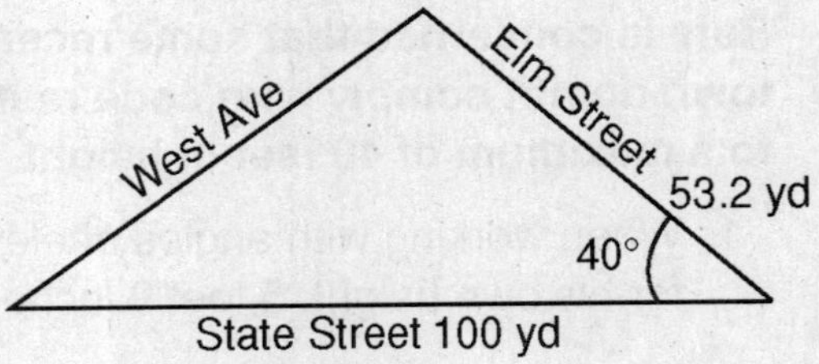

1. Hoa would like to know the area of the pocket park.

   a. Write a formula for the area of the pocket park using the given dimensions.

   ____

   b. What is the area of the pocket park to the nearest tenth of a square yard? ____________

2. Cat determines that the total distance around the pocket park is 221.6 yards.

   a. Write and evaluate an expression for the length of the park along West Avenue. ____________

   b. Use the Law of Sines to find $\angle S$ to the nearest degree, the angle that West Avenue makes with State Street. ____________

   c. Write an expression for the angle that West Avenue makes with Elm Street. ____________

____

3. West Avenue makes angles of 55° with Main Street and 80° with Third Street. The distance from Main to Third along West Avenue is 40 yards. Hoa contracts to design a pocket park for the acute-angled triangular area enclosed by these streets.

   a. What is the measure of the third angle of the triangular area? ____________

   b. Write and evaluate an expression for the distance from West Avenue to Third Street along Main Street. ____________

Choose the letter for the best answer.

4. Hoa wants to plant palm trees 8 feet apart along the side of the park on Third Street. Which expression gives the number of trees she will need?

   A $\dfrac{40 \sin 55°}{\sin 45°}$ C $\dfrac{5 \sin 45°}{\sin 55°}$

   B $\dfrac{5 \sin 55°}{\sin 45°}$ D $\dfrac{40 \sin 45°}{\sin 55°}$

5. What is the area of the new pocket park that Hoa is designing?

   F 913 yd^2

   G 1004 yd^2

   H 1207 yd^2

   J 1398 yd^2

Name ______________________ Date ______________ Class ______________

LESSON 10-6

Problem Solving

The Law of Cosines

Standing on a small bluff overlooking a local pond, Clay wants to calculate the width of the pond.

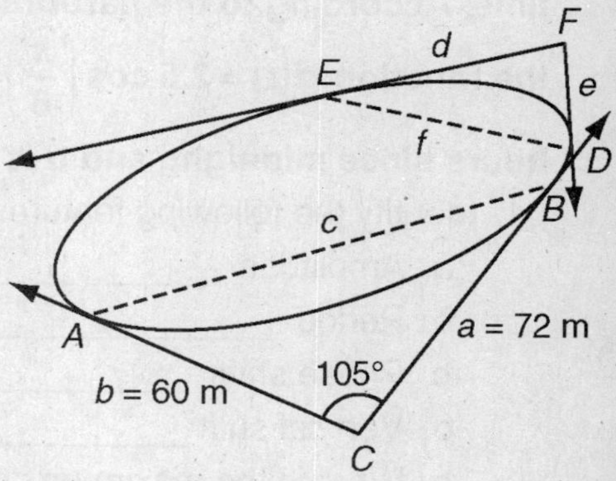

1. From point *C*, Clay walks the distances $\overline{CA}$ and $\overline{CB}$. Then he measures the angle between these line segments.

   a. Use the Law of Cosines to write an equation for the distance $\overline{AB}$.

   ____

   b. What is the distance to the nearest meter from *A* to *B*?

   ____

2. From another point *F*, Clay measures 20 meters to *D* and 50 meters to *E*. Reece says that last summer this area dried out so much that he could walk the 49 meters from *D* to *E*.

   a. Use the Law of Cosines to write an equation for the measure of the angle between $\overline{DF}$ and $\overline{EF}$. ______________________________

   b. What is the measure of this angle? ______________________________

3. Reece tells Clay that when the area defined by Δ *DEF* dries out, it becomes covered with a grass native to this area of the country. Clay wants to know the area of this section.

   a. Use Heron's Formula to write an expression for the area. ______________________________

   b. Find the area to the nearest tenth of a square meter. ______________________________

A local naturalist says that a triangular area on the north sides of the pond is a turtle habitat. The lengths of the sides of this area are 15 meters, 25 meters, and 36 meters. Choose the letter for the best answer.

4. What is the area of this triangular turtle habitat?

   A 150.7 m^2

   B 213.2 m^2

   C 1012.9 m^2

   D 3075 m^2

5. Which expression gives the measure of the angle between the sides of the habitat that measure 15 meters and 25 meters?

   F $\cos^{-1}(-0.595)$

   G $\cos(-0.595)$

   H $\cos(0.595)$

   J $\cos^{-1}(0.595)$

Name ______________________ Date ______________ Class ______________

LESSON 11-1

Problem Solving

Graphs of Sine and Cosine

As a result of the tide, the depth of the water in the bay varies with time. According to the harbormaster, the depth can be modeled by the function $d(t) = 2.5\cos\left(\frac{\pi}{6}\right)(t - 2) + 4$, where t is the number of hours since midnight, and d is the depth in meters.

1. Identify the following features of the graph of the function.
   a. Amplitude ______________
   b. Period ______________
   c. Phase shift ______________
   d. Vertical shift ______________
   e. What is the maximum depth and when does that occur?
   ____
   f. What is the minimum depth and when does that occur?
   ____

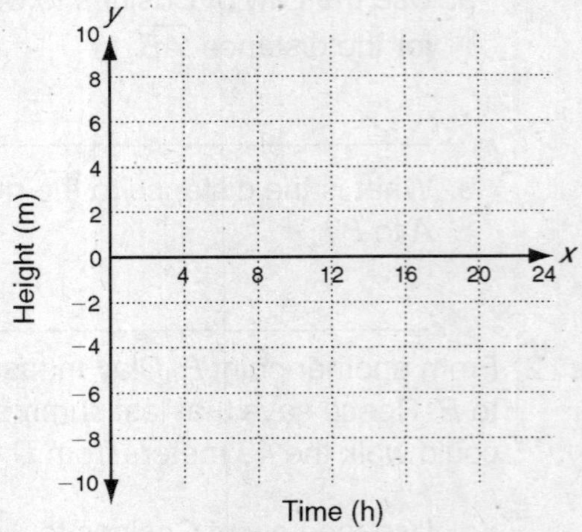

2. Graph the function for 24 hours.
3. How many high tides occur in 24 hours? ______________
4. Jim thinks that the amplitude and the vertical shift should be reversed.
   a. Write the equation for this new function. ______________
   b. Explain how water depth and frequency of tides would change using Jim's function.
   ____
   ____
5. Petra thinks that the original function is correct, except for the period, which should be 24. If so, how many hours after midnight would the first high and low tides occur? ______________

Jim looks at equations for the depth of water in different locations. Choose the letter for the best answer.

6. Which function represents a location that will dry out?
   A $d(t) = 5\cos\frac{\pi}{12}(t - 1) + 4$
   B $d(t) = 4\cos\frac{\pi}{8}(t - 2) + 4.5$
   C $d(t) = 3\cos\frac{\pi}{6}(t - 3) + 5$
   D $d(t) = 2\cos\frac{\pi}{4}(t - 4) + 5.5$

7. How deep is the water at 1:00 A.M. in a location where the water depth t hours after midnight is modeled by $d(t) = 1.25\cos\frac{\pi}{12}(t - 1) + 6$?
   F 4.75 m
   G 5.75 m
   H 7.25 m
   J 8.25 m

Name ______________________ Date ______________ Class ______________

LESSON 11-2

Problem Solving

Graphs of Other Trigonometric Functions

As the sign outside the community youth center rotates, the light on it traces a path on the center's wall. The distance in feet of the light to the point on the wall where it shines varies with time, *t*, and can be modeled by the function $g(t) = 9 \csc\left(\frac{3\pi}{4}t\right)$, where *t* is measured in seconds.

1. Identify the period of the function.
   a. What is the coefficient of *t* in the equation of the function? ______
   b. Write and evaluate an expression for the period of the function. ______
   c. Explain what the period of the function means in terms of the time for one rotation of the light.
   ____
   d. How does the graph of the function vary based on the period?
   ____

2. a. This function has asymptotes at points where what other function is equal to 0?
   ____
   b. What are the asymptotes of the function?
   ____

3. What is the significance of 9 in the equation for the function?
   ____

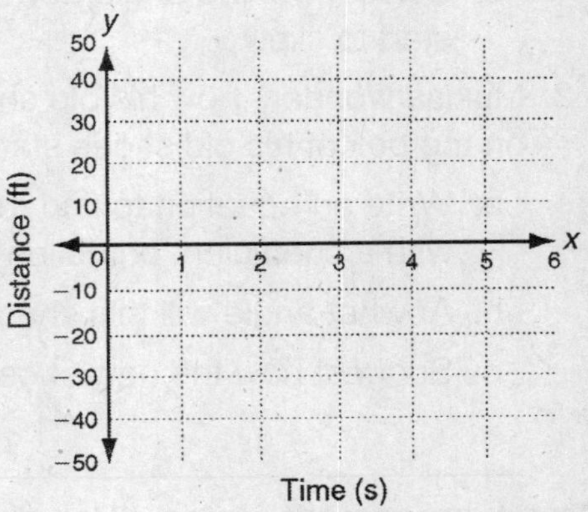

4. Graph the function using all the information about the function.

Toni changes the rotation rate of the light so that it rotates once every 4 seconds. Choose the letter for the best answer.

5. Which equation represents the distance of the light to the point on the wall where it shines, as a function of time, *t*?

   A $g(t) = 9 \csc\left(\frac{\pi}{4}t\right)$

   B $g(t) = 9 \csc\left(\frac{\pi}{2}t\right)$

   C $g(t) = 9 \csc(2\pi t)$

   D $g(t) = 9 \csc(4\pi t)$

6. Which pair of parameters describes this new function?

   F period: 4 s; vertical asymptotes at $\pm 2n$ s

   G period: 2 s; vertical asymptotes at $\pm n$ s

   H period: 2 s; horizontal asymptotes at $\pm 2n$ s

   J period: 4 s; horizontal asymptotes at $\pm n$ s

Name ______________________ Date ______________ Class ______________

LESSON 11-3

Problem Solving

Fundamental Trigonometric Identities

The advertisement for a new shoe promises runners less slip. The coefficient of friction (μ) between concrete and a new material used in the sole of this shoe is 1.5. The force of friction that causes slip is equal to $mg \sin \theta$, where m is a runner's mass and g is the acceleration due to gravity. The force that prevents slip is $\mu mg \cos \theta$.

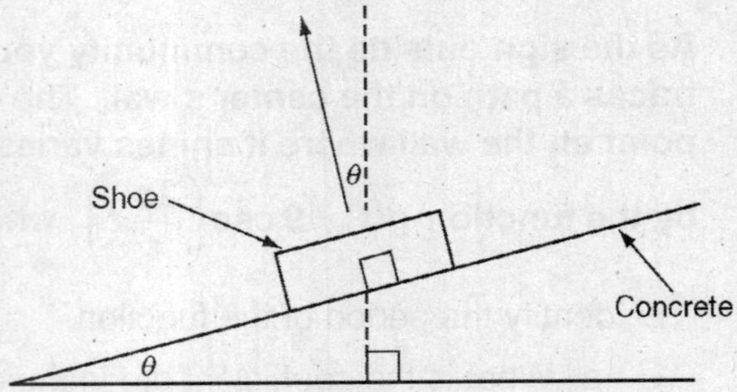

1. Mukisa wants to know what this new shoe will do for his performance.
   a. At the instant of slip, the force that causes slip is equal to the force that prevents it. Write an equation to show this relationship. ______________
   b. Rewrite the equation with trigonometric expressions on one side of the equation, and substitute the coefficient of friction for the new material. ______________
   c. Use a trigonometric identity to rewrite the equation using only the tangent function. ______________
   d. Solve for θ, the angle at which the new shoe will start to slip. ______________
2. Mukisa wonders how his old shoes compare to these new shoes. The label on the box of his old shoes states that the coefficient of friction is 1.3.
   a. Write an equation to find the angle at which a shoe with a coefficient of friction of 1.3 will slip. ______________
   b. At what angle will this shoe start to slip? ______________
   c. Suggest how the new shoes might improve Mukisa's performance.

____

An advertisement states, "Use this wax and your skis will slide better than silk on silk!" The coefficient of friction for silk on silk is 0.25. The coefficient of friction for waxed wood on wet snow is 0.14. The equation $mg \sin\theta = \mu mg \cos\theta$ can be used to find the angle at which a material begins to slide. Choose the letter for the best answer.

3. Which expression gives the angle at which silk begins to slide on silk?
   A $\cos^{-1}(0.25)$
   B $\sin\left(\frac{1}{0.25}\right)$
   C $\tan\left(\frac{1}{0.25}\right)$
   D $\tan^{-1}(0.25)$
4. At what angle would a waxed wooden ski begin to slide on wet snow?
   F 2°
   G 8°
   H 12°
   J 14°

Name ______________________ Date ______________ Class ______________

LESSON 11-4

Problem Solving

Sum and Difference Identities

Caitlin is designing a rotating graphic for her website. She explores what it will look like if it flashes in different positions.

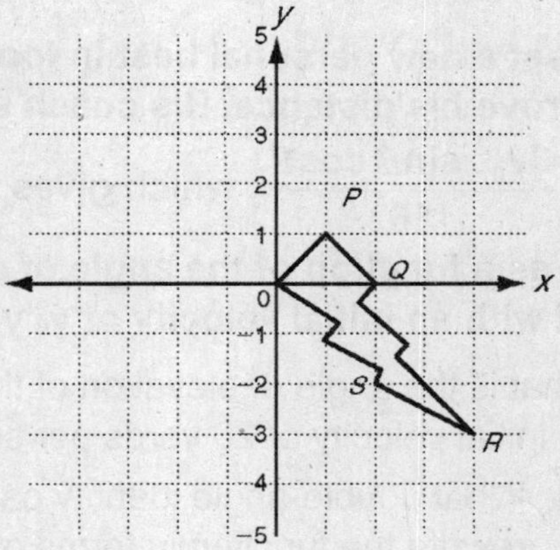

1. Use rotation matrices to find the coordinates of the figure *PQRS* after a 60° rotation about the origin.

   a. Write matrices for a 60° rotation and for the points *P*, *Q*, *R*, and *S* in the figure.

   $R_{60^\circ} = [\quad]$

   $PQRS = [\quad]$

   b. Find the matrix product. $R_{60^\circ} \times PQRS \approx [\quad]$

   c. Name the coordinates of *P*′, *Q*′, *R*′, *S*′ to the nearest hundredth after a 60° rotation.

   ____

2. a. Write the matrix product that gives the coordinates of the figure after a rotation of 150°.

   $R_{150^\circ} \times PQRS = [\quad]$

   b. Name the coordinates of *P*″*Q*″*R*″*S*″ to the nearest hundredth.

   ____

3. Graph the two rotations on the plane above to see where Caitlin's rotating graphic will flash. Label *R*′ and *R*″.

Choose the letter for the best answer.

4. Which expression gives the exact value of sin150°?

   A sin90°cos60° + cos90°sin60°

   B sin90°cos60° − cos90°sin60°

   C cos180°cos30° + sin180°sin30°

   D cos180°cos30° − sin180°sin30°

5. What is the exact value of cos75°?

   F $\frac{\sqrt{2}-\sqrt{6}}{2}$

   G $\frac{\sqrt{6}+\sqrt{2}}{4}$

   H $\frac{\sqrt{6}-\sqrt{2}}{4}$

   J $\frac{\sqrt{6}+\sqrt{2}}{2}$

Name ______________________ Date ______________ Class ______________

LESSON 11-5

Problem Solving

Double-Angle and Half-Angle Identities

Chris set a new personal best in football with a 35-yard kick. He wants to improve his distance. His coach suggests using the formula $d(\theta) = \dfrac{3v_0^2 \sin\theta \cos\theta}{16}$, which gives the horizontal distance, *d*, in yards, as a function of the angle of elevation, *θ*, at which the ball is kicked with an initial velocity of v_0 yards per second.

1. What is the angle of elevation of the ball when Chris kicks it with an initial velocity of 20 yards per second and the ball covers 35 yards.
   a. What double-angle identity can you use to rewrite the function in terms of $\sin 2\theta$? ______________
   b. Rewrite the function in terms of $\sin 2\theta$. ______________
   c. Substitute the known values in the equation. ______________
   d. Solve for $\sin 2\theta$. ______________
   e. What is the angle at which he kicked the ball? ______________
2. Chris wonders how the horizontal distance would change if he kicked the ball with the same velocity but at a different angle.
   a. Complete the table to show the horizontal distance, to the nearest hundredth yard, for the given angles.
   b. At what angle must Chris kick the ball to cover the greatest horizontal distance?

   ____

Angle of Elevation (°)	Horizontal Distance (yd)
15	
25	
35	
45	
55	

3. What is the least angle at which Chris must kick the ball if he wants to cover at least 30 yards horizontally?

   ____
4. Chris thinks he can kick the ball with an initial velocity of 18 yards per second and make a horizontal distance of 40 yards. Is he correct? Explain.

   ____

Choose the letter for the best answer.

5. If Chris kicks the ball with an initial velocity of only 15 yards per second and an angle of elevation of 45°, what is the maximum horizontal distance the ball will cover?

   A 12.06 yd　　C 21.09 yd
   B 14.92 yd　　D 29.83 yd
6. At what angle can Chris kick the ball to cover a horizontal distance of 36 yards, if he kicks the ball with an initial velocity of 20 yards per second?

   F 18.5°　　H 44.1°
   G 36.9°　　J 73.7°

Name ______________________________ Date ______________ Class______________

LESSON 11-6

Problem Solving

Solving Trigonometric Equations

Jon watches his sister Jessica skateboard. When she jumps and launches herself into the air with an initial speed of v_0 feet per second, her path in terms of time, *t*, in seconds, is represented by these equations.

Equation 1 $x(t) = v_0 t\cos\theta$

Equation 2 $y(t) = v_0 t\sin\theta - 16t^2$

The first equation models the horizontal distance, *x*(*t*), that the skateboarder travels, and the second equation models the vertical height, *y*(*t*), that the skateboarder attains.

1. Jessica attains a height of 4.7 feet above the launch and landing ramps after 1 second. Her initial velocity is 25 feet per second. Find the angle of her launch.

   a. Which equation can you use with the given information to solve for θ? ______________

   b. Substitute the known values and solve for θ. ______________

   c. What is Jessica's height above the launch and landing ramps after 0.5 second? ______________

   d. What distance has Jessica traveled after 1 second? ______________

2. Jon attains a height of 5.2 feet above the launch and landing ramps after 1 second. His initial velocity is 28 feet per second. Find the angle of his launch.

   a. Write and evaluate an expression for Jon's launch angle.

   ____

   b. Write and evaluate an expression for his height above the launch and landing ramps after 0.5 second.

   ____

Choose the letter for the best answer.

3. How far does Jon travel in 1 second?

   A 14.5 ft C 18.3 ft

   B 16.7 ft D 21.2 ft

4. Jessica increases her initial velocity to 30 feet per second. She attains a height of 5.5 feet after 1 second. Which expression represents her launch angle?

   F $\cos^{-1}\left(\frac{10.5}{30}\right)$ H $\sin^{-1}\left(\frac{10.5}{30}\right)$

   G $\cos^{-1}\left(\frac{21.5}{30}\right)$ J $\sin^{-1}\left(\frac{21.5}{30}\right)$

Name ______________________ Date ______________ Class ______________

LESSON 12-1

Problem Solving

Introduction to Conic Sections

Hunter and Max draw a grid over a map of their town so that they can determine precisely where to set up a broadcast station. Hunter decides that locations *A* and *B* should be the endpoints of the diameter of a circle around the broadcast station.

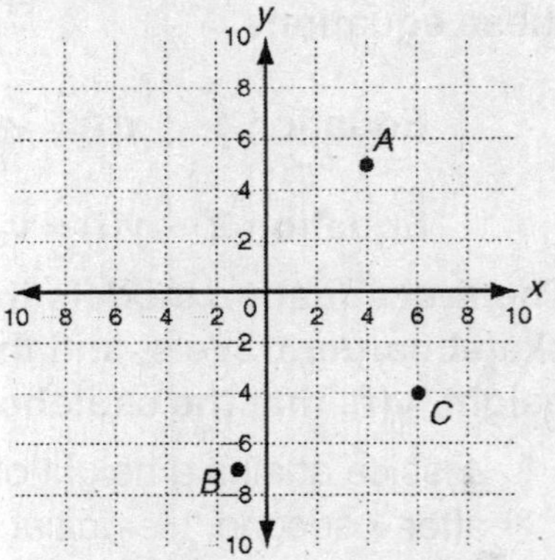

1. Locate the center of the circle using the Midpoint Formula and points *A* and *B*.

____

2. Find the radius and the circumference of the circle.

   a. Name the coordinates of two points you can use with the Distance Formula to find the radius.

   ____

   b. Use the Distance Formula to find the radius. _______________

   c. What is the circumference of the circle? _______________

3. Hunter says that point *C* is within the circle. Max says that point *C* is on the circumference of the circle.

   a. Explain how they can use the Distance Formula to determine the answer.

   ____

   b. Who is correct? Why?

   ____

A broadcast station is set up at the location with coordinates (0, 2). The transmissions just reach a location with coordinates (8, 8). Choose the letter for the best answer.

4. Which point is farthest from the point (8, 8) and still within range of the broadcast station?

   A (–8, –4) C (0, 10)

   B (–8, –8) D (10, 2)

5. What is the maximum distance the broadcast transmissions will reach?

   F 6 units

   G 8 units

   H 9 units

   J 10 units

6. What is the area the broadcast transmissions will cover?

   A 20π C 100π

   B 64π D 196π

7. The broadcast transmissions just reach the point (x, 0). What is the value of x?

   F 8.4 H 9.2

   G 8.8 J 9.8

Name ______________________ Date ______________ Class ______________

LESSON 12-2

Problem Solving

Circles

When Claire started her consulting business, she decided not to accept any clients located more than 10 miles from her home. On the graph below, her home is located at (5, 1), and her prospective clients are represented by the letters *P* through *W*.

1. Claire needs to know which prospective clients are located within a 10-mile radius of her home.

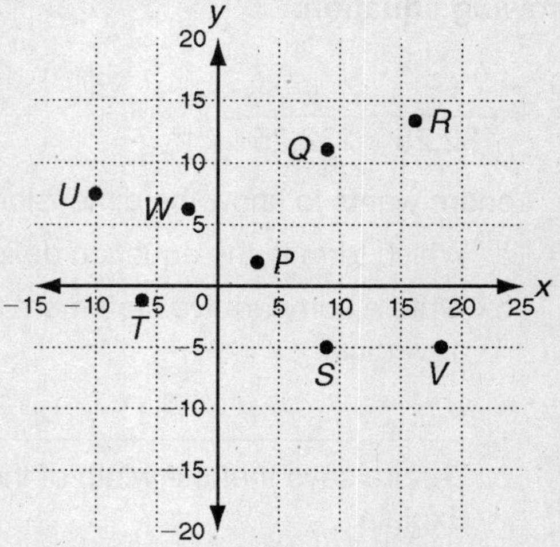

   a. Write the equation of a circle with center (5, 1) and radius 10.

   ____

   b. Which prospective clients are located within 10 miles of Claire's home?

   ____

   c. Which prospective clients are located more than 10 miles from Claire's home?

   ____

2. Claire finds that she isn't earning enough to pay the expenses from her consulting business and she needs to find some additional clients. She decides that she will drive up to 15 miles from her home to visit a client. Which prospective clients are within a 15-mile radius of her home?

   a. Write the equation of a circle with center (5, 1) and radius 15. ______________________

   b. Which prospective clients are located within 15 miles of Claire's home? ______________________

   c. How far away is a prospective client located at (10, 15)? ______________________

Claire rents an office at location (–2, –3). Choose the letter for the best answer.

3. Which of the prospective clients *P* through *W* are located more than 15 miles from Claire's office?

   A *R, V*

   B *R, S, V*

   C *Q, R, V*

   D *Q, R, S, V*

4. Which location is within 5 miles of Claire's office?

   F Post office at (2, 3)

   G Library at (2, –3)

   H Marina at (–3, 2)

   J Swimming pool at (–2, 3)

Name ______________________ Date ______________ Class ______________

LESSON 12-3

Problem Solving

Ellipses

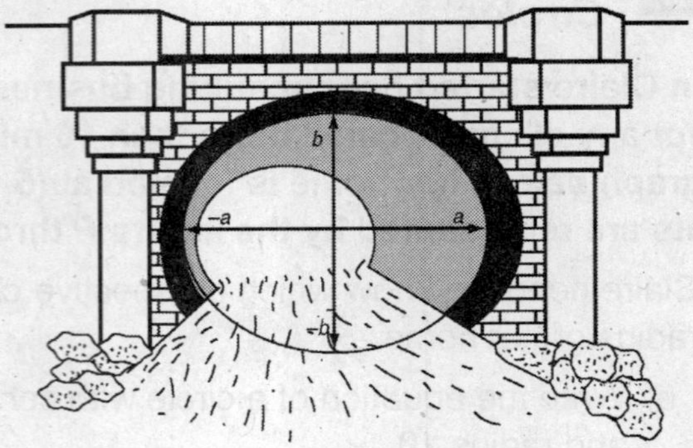

Lenore and Zane study a drawing of an ornamental bridge such as the one shown at right. It shows an elliptical arch that spans a narrow strait of water. The arch they are studying can be modeled by the following equation.

$$\frac{x^2}{182.25}+\frac{y^2}{132.25}=1$$

1. Lenore wants to know the dimensions of the arch.
   a. Which term in the equation defines the horizontal axis? ______________
   b. Write a comparative statement to show whether the major axis of the arch is horizontal or vertical.

   ____

   c. Lenore says that the width of the bridge is 13.5 feet. Is she correct? Explain.

   ____

   d. Write an expression for the height of the bridge. ______________
2. Zane notes that this bridge is hardly high enough to pass under while standing up in a moderate-size boat. If he were to build a bridge, it would be at least 1.3 times as wide and twice as high.
   a. Find the vertices and co-vertices of Zane's bridge design.

   ____

   b. Write an equation for the design of Zane's bridge using his minimum dimensions. ______________

Lenore finds architectural drawings for other bridges. Choose the letter for the best answer.

3. The equation for the arch of a bridge at the entrance to a wildlife park is $\frac{x^2}{225}+\frac{y^2}{324}=1$. What is the width of this bridge?

   A 36 ft

   B 30 ft

   C 18 ft

   D 15 ft

4. The width and the height of one arch leading into part of an old town are both 17 feet. What is the equation for this bridge?

   F $\frac{x^2}{72.25}+\frac{y^2}{289}=1$

   G $\frac{x^2}{72.25}+\frac{y^2}{72.25}=1$

   H $\frac{x^2}{289}+\frac{y^2}{72.25}=1$

   J $\frac{x^2}{289}+\frac{y^2}{289}=1$

Name ______________________ Date ______________ Class ______________

LESSON 12-4

Problem Solving

Hyperbolas

A brochure for a new amusement park describes the design of the towers that characterize the park. The outline of the central and largest tower can be modeled by the hyperbola $\frac{x^2}{625} - \frac{y^2}{2025} = 1$, with dimensions in feet. The smaller towers are scaled-down versions of the central tower, and so their dimensions are in proportion to those of the central tower.

1. What is the diameter of the central tower at its narrowest part?
   a. Explain how to determine whether the transverse axis of a hyperbola is horizontal or vertical.
   ____
   b. Find the vertices and co-vertices.
   ____
   c. How can you use these data to answer the question?
   ____
   d. What is the diameter of the tower at its narrowest part? ______________
2. The vertices of a smaller tower are (10, 0) and (–10, 0).
   a. Name the coordinates of the co-vertices. ______________
   b. What is the equation for the outline of the smaller tower? ______________
3. How do the asymptotes of the hyperbolas of the larger central tower and the smaller tower compare?
   a. Find the asymptotes of the two towers. ______________
   b. Compare the asymptotes of the two towers. ______________

Choose the letter for the best answer.

4. The hyperbola that models a third tower has vertices (0, 9) and (0, –9) and focus (0, 15). The solution to which of the following equations gives the denominator of the y^2 term in the equation of the hyperbola?
   A $15^2 = a^2 - 9^2$
   B $15^2 = a^2 + 18^2$
   C $15^2 = b^2 + 9^2$
   D $15^2 = b^2 - 18^2$
5. The outline of a tower at the park's Welcome Center can be modeled by the equation $\frac{x^2}{25} - \frac{y^2}{81} = 1$. What are the asymptotes of the hyperbola?
   F $y = \pm 0.31x$
   G $y = \pm 0.56x$
   H $y = \pm 1.8x$
   J $y = \pm 3.24x$

Name ______________________ Date ______________ Class ______________

LESSON 12-5

Problem Solving

Parabolas

Rodrigo and Juan are constructing a model of the mirror grid in the solar wind concentrator used during the Genesis space mission to collect charged solar particles. They know that a cross section of the mirror grid can be modeled by the equation $y = \frac{x^2}{80}$, with dimensions in centimeters.

1. Draw a graph of the cross-sectional shape of the mirror grid.
   a. What are the coordinates of the vertex of the parabola? ______________
   b. Find the distance, p, from the vertex to both the focus and the directrix of the parabola. Write an equation for p. ______________
   c. Write an equation to represent the axis of symmetry.

      ____
   d. Find the coordinates of the focus.

      ____
   e. Write an equation to represent the directrix.

      ____
   f. Sketch a graph of the cross section of the mirror grid including the focus and the directrix.

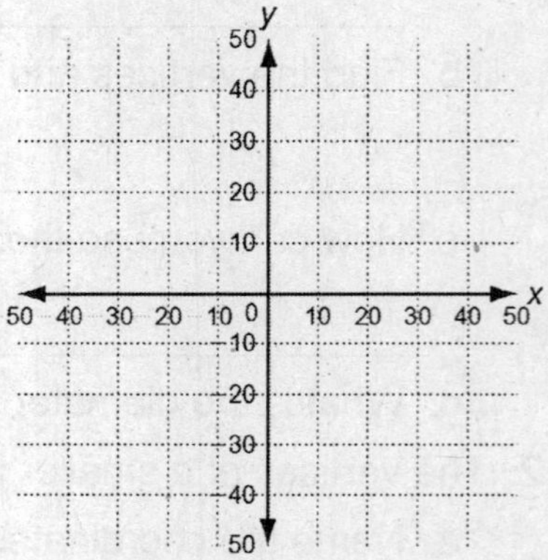

2. Juan wants to construct a different parabolic mirror grid. He changes the focus to (0, 5) and the directrix to $y = -5$.
   a. Explain why you can use the Distance Formula to find the equation for this parabola.

      ____
   b. Find the equation for the new parabola.

      ____

Choose the letter for the best answer.

3. Juan writes an equation for a parabola with vertex (0, 0) and directrix $x = -4$. Which equation could he have written?

   A $x = \frac{y^2}{16}$ C $y = \frac{x^2}{16}$

   B $x = \frac{y^2}{4}$ D $y = \frac{x^2}{4}$

4. If the equation of the mirror grid in the Genesis solar wind concentrator is $y - 2 = \frac{1}{15}(x - 3)^2$, where is the vertex of the parabola?

   F (2, 3)

   G (2, –3)

   H (–3, 2)

   J (3, 2)

Name ________________________ Date ____________ Class____________

LESSON 12-6

Problem Solving

Identifying Conic Sections

At a bungee-jumping contest, Gavin makes a jump that can be modeled by the equation $x^2 - 12x - 12y + 84 = 0$, with dimensions in feet.

1. Gavin wants to know how close he came to the ground during his jump.

   a. Classify the shape of his path. Identify the values for the coefficients of each term, and determine what conic section models his path.

   ____

   b. Write the equation of his path in standard form by completing the square.

   ____

   c. Which point on the path identifies the lowest point that Gavin reached? What are the coordinates of this point? How close to the ground was he?

   ____

2. Nicole makes a similar jump that can be modeled by the equation $x^2 - 4x - 8y + 84 = 0$. She wants to know whether she got closer to the ground than Gavin and by how much.

   a. Write the equation of Nicole's path in standard form.

   ____

   b. How close to the ground did she get? ____________

   c. Did Nicole get closer to the ground than Gavin? ____________

The design for a new auto racetrack can be modeled by the equation $x^2 + 4y^2 - 20x - 32y + 160 = 0$, with dimensions in kilometers. Tracey tests the track. Choose the letter for the best answer.

3. What is the standard form of the equation for the path of the racetrack?

   A $\frac{(x-10)^2}{1^2} + \frac{(y-4)^2}{2^2} = 1$

   B $\frac{(x-10)^2}{2^2} + \frac{(y-4)^2}{1^2} = 1$

   C $\frac{(x-4)^2}{2^2} + \frac{(y-10)^2}{1^2} = 1$

   D $\frac{(x-4)^2}{1^2} + \frac{(y-10)^2}{2^2} = 1$

4. While driving around the track, what is the greatest distance that Tracey will reach from the center of the track?

   F 1 km

   G 2 km

   H 10 km

   J 16 km

Name ______________________ Date ______________ Class ______________

LESSON 12-7

Problem Solving

Solving Nonlinear Systems

Jim sets a course in his fishing boat that can be modeled by the equation $4x^2 + 9y^2 = 36$. Janice has her sailboat on a path that can be modeled by the equation $x - 2 = \left(\frac{1}{8}\right)y^2$.

1. Janice wonders whether there is a danger of them colliding.
   a. Explain which conic section models each boat's path and why.

   ____

   b. What is the maximum number of points of intersection between two such paths? ______________

   c. To solve this system of equations using the quadratic formula, what expression can be substituted for y^2 in the equation of the path of Jim's boat? ______________

   d. Rewrite the equation of the path of Jim's boat in terms of x. ______________

   e. Solve for x using the quadratic formula.

   ____

   f. Is there a possibility of collision? If so, name the coordinates of the point(s) of intersection.

   ____

2. Janice changes course so that her sailboat now follows a path modeled by the equation $\frac{y^2}{4} - x^2 = 1$ in quadrants I and II. Is there now a possibility of collision?
   a. Sketch the system of equations represented by Jim's boat's course and Janice's boat's new course.
   b. Use your graph to determine if there is now a possibility of collision. If so, give the coordinates of the point(s).

   ____

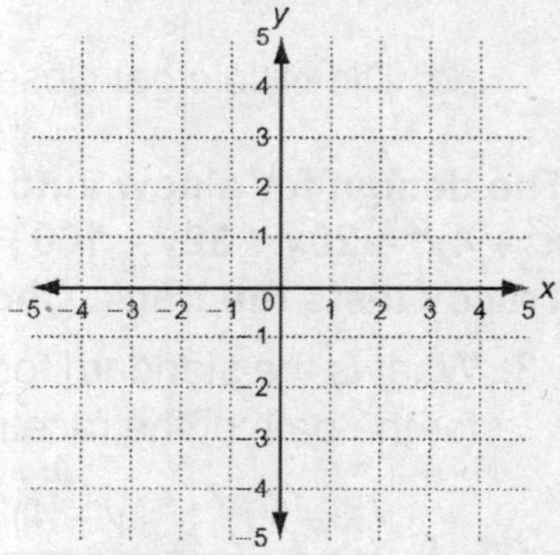

A trawler is on a course modeled by the equation $2x + y + 3 = 0$. Choose the letter for the best answer.

3. Which solution set represents possible points of collision between Jim's boat and the trawler's course?

   A (–2.2, 1.37)

   B (–0.5, –2)

   C (–2.2, 1.37); (–0.5, –2)

   D There is no possible collision point.

4. Janice sees the trawler. Which equation models a path that avoids a possible collision of her boat with the trawler?

   F $x - 1 = 0.5y^2$

   G $y = 0.5x + 2$

   H $y^2 - x^2 = 1$

   J $4x^2 + 3y^2 = 12$